ED L2

Fine DIY prote
adhesive cove

CW00671700

The Battle of Beecher Island
and the Indian War of 1867–1869

John H. Monnett

The Battle of Beecher Island
and the Indian War
of 1867–1869

University Press of Colorado

10 9 8 7 6 5 4 3 2 1

Jacket: *Battle of Beecher Island.* Oil painting by Robert Lindneux.
Courtesy Colorado Historical Society, Denver, Colorado.

The University Press of Colorado is a cooperative publishing
enterprise supported, in part, by Adams State College, Colorado
State University, Fort Lewis College, Mesa State College,
Metropolitan State College of Denver, University of Colorado,
University of Northern Colorado, University of Southern
Colorado, and Western State College.

Library of Congress Cataloging-in-Publication Data

Monnett, John H.
    The Battle of Beecher Island and the Indian War of 1867–
1869 / John H. Monnett.
        p.   cm.
    Includes bibliographical references (p.   ) and index.
    ISBN 0-87081-267-x (cloth: alk. paper)
    1. Beecher Island, Battle of, 1868. 2. Cheyenne Indians —
Wars — 1868–1869. I. Title.
E83.868.M65   1992
973.8'1 — dc20   92-29121
                                                      CIP

The paper used in this publication meets the minimum
requirements of the American National Standard for
Information Sciences—Permanence of Paper for Printed Library
Materials. ANSI Z39.48–1984

∞

For Darren

May you choose to know the joys of history
as I enjoyed them with my dad

Contents

Acknowledgments

No book of this nature would be complete without the contributions of others. My father, the late Howard N. Monnett, a longtime resident of Kansas City and a pretty good Civil War historian, instilled in me an appreciation of history, which has since formed the basis of my chosen profession. The late George L. Anderson, former chairman of the Department of History at the University of Kansas and my early mentor, showed me there are many dimensions to the Indian wars that transcend mere troop movements and engagements. Edwin C. Bearss of the National Park Service, with whom my father and I tramped many a battlefield in my youth, first made the nineteenth-century army come alive for me.

I wish to express my gratitude to the State Historical Societies of Kansas, Colorado, Nebraska, and Oklahoma for their assistance. This book could not have been written without them. To all the helpful people at the Western History Department of the Denver Public Library, the Norlin Library of the University of Colorado at Boulder, the Denver Auraria Library, and the National Archives in Washington, D.C., Kansas City, and Denver, a very special thanks. Thanks to my friend Jerry Keenan for reading the manuscript and offering suggestions. Finally, to my wife, Linda, and my son, Darren, who suffered with me through the completion of the project. I love you both in more ways than I can count.

JOHN H. MONNETT

The Battle of Beecher Island
and the Indian War of 1867–1869

Introduction: The Forsyth Scouts, American Indians, and Writing Western History

General Nelson A. Miles called the Battle of Beecher Island "one of the most remarkable affairs with Indians in the history of the American frontier."[1] But to the Oglala and Brulé Sioux, the Cheyenne Dog Soldiers, and the Northern Cheyennes and Arapahoes who participated in the engagement, it was considered only a minor fight.[2] To be sure, the action has been portrayed as a heroic stand made by a handful of civilian scouts facing overwhelming numbers of plains warriors. In that respect it has held an esteemed place in white histories of the Indian wars. Yet in most accounts the Beecher Island fight is treated as an isolated incident having little impact on the events that followed it. Considering the rather sensational nature of the stand on the Arickaree, it is surprising that the battle, and its relationship to the Indian War of 1867–1869, have never been the subject of in-depth critical inquiry.[3]

The fight took place far out on the shortgrass prairie of the central plains in the middle of the Arickaree Fork of the Republican River. The site is located in extreme eastern Colorado, in Yuma County, near the present town of Wray, five miles west of the Kansas state line.[4] On the early morning of September 17, 1868, a force composed principally of Cheyenne Dog Soldiers and Sioux, whose numbers have been estimated in the literature to be anywhere from two hundred to over one thousand warriors, attacked about fifty citizen scouts under the command of Major George A. "Sandy" Forsyth, a member of Major General Philip Sheridan's staff since the dark days of the Civil War.[5]

The whites, surrounded and cut off, took refuge and entrenched themselves on a small, sparsely vegetated sandbar island in the middle of the mostly dry Arickaree Fork. There, on the 17th, armed with seven-shot repeating Spencer rifles and Colt revolvers, they held off several dramatic charges upon their position by the determined warriors. Tied to their wounded, the command was on the island for nine consecutive days, where they were forced to sustain themselves upon the decayed flesh of their horses. Scouts sent through the Indian lines under the cover of darkness were finally able to bring relief forces to the beleaguered command on the 25th. By then the Indians had given up the fight and departed the vicinity.

Forsyth's command sustained losses of five men killed and about eighteen wounded, or approximately 45 percent casualties. Among those killed was Forsyth's second in command, First Lieutenant Frederick H. Beecher, 3rd Infantry, in whose memory the island was named. The number of Indian losses has become the subject of controversy. Forsyth officially reported that he personally counted thirty-two dead. But George Bird Grinnell, who knew the Cheyennes well, wrote that the Indians themselves could identify only nine killed. In later years some Brulé Sioux told the aging George A. Forsyth that seventy-five Indian people lost their lives at Beecher Island. In the highly nationalistic, early prerevisionist secondary sources, which were written from the white point of view, the number of Indian casualties escalated into the hundreds.[6]

No wonder. Beginning almost immediately after their rescue a jingoistic national press dramatized the actions of the Forsyth Scouts. With descriptions of a tearful Commanding General Sheridan traveling to Fort Wallace, Kansas, to attend the bedside of his fallen aide (Forsyth sustained three wounds, at least one of which was life threatening), both easterners and westerners began the task of exalting Forsyth and his men as national heroes. By 1868, the mainstream of American society was weary with memories of the Civil War; it was preoccupied with the ills of military Reconstruction and soon was engrossed with the embarrasing impeachment of President Andrew Johnson. Indeed, the memory of militia colonel John M. Chivington's slaughter of Southern Cheyenne women and children at Sand Creek (Colorado) in 1864 still burned vividly in the minds of reformers and people of the East who championed a peaceful, civilized approach that was divorced from the military for dealing with the so-called Indian problem in the West.

A less-than-successful show of military force on the plains the previous year by Major General Winfield Scott Hancock had, in the estimation of many, touched off the hostilities with the volatile Dog Soldiers, one of the most renowned of the Cheyenne warrior societies. During the summer of 1867 Lieutenant Colonel (Brevet Major General) George Armstrong Custer's newly formed 7th U.S. Cavalry could do little to catch the elusive Dog Soldiers and their allies. A protracted war with the Sioux under Red Cloud on the northern plains had led to the extermination of Captain William Fetterman's command near Fort Phil Kearny in December 1866. In essence, white settlers in the West, and the military establishment in Washington, needed a group of symbolic heroes on the Indian frontier.[7]

In actuality, the Battle of Beecher Island had an emotional impact on policymaking that went beyond what most histories reveal. This reverberation had its most important effects shortly after the fight when it became obvious that current treaty efforts had failed. During the summer and fall of 1867 a "Blue Ribbon" Peace Commission, composed of important officials in the Indian Bureau, members of the national legislature, and high-ranking generals of the army, had succeeded in persuading some of the peace chiefs of the southern plains tribes to sign the Treaties of Medicine Lodge.

A major objective of this commission was to separate the northern and southern tribes by restricting their camps between the Platte and Arkansas rivers. Above and between these streams, the Union Pacific main line and Union Pacific Eastern Division (eventually renamed the Kansas Pacific) were laying steel rail in a race toward the one-hundredth meridian and the right to link with the Central Pacific Railroad in the Great Basin. Many civilian members of the commission felt that the treaty would free this "central plains corridor" for unmolested travel by whites, remove the causes of the Indian wars, and thus silence demands by the military that the Indian Bureau be reorganized as part of the federal War Department.

However, many young warriors from all the southern tribes, especially the Dog Soldiers, refused to recognize the treaty and continued their raids on the Kansas settlements during the following summer of 1868. In October 1868 the Peace Commission met in Chicago. Sitting in on the meeting was Republican presidential candidate Ulysses S. Grant. "Fresh in the minds of all," wrote historian Robert M. Utley, "was Forsyth's bloody stand at Beecher's Island. . . . The Medicine Lodge Treaty seemed dead."[8] In the minds of candidate Grant and the army generals present at the discussion, any further notions of trusting Indian matters to a civilian-controlled Indian Bureau were not desirable. "Too many scalps have disappeared from the heads of their legitimate owners," General William T. Sherman, commander of the Division of the Missouri, told a reporter, "to make it safe to prolong this policy."[9]

Although future events would prevent him from doing so, it is highly likely that during this gathering in Chicago Ulysses S. Grant decided that he would move the Indian Bureau to the War Department if he were elected president. In addition, the commission went on record as expressing the belief that the federal government should quit recognizing indigenous societies as "domestic dependent nations," except as already established in existing treaties, and to henceforth make Indians individually subject to American laws.[10] With that, and while Major George A. Forsyth was still recovering from his multiple wounds, the Peace Commission adjourned, never to reconvene. Major General Philip Sheridan pushed on with preparations for the army's winter campaign to punish the Southern Cheyennes for summer raids. But after Beecher Island, the reorganized scout unit was not used independently in offensive operations against Indians.[11]

Nevertheless, throughout the later years of the nineteenth century, and the early decades of the twentieth, the exploits of the scouts were told. George A. Forsyth in particular, breveted a brigadier general because of his leadership during the engagement, was upheld as the ideal soldier. He was revered by vainglorious commanders at a time when the officer corps of the regular army found competition for promotions intense and usually measured in terms of seniority combined with combat experience against Indians, encounters that were all too ephemeral and rare.

George Armstrong Custer became one of Forsyth's greatest admirers. Custer called Forsyth's actions at Beecher Island "one of the most remarkable and . . . successful contests in which our forces on the Plains have ever been engaged; and the whole affair . . . was a wonderful exhibition of daring courage, stubborn bravery, and heroic endurance, under circumstances of greatest peril and exposure. In all probability," Custer continued, "there will never occur in our future hostilities with the savage tribes of the West a struggle the equal of that in which were engaged the heroic men who defended so bravely 'Beecher's Island.' Forsyth, the gallant leader, after a long period of suffering . . . finally recovered from the effects of his severe wounds, and is now [circa 1871], . . . contentedly awaiting the next war to give him renewed excitement."[12]

In later years, the actions of Forsyth and the scouts were not uncommonly cited as examples of appropriate behavior for officers whose commands were forced to make a defensive stand. Captain Robert G. Carter of the 4th U.S. Cavalry, who was a veteran of the Indian wars, deplored the indecisiveness exhibited by Major Marcus A. Reno at the Battle of the Little Bighorn. Writing to author W. A. Graham in 1925, Carter unabashedly gave his assessment of the soldier Reno *should* have emulated: "What a force of good fighting . . . troops needed more than anything else," he stated, "was a leader with guts, fighting spirit, resourcefulness, and a cabeza on him that was not afflicted with 'nervous timidity.' Such was 'Sandy' [George A.] Forsythe [*sic*]."[13] Like Carter, others, particularly James B. Fry, Cyrus Townsend Brady, and Nelson A. Miles, further exploited the actions of the Beecher Island defenders.

Lost in this sensationalism was an evaluation of Sheridan's objective for organizing the Forsyth Scouts and sending them out in the field on the trail of large numbers of Indians. In actuality, Sheridan's Department of the Missouri suffered from a severe shortage of troops in the summer of 1868. Until Sheridan could justify the need for additional companies, he hoped that the swift-moving "ranger unit," created on the model of those he had used in the Civil War, could keep the Indians on the move and deep in their own territory, thus preventing them from raiding the Kansas settlements, railroad construction sites, and stage stations. In this regard Sheridan and Forsyth both succeeded and failed. The Battle of Beecher Island did not stop the raids. The Dog Soldiers stayed in Kansas during the fall and winter of 1868–1869 and continued their attacks on the whites. The defensive stand on the Arickaree did, however, call public attention to the need for additional troops and ensured that popular opinion would generally support Sheridan's projected winter campaign, which culminated with the Battle of the Washita in November.[14]

In September 1898, two survivors of the battle, Chalmers Smith and H. H. Tucker, and a former member of one of the three columns that came to the relief of Forsyth's command, James J. Peate, traveled by train from their homes near Beverly, Kansas, to Goodland, where they took a wagon the final distance to the site of the engagement. Barely recognizing the island at first, the three men sat down on the banks of the Arickaree, reminisced about the events of thirty years previous, and vowed to hold a reunion each year thereafter.[15] Thus was the genesis of the "Beecher Island Battle Memorial Association," officially incorporated August 7, 1903. As long as surviving scouts were able, reunions were held. George A. Forsyth attended the event in 1905 and gave a stirring speech for the dedication of a monument. Commemorations at the battlefield site have been held annually far into the twentieth century.[16]

With the help of Robert Lynam of Wray, Colorado, *The Beecher Island Annual* was published in 1905. When they could be found, surviving scouts were contacted and each was asked to contribute his story of the Beecher Island fight for the most recent printing of the *Annual*. Forsyth's somewhat zealous account, excerpted from his book, *Thrilling Days in Army Life* (1900), was reprinted in the *Annual*, as was an autobiography of Sigmund Shlesinger, the youngest member of the scouts who first told his story of the fight to E. A. Brininstool, one of the most prolific prerevisionist chroniclers of the Indian wars. Soon others were recording the scouts' tales for publication in books and journals. The siege at Beecher Island inspired two illuminating battlefield diaries, one a brief scribbled set of notes by Sigmund Shlesinger and the other a more detailed, articulate record by Chauncey B. Whitney. Until the present study, however, all of the available scout stories have not been examined together in a single work.

Although most of the scouts' reminiscences of the circumstances surrounding the battle are fairly objective, with major episodes effectively corroborated and the events reconstructed as the participants honestly remembered them, the rhetoric is predictably nationalistic in tone and has little consideration for the possibility of an indigenous point of view. Although the Battle of Beecher Island was fought in Colorado, the battle is inextricably linked to the struggle of whites to settle the rich lands of

Kansas. A majority of the Forsyth Scouts were settlers on the high plains and many were from the Saline Valley in western Kansas, the frontier line as it existed in 1868, where Kansas governor Samuel J. Crawford, a self-avowed Indian hater, had made monumental strides in boosting settlement in the 1860s despite raiding by the Cheyennes after the Sand Creek Massacre and the prolonged war with Red Cloud and the Sioux. Unlike many men in the regular army, stationed only temporarily in Indian country, these civilians reflected the extreme prejudices held by a majority of westerners of that time. These attitudes ran the gamut from advocating removal of recalcitrant Indians to reservations to their total extermination.

It seems that a number of the scouts, in later life, became enamored with the hero status that journalists and other writers heaped upon them. Forsyth and his men became, to some degree, symbols of glory to an appreciative, second-generation, white audience. That new audience actually grew in number over the years as the old veterans died. The Indian wars temporarily faded from memory but were then resurrected full-blown in popular legend for the entertainment of citizens born too late to participate in them. Consequently these tales of battle became integrated as one of the most, if not the most, central attractions of the colorful western myth.

If the two major army defensive actions of the post–Civil War Indian conflict, the Battle of the Little Bighorn in 1876 and the Fetterman Fight near Fort Phil Kearny a decade earlier, had not ended in the annihilation of the soldiers, it is doubtful that George A. Forsyth and the Battle of Beecher Island would have ever held such high esteem among those who remembered the Indian wars.

As early as 1913, objective criticism found its way into print. In that year, an article appeared in *Harper's Weekly* retelling the deeds and circumstances of the Battle of Beecher Island. Well written by correspondent Arthur Chapman, it was published complete with illustrations of Forsyth's defenses drawn by budding illustrator Maynard Dixon. Although he generally applauded the actions of the Forsyth Scouts, Chapman nevertheless stated, "It was due to the fact that the scouts were able to make a stand on slightly depressed ground, instead of on a hill, that

Forsyth's command was not annihilated, like the commands of Custer and Fetterman."[17]

Chapman applauded Forsyth's decision to retreat from his original position on the bank of the Arickaree and onto the island, but he inferred that from then on Forsyth was lucky. "Had Forsyth been caught on any of the high cliffs overlooking the Arickaree Valley," he wrote, "his defense, to use the words in which the Indians described Custer's fight, would have lasted 'about as long as it takes a hungry man to eat his breakfast.' "[18]

But in another sense Chapman's article had the effect of setting up Forsyth and the events of Beecher Island as a model for comparative evaluation of campaigns that were more controversial but less successful (for whites) in the Indian wars. That pattern of interpretation has continued somewhat, and the Beecher Island fight has emerged with a stereotype of being unique, desperate, and of course heroic.[19]

In his book *The Fighting Cheyennes* (1915), George Bird Grinnell, who had personally interviewed many of the old warriors, attempted to place the Beecher Island fight in a different perspective — that of the Cheyenne Dog Soldiers who fought there. Grinnell states that for the plains Indians "fights such as this were of frequent occurrence. Sometimes they were successful; sometimes they lost men, were beaten, and ran away. Whatever the event, they manifested neither special triumph in success, nor mortification at failure." The Forsyth Scouts were fighting against tremendous odds and thus, according to Grinnell, their points of view made the Battle of Beecher Island out to be a "vivid and thrilling story." But the "Cheyenne story," he asserted, "is quite different."[20]

Grinnell's main argument with the scouts' reminiscences was that the whites grossly exaggerated the number of Indian casualties. Early twentieth-century secondary sources presented readers with vivid accounts of disciplined and deadly accurate rifle fire from Forsyth's men in breaking the Indians' charges on the island, with only passing mention that the command possessed weaponry vastly superior to that of the Indians in the form of seven-shot Spencer carbines. The Cheyennes told Grinnell, however, that only nine warriors were killed from the various tribes participating in the battle. One must consider that a major factor contributing to the survival of Forsyth's command was the scouts' timely manner of entrenching themselves in rifle pits dug deep in the soft sand of the island. From that point the Indians pinned down the command until they finally broke off the action. Perhaps the most honest insight into the matter of Indian casualties rendered by a Forsyth Scout came from one of the late memoirs of Sigmund Shlesinger:

> I have often been asked whether I have killed any Indians, to which my answer must truthfully be, that I do not know. The conditions were such ... that I did not consider it safe to watch the results of a shot, the Indians being all around us, shooting at anything moving above ground. At one time I threw a hatful of sand [from] my pit to the top of the excavation, exposing myself more than usual, when a hail of bullets struck my hill ... almost blinding me. This will explain why I did not look for results![21]

We will probably never know how much of the source material collected by Grinnell actually came from the letters of George Bent, the mixed-blood son of trader William Bent and his Cheyenne wife, Owl Woman, but it is likely substantial, considering that Bent was one of Grinnell's important informants. A fairly literate writer, Bent gathered many stories from the old ones among his Cheyenne people on the reservation; he had, himself, participated in many episodes of the Indian wars. From 1905 almost until his death in 1918, Bent sent these letters to George E. Hyde, who eventually included much of the material in a manuscript that he sold to the Denver Public Library in 1930. Almost forty years later Savoie Lottinville edited and published the manuscript as *The Life of George Bent: Written From His Letters* (1968). Together with Grinnell's work, and a few stories collected by Cheyenne historian John Stands in Timber, we are fortunate indeed to have a highly respectable original portrait of the Battle of Beecher Island from the Indian perspective.

Bent concurred fully with Grinnell. "The whites," Bent asserted, "give this fight much importance, but the Indians take it as an ordinary incident." Like Grinnell, he placed the number of Indians killed in the battle at nine.[22] The most significant casualty, Bent wrote, was the highly respected Northern Cheyenne warrior Roman Nose, who was almost legendary as a brave man among his people even before his death at Beecher Island. Roman Nose hated the whites with a passion, having fought them in the Powder River country. In the spring of 1867 he had to be restrained by the Dog Soldiers from carrying out a boast to personally kill Major General Winfield Scott Hancock because he thought the officer too arrogant for his liking.

Despite a serious break in his "medicine" (protective benediction) before the Battle of Beecher Island (he unwittingly had eaten food touched by a metal fork, which he knew would result in his imminent death), he nevertheless led one of the charges on the scouts' position in the Arickaree. As foretold, the charge proved fatal. Recounting in oral tradition the story of the great warrior's broken medicine and the inevitable result, many Cheyennes afterward called the battle of Beecher Island "Where Roman Nose Was Killed."[23] Thus the esteemed Northern Cheyenne died fighting to protect the lands of his southern friends, the Dog Soldiers. In one sense, the current work is an integrated examination of the Dog Soldiers' struggle to retain their traditional hunting grounds and homelands in the Smoky Hill, Solomon, and Republican valleys of western Kansas and eastern Colorado.

By the 1960s and 1970s, studies of the Indian wars stressing the indigenous point of view were becoming common. In one sense, during that era of revisionism, which was fueled by the Vietnam controversy and an awakened Red power movement, popular points of view challenged the tone of the earlier, nationalistically inspired white writers. But in another sense, these studies merely echoed emotional pro-Indian sentiment first expressed by such early reformers as Helen Hunt Jackson. In essence, these new histories treated the vexing subject of Indian-white relationships with the same methodology as the old histories: by drawing conclusions expressed in moral and judgmental terms. The heroes and villains were simply reversed.[24] According to historian David Fridtjof Halaas, it was not only unpopular but unwise to write about the subject in terms other than pro-Indian. "Ubiquitous in these [revisionist histories]," he stated, "was the by-now obligatory litany of sins committed by white missionaries, Indian agents, politicians, military leaders, and Protestant reformers. Evil and sinister motives lurked behind every white action, while the Indians were seen as helpless victims of a superior technology. To write otherwise was to invite charges of racism."[25]

During this time, Beecher Island fared well compared with events such as the Sand Creek Massacre, which more defensibly cast whites as transgressors. Nevertheless, the scouts' tales were overshadowed in favor of the Indians' side of the story. One of the more balanced accounts of the battle written during this period is found in Donald J. Berthrong, *The Southern Cheyennes* (1963). William H. Leckie aimed at objectivity in *The Military Conquest of the Southern Plains* (1963). Unfortunately, because these scholars' books survey much broader topics, their accounts of the Beecher Island affair and associated events are all too brief considering the wealth of interesting original material available to them.

In the wake of the Vietnam era, the Indian wars as a topic of inquiry fell on hard times, both critically and in terms of the numbers of high-quality original works produced. Instead, scholars favored and welcomed much-needed interpretations of Indian history that examined topics other than warfare between Indian warriors and white soldiers. In essence "Indian history" and "western military history," for all practical purposes, became two distinct fields of study, with the former having, on balance, a bit more serious interest and respect among scholars.

To be sure, a few highly regarded historians such as Robert M. Utley, Francis Paul Prucha, Jerome Greene, and, more recently, Paul Andrew Hutton have kept the story of the frontier army and its conflict with Native Americans alive. They have integrated well the significance of the conflict into western history with their well-balanced, scholarly research. Overall, these scholars have avoided judgmental interpretations of their subjects yet have extended the scope of the topic to include congressional and Indian Bureau politics and policymaking.[26] Prucha in particular, wrote David Fridtjof Halaas, "dared to challenge the Indian history revisionists and their underlying assumptions of Native American good-ness and white badness . . . Prucha was fighting for a principle that should have been established long before the right to see beyond simplistic moral judgements and to write to understand, not condemn, the actions of both whites and Indians in the nineteenth century."[27]

In the late 1980s, a new wave of revisionism began to overtake the field of western history. Dubbed the "New Western History," this point of view, which might now be categorized fairly as a legitimate school of interpretation, stresses a continuity between frontier history and the directions that the region has developed or continued through the twentieth century. Beliefs central to this thesis are that the West is a place rather than a process and that Frederick Jackson Turner's ethnocentric, highly nationalistic Frontier Thesis is inadequate in explaining the diversity of directions initiated by a multiplicity of cultural and ethnic groups and women in the West, beginning in the nineteenth century and continuing into the twentieth. Although to conceive of western history as a continuum (thus eliminating the sharp division of "frontier" and modern history marked by the year 1890) may be an innovative approach, to point out Turner's shortcomings, and the extensive list of atrocities committed by pioneers against the environment, is nothing new, as the name of this interpretative field suggests. It is too soon to know what impact, if any, this new wave of revisionists will have in the long run on the views of western history and the military frontier.[28]

One transcending aspect of western history, however, is the continued presence of Native Americans. Like Turner, Indians remain somewhat of an enigma and always will. Neither did Indians totally assimilate during the twentieth century, as many thought would happen. Thus in a very different, nonviolent, yet equally significant way, a number of the yet unsolved "Indian problems" facing Indian-white relations today are not all that far removed from those differences that separated Roman Nose from George A. Forsyth on the Arickaree in September 1868. The New Western historians stress the importance of cultural relativism, and they warn us not to be ethnocentric. Indeed, the field of Indian-white relations, especially military history, has been both intentionally and unintentionally riddled with ethnocentric studies. Well-meaning white scholars, sincerely intent on presenting an unbiased viewpoint, or the Indian side of the story, frequently do not possess the cultural perspective of a long relationship or acculturation with indigenous societies to accomplish the task adequately.

What then of the Native American scholar? A New Western historian wrote,

> What if Indian people are now so certain of their injuries that they want condemnation and blame explicit in the writing of their history? . . . The historian, annoyed by the ethnocentricity of earlier frontier history, might still have the impulse to 'take the Indian's side.' But the impulse offers no escape from ethnocentricity; the very notion of 'the Indian side of the story' requires one to hold resolutely to the Euro-American angle of vision, by which Indian diversity flattens out into one, simple story. . . . When tribe fought tribe, with or without whites in the picture, where was 'the Indian side' to be found?[29]

The challenge to reexamine traditional sources and to question old conclusions on a nonjudgmental basis requires historians to set aside the outworn simplistic assumptions of barbarism versus the concept of the noble savage as a basis for understanding and evaluating the motivations of both Indians and white frontiersmen. These notions, in one way or another, have traditionally crept into many interpretations of the Indian wars. Such notions, believes Francis Paul Prucha, are misleading in the present day: "While no one seems to doubt that Indian culture was distinctly different from that of whites," Prucha wrote, "precious few writers have acknowledged that nineteenth-century white culture was significantly different from that of the present. To begin to comprehend the nature of white-Indian relations, it is necessary to understand *two* quite different cultures from our own."[30]

Two revisionist historians of the 1980s and 1990s, William Cronon and Richard White, likewise attempt to understand Indian ways rather than adhere to old judgmental beliefs. The Euro-American idea that the Indian lived "in harmony with nature," they assert, denies to Indian people certain attributes of the human cultural condition. They point to how Indians utilized fire to reshape the landscape for agriculture and other cultural activities. "The Indians *killed* animals," stated White. "They often overhunted animals. . . . What's hardest for us to understand . . . is the Indians' different way of making sense of species and the natural world in general . . . we have to move beyond these notions of 'noble savages' and

'Indians as the original ecologists,' " Cronon added. "We have to look instead to how they actually lived."[31] Halaas concurred: "The public's current image of the saddened Indian," he wrote, "eyes glistening with tears while viewing white-caused pollution, may have as little to do with reality as did the Indian head nickel [the portrait of the noble savage] of nineteenth-century fame."[32]

A more recent work of monumental proportions that incorporates new themes is Father Peter John Powell's two-volume study *People of the Sacred Mountain:A History of the Northern Cheyenne Chiefs and Warrior Societies, 1830–1879, With an Epilogue, 1969–1974* (1981). "Moral judgements have little place in Powell's account," wrote Halaas. "The Cheyennes fight as they know how, while the whites and other enemies of the People [the Cheyenne name for their tribe] fight according to their standards of combat."[33]

As the lives and culture of Indian people are currently being reexamined on a nonjudgmental basis, so too are the roles of white soldiers in the Indian wars. A study of importance is Sherry L. Smith's *The View From Officer's Row: Army Perceptions of Western Indians* (1990). Smith concluded in her study that officers, and their wives, did not share monolithic and negative views of the Indians they fought. Instead, many officers developed great respect for Indian people and their cultures; some, like George Crook, came to question Indian policy, some expressed personal misgivings about their roles in the Indian wars, and some even openly sympathized with their old enemies.

However, Smith concluded, these officers saw themselves as "civilization's guardians," who not only protected whites from Indians but also protected Indians from "the white world's own baser elements, who, if left unchecked, would wipe out the Indians."[34] Of major importance here is the philosophy of Social Darwinism, which made its way west during the later years of the nineteenth century. This belief helps explain frightened settlers' demands for Indian extermination and motivations for reformers' costly programs for assimilation. It also illuminates the reasoning of the military in their insistence to "take up the White man's burden," as Kipling delineated that aspect of Social Darwinism, and fight Indians for the purpose of protecting their race while simultaneously destroying their native culture. Viewing themselves as the vanguard of civilization in the wilderness, frontier officers stood together in their belief that the Indian was an impediment to "progress" as white industrializing America defined it.

The "classic statement of this view," Smith wrote, was provided by none other than Lieutenant Colonel George A. Forsyth when he asserted around the turn of the century that although "the Indian has been wronged, and deeply wronged, by bad white men, it must always be borne in mind that, cruel as the aphorism is, 'the survival of the fittest' is a truism that cannot be ignored nor gainsaid and barbarism must necessarily give way before advancing civilization."[35] Unfortunately, much of the casual interpretation of the Indian wars has been an unilluminated attempt to either justify or dispute Forsyth's words.

But the Indian wars were not solely a contest among policymakers in Washington and on the reservations and among soldiers and Indians on the battlefield. The conflict also involved the beliefs and actions of settlers, whose attitudes and prejudices toward Indians were often far more passionate than those of the military. Often these settlers have been pictured as innocent victims of the Indian wars — conflicts in large part begun because of their presence. Indeed, the fears of the isolated settlers in prereservation years were very real, and from their point of view Indian removal or extermination were acceptable alternatives to remedy that fear.

The Battle of Beecher Island and the Indian War of 1867–1869 in general serve as an excellent case study for a fresh look at the Indian wars. There is indeed a wealth of journalism from various times portraying the exploits of Forsyth and his scouts over the nine grueling days on the Arickaree. In addition, the public reaction to the fight inspired many personal reminiscences by original participants, both Indian and white. For this reason, and whenever possible, I have endeavored to let the original participants speak for themselves in this work. Inherent will be their biases and prejudices, their view of politics and the environment, and the diverse futures both societies envisioned for the world around them. Their struggle was not one of good versus evil but rather one of opposite viewpoints, both practical and cultural, in regard to the course of that future.

Historian Gerald Nash argues that each generation of western historians since 1890 has interpreted western history in terms of its own prejudices and biases. He asserts that these interpretations are as important in shaping the mythology of western history as the historical events they have written about. The result is a judgmental view of the past that is highly ethnocentric when the differences in values between nineteenth-century and twentieth-century Americans are considered.[36] It is my intent that the reader understand not only events but also the motivations of soldiers and Indians as well as each civilian group of participants. For this reason I view the human interest of my subject in a somewhat categorical manner and consequently do not always adhere to a strict chronological approach, favoring instead a presentation of the experiences of each group over the span of the Indian War of 1867–1869. Although actions undertaken by individuals and groups are evaluated as to their effectiveness, I do not consciously seek to *judge* the overall cultural mores and values of the antagonists in this conflict.

Many of the events preceding the Battle of Beecher Island, such as the so-called Hancock-Custer Campaign of 1867, and the events following the fight on the Arickaree, such as the Battles of the Washita and Summit Springs, have been well documented by others. It is not my intent to rehash them in minute detail. Instead I have stressed their relationships to the Dog Soldiers' struggle to retain their lands in western Kansas, to the causes and effects of the Battle of Beecher Island, and in respect to the backgrounds of some of the antagonists who fought in that engagement.

My understanding of things Indian is necessarily filtered through Caucasian eyes, and any and all errors are completely mine. The main challenge I have posed for myself is this: How can we come to understand events of the past more completely if we do not, on occasion, attempt to view those events in new and different ways? Historian Patricia Nelson Limerick once wrote that, "of course, Indian people can and should write their own histories according to their traditions, just as pioneers and their descendants have every right to publish books enshrining their own versions of the past. For the sake of national and regional self-understanding, however, there should be a group of people reading all these books and paying attention to all these points of view. In that process,

Western historians will not reach a neutral omniscient objectivity. On the contrary," Limerick emphasizes, "the clashes and conflicts of western history will always leave the serious individual emotionally and intellectually unsettled. In the nineteenth-century West, speaking out for the human dignity of all parties to the conflicts took considerable nerve. It still does."[37]

It is in this spirit that I have endeavored to undertake this study.

The Road to War   1

I have heard that a great many Indians want to fight; very well, we are
here, and are come prepared for war.

— MAJOR GENERAL WINFIELD SCOTT HANCOCK
addressing the headmen of the Dog Soldiers
Fort Larned, Kansas, April 12, 1867

On a warm evening in late September 1868, Major Henry Inman
sat quietly in his office at Fort Harker, Kansas, "musing over a pipeful of
'Lone Jack.' "[1] He was thinking about Major General Philip Sheridan's
impending winter campaign against the southern plains tribes, some
details of which had been planned in the seclusion of Inman's quarters
the previous night. Darkness was slowly falling over the unbroken Kansas
prairie, flanking the Smoky Hill River in present-day Ellsworth County.
Nothing that evening save the monotonous clicking of the telegraph relay
in the next room had disturbed Inman's revery. With little to do he sat
watching out his window as the last tinge of purple twilight departed the
western sky. His mind wandered off to rivers farther south — the Arkansas,
the Cimarron, the Canadian — that were so soon to be the scene of
military operations. Off in the distance the "dismal howl of a hungry wolf
[was] borne upon the still air from the timbered recesses of the Smoky."[2]

Suddenly the clicking from the telegraph speeded up and then became
frantic. "My God! Major, what's this?" the excited clerk shouted.

"What is what?" Inman said, jumping from his chair and rushing to
his side.[3]

The clerk quickly lit another oil lamp, seized a pencil, and — with
Major Inman looking over his shoulder — began writing down the
incoming message, as the clicking of the relay "grew more convulsive."[4]

"Forsythe [*sic*] surrounded by Indians on the Republican," he wrote. "Lieut. Beecher, the doctor, and many of the scouts killed; nearly the entire command, including [Forsyth], wounded. Stillwell, one of the scouts, ran the gauntlet of the savages, and brings report. Col. Carpenter, Tenth Cavalry, and his command, leave immediately to relieve them."[5]

Shortly the story of the Beecher Island fight found its way into eastern newspapers. Readers marveled at reports avowing the courage of fifty civilian scouts from the Kansas settlements and their commander, Major George Alexander Forsyth. Reports described how this highly mobile but small ranger unit had been assigned the momentous task of seeking out bands of Indian warriors, possibly many times their own size, and keeping them on the move in such a way as to prevent them from raiding settlements on the central plains frontier. An appreciative public learned how the little command, on September 17, had been attacked by hundreds of Indians. They read the story of how the scouts had taken refuge on a small sand island in the middle of the Arickaree Fork of the Republican River in northeastern Colorado Territory and there held off several concerted charges from a combined force of Sioux, Dog Soldiers, and a few Northern and Southern Cheyennes and Arapahoes.

For nine arduous days the brave little group was pinned on the island with their wounded. Casualties approached 45 percent. Forsyth himself had sustained three wounds but had not failed to do his duty. The surgeon, Dr. J. H. Mooers, and First Lieutenant Frederick H. Beecher had been mortally wounded early in the fight. By the end of the siege, the men had been reduced to eating the putrefied flesh of their horses, which had been killed early in the engagement. Rescue came only after two separate pairs of scouts had made their way through enemy lines for over one hundred miles to Fort Wallace. On at least one occasion, two of the men hid for the daylight hours inside the rotting carcass of a buffalo to avoid certain detection by nearby warriors. Following their rescue, Forsyth and the other wounded men were hospitalized at Fort Wallace, Kansas. It was the stuff of heroism.

In 1868 there were few war correspondents in the nation better qualified to scoop such a dramatic tale from the battlefield than DeBenneville Randolph Keim. At age twenty-seven, Keim was already a veteran newspaperman for the prestigious *New York Herald*. During the Civil War he had witnessed and reported on no less than twenty-six battles for the *Herald*. He had been with Grant at Vicksburg and developed a close friendship with the famous general. He had marched with Sherman during the Atlanta campaign and had been there before Richmond in 1865 to report on the final engagements.[6]

Born to an old and distinguished Pennsylvania family, Keim chose his profession early in life, even dropping out of college because he considered excessive education to be detrimental to becoming a journalist. Allegedly he once quipped to some colleagues that he never read Shakespeare because he feared that the great playwright's prose would impede his own writing style.[7] Confident, self-assured, and opinionated, Keim complemented the thoroughly Victorian personalities of the many career officers that he followed into battle for the *Herald*.

There is no question that Keim was in agreement with the sentiments of his editor and publisher, James Gordon Bennett, Jr., regarding the necessity of a military solution to the "Indian problem" on the western plains. Consequently, in modern terms the reader recognizes his rhetoric about Indians as patronizing and racist. Keim held to a strict, almost Calvinistic belief in the conquest of savagery by civilization. Such notions were viewed not only as morally right but inevitable. And in his convictions as well as his journalism Keim mirrored the attitudes of most non-Indian Americans of the mid-nineteenth century.[8]

Assimilation or extermination of native tribesmen was the only realistic alternative to the "problem," with the former holding much greater weight in the post–Civil War years among those citizens living in the East or apart from the frontier. The only question was, who should administer the policy of assimilation: the civilian Indian Bureau or the War Department? The answer was obvious as far as Keim was concerned. He had made too many friends and acquaintances in the great encampments of his nation's greatest war. Soldiers, not politicians, were his heroes, and he portrayed them as such in his writing. The evidence that military power had been necessary for the industrial forces of modern civilization inevitably to displace forever the archaic slave establishment of the backward-looking South was both cause and justification for Keim and men like him to advocate a similar solution in dealing with the last impediments to Judeo-Christian progress — the Indians of America's final frontier. In essence, the military in the West had nothing to fear from the pen of DeB. Randolph Keim.[9]

A week after the rescue of the Forsyth Scouts, Keim hurriedly made his way west from Fort Hays to interview them. Officially he was in Kansas to cover Sheridan's impending winter campaign, but a chance for a firsthand interview with the scouts sent him to Fort Wallace. On the trip west from Hays, Keim became enthralled with the sights and sounds of the frontier. But of his fellow passengers aboard the Union Pacific Eastern Division coach, which included two army wives, he wrote, "A fiercer, hirsute, and unwashed set I never saw."[10]

Fifteen miles west of Hays, Keim observed from the coach that the grasslands were blackened with buffalo. The sound of the wood-burning locomotive startled the animals, causing them to stampede across the tracks. One bull didn't make it. The locomotive's cowcatcher struck the angry buffalo head on and tossed the beast into a trackside ditch. Turned on its back, the struggling animal began kicking furiously. The train then stopped to allow passengers the opportunity to cut choice meaty humps from other animals they had shot from the windows of the moving train. With several other passengers, Keim started down the tracks to finish the wounded bull, which was now enraged and still pawing frantically in the ditch. One shot brought the angry beast to its feet. Putting its head down, and bleeding at the mouth, the bull charged the passengers. Taking cover in the trackside ditch, Keim's party put enough bullets into the animal to finally kill it. By then the conductor signaled that it was time to leave, and the animal was left where it fell.[11] Back aboard the coach, Keim recorded that he felt "a pang of shame" that the carcass was left on the prairie — a "useless waste."[12] But if the correspondent entertained any thoughts that similar, more extensive, slaughter of the buffalo might have been a contributing cause to the current Indian war, he did not write about it.

The next day Keim arrived at Fort Wallace, where a visit from such a representative from civilization was viewed as "a rare and important event in the daily routine of the garrison."[13] Soon he was at Forsyth's bedside conducting an interview. Then he moved on to the scouts' camp and took down their story of the recent fight. Keim's report of the battle agrees with Forsyth's later accounts, although there is considerable variation in the sequence of events.[14] Keim, the first acclaimed writer to tell the Beecher Island story to the outside world, initiated a popular fascination with the battle. He began the process of enshrining the Forsyth Scouts as heroes, a trend that would continue for at least the next century, and in so doing played down any other historical significance this relatively minor military engagement may have had in the chronicle of the Indian wars on the central plains.[15]

Keim called Forsyth's defensive victory a "brilliant and heroic achievement" and an illumination of the "desperate character of warfare on the plains."[16] On October 6, Major General Philip Sheridan arrived at Fort Wallace to personally offer his congratulations to Forsyth. According to witnesses, the commander of the Department of the Missouri could not hold back his emotions as he sat at the bedside of his trusted aide.[17] After spending some time with Sheridan, Keim recognized the immediate significance of the Beecher Island fight: "The warm reception which greeted Forsyth's little band . . . had the effect of increasing, to the highest degree, the determination of the Commanding General to punish the refractory tribes . . . to reduce them to such a condition of feebleness and fear that they would see the folly of opposition and be content to remain upon their reservations."[18] After Beecher Island, Sheridan, and probably a sizable proportion of the public as well, had no doubt that a winter campaign against the warring bands of Indians was justified because the campaign would take place at a time of year when the Indians' food was scarce and their ponies weak.

The 7th Cavalry's subsequent victory at Black Kettle's village on the Washita River in November (vividly reported by DeB. Randolph Keim), combined with Major Eugene Asa Carr's resounding destruction of the Dog Soldiers at Summit Springs, Colorado, on July 11, 1869, went far in breaking Indian resistance on the central and southern plains. Only the Red River War in 1874 and 1875, and the dramatic Dull Knife and Little Wolf raids through Kansas in 1878, would again occupy such attention south of the Platte as did the campaigns of 1868 to 1869.[19]

Indirectly, these offensive campaigns sputtered into action when the Forsyth Scouts took the field to seek out Indian raiders in the autumn of 1868 and when an ill-fated expedition against the Southern Cheyennes south of the Arkansas was led by Lieutenant Colonel (Brevet Brigadier General) Alfred Sully of the 7th Cavalry. Although the subsequent winter foray culminating with the Battle of the Washita was not totally decisive, the major goals were nevertheless well on their way to being achieved. With the Republican River Expedition the following summer, which came to a head with the Battle of Summit Springs on July 11, whites finally expelled the Indians (most importantly the Dog Soldiers) from the central corridor in Kansas and Colorado between the Platte and Arkansas rivers, thus providing security for settlers and construction crews on the Pacific railroads.

After Washita especially, never again would any warrior on the plains feel safe from attack during the winter months. Although it is likely that these events would still have occurred had the Battle of Beecher Island never been fought, the engagement on the Arickaree nevertheless served as an emotional catalyst to justify them, and to persuade many that a vigorous military policy supported by a revamped Indian Bureau, under the control of the War Department, was the solution to the so-called Indian problem.[20]

From the emotional viewpoint of the white soldiers, Beecher Island was in a sense the genesis of conclusion to the raiding and warfare that raged in Kansas and Colorado between the Platte and Arkansas rivers between 1867 and 1869. But what of the war's origins, the events that touched off the hostilities beginning in 1867 and a year later brought Major George A. Forsyth with Lieutenant Beecher and fifty civilian scouts to the headwaters of the Republican River?

As proved true with so many other currents in American history, the Civil War was the great watershed for the nation's final thrust westward during the last decades of the nineteenth century, and with it the ultimate demise of the plains tribes. During the war years, Congress passed two pieces of legislation that proved catastrophic for nomadic indigenous societies. First was the Homestead Act of 1862, which evidenced the belief that the remaining frontier would be settled in 160-acre plots. This assumption was highly optimistic from a scientific viewpoint given the aridity of the country roughly west of the one-hundredth meridian. But its emotional impact was far greater than its scientific reality.

In the thirty years after the Civil War, more land became peopled and put into cultivation than in all of America's previous history. As northern industry turned from wartime to peacetime production, agricultural technology rapidly advanced and became affordable for the average farmer faced with the reality of having to cultivate greater acreage in the arid West in order to achieve an adequate crop yield. With free land, inexpensive equipment, and ready markets back East, incentives existed for what became one of the great movements of peoples in world history.[21]

The second important piece of legislation passed by Congress during the war was the Pacific Railroad Act of 1862 (amended in 1864). That fateful bill, long blocked by the passions of sectionalism, provided the most important stimulus for westward migration by linking would-be settlers to their markets. In essence, the railroad law, along with the Homestead Act, opened extensive settlement of the Great Plains by simply legislating out of existence, at least psychologically, the notion of an uninhabitable land that explorer Stephen Long once called "the Great American Desert."[22]

Not only the federal government but also the railroads, the state, and private land companies all beat the drums to boost settlement. During the 1860s settlers filed on about six million acres in Kansas.[23] By 1870, the population of Kansas had increased 239.9 percent over the preceding decade. Population density was up from 1.3 persons per mile to 4.5. West of the ninety-sixth meridian, five counties had a density ratio above 5. Between 1861 and 1873, a total of thirty-five new counties were added to the map of Kansas, as pioneers crept ever closer to the one-hundredth meridian.[24]

In 1867 the frontier line in northwestern Kansas lay roughly halfway between the ninety-eighth and ninety-ninth meridians with the counties of Jewell, Mitchell, Lincoln, and Ellsworth all being created in that year on a north-to-south axis.[25] In Mitchell County, some twenty miles southeast of the settlements at White Rock, there was a salt and mineral spring, more than sixty feet in diameter, located in a mound that rose more than thirty feet above the surrounding prairie. The Pawnees knew it as Waconda Spring, and it was sacred to them as well as their enemies, the Cheyennes and Arapahoes.[26] It was called the "Spirit Spring" by some of the Indians and came to serve as a symbolic dividing line between eastern and western Kansas. The spring became a point of contact for the Sioux and Northern Cheyennes to the north, the Southern Cheyennes and Southern Arapahoes to the south and west, and the Pawnees to the east. West of Waconda Spring were the Solomon, Saline, and Republican valleys, the favorite camping grounds of the Dog Soldiers and the roving bands of Sioux and other northern plains tribes who befriended them.

By 1868 fingers of white settlement protruded up the Saline and Solomon river valleys to the forks of the Republican, and it is entirely possible that the Cheyennes, Arapahoes, and Sioux declared a "deadline" to further westward intrusion by whites along this line of counties, as they had done long previous for their traditional enemies the Pawnees, Kaws, and Osages. The deadline ran to the Arkansas River in the south and to the land of the Kiowas and Comanches.[27]

Indeed, the vast majority of Indian raids in the state between 1867 and 1869 occurred in this northwestern quadrant of Kansas, from White Rock Creek on the east to the forks and upper reaches of the Smoky Hill, Saline, Solomon, and Republican rivers to the west.[28] To protect advancing settlement, the military in Kansas added to the already existing military posts of Forts Leavenworth, Riley, Zarah (1864), Kirwin (1865), Harker (1864), Hays (1865), and Wallace (1865), the last three being located near the Smoky Hill route of the projected Union Pacific Eastern Division Railroad. Down in the Arkansas Valley were Forts Larned (1859) and Dodge (1865), and New Fort Lyon (1867) across the state line in Colorado Territory.[29] North, in Nebraska along the Platte River, Forts Kearny (1848) and McPherson (1863) ostensibly would protect construction of the Union Pacific main line building west from Omaha.[30]

Even before the agricultural frontier pushed into western Kansas, the rush for "Pike's Peak Gold," the birth of Denver City in 1858, and the eventual establishment of Colorado Territory in 1861 had created a swift and formidable barrier against the plains tribes. After the Treaty of Fort Wise in 1861, Denver's agricultural hinterland gradually pushed eastward.

The Cheyennes and Arapahoes found themselves caught between the settlers pushing westward from Kansas and a similar group of homesteaders who found their markets in the mining camps and service towns of Colorado Territory pushing from the opposite direction. The Colorado immigrants took out choice homesteads along the rich strip of real estate flanking the front range of the Rockies, a country blessed by temperate winter chinooks, a land that attracted both the buffalo and the Indians during the harsh seasons of the year.[31]

During the earliest years of the Colorado gold rush, the Indians let emigrants to the mining camps move relatively unmolested across the central plains corridor. But, as was bound to happen, misunderstandings took place. As passenger traffic increased along both the South Platte Trail into Denver from Nebraska, and later across the Smoky Hill route in Kansas, tensions increased. Freighters from the towns along the Missouri River literally kept Denver alive before the arrival of the railroad in 1870. Supplies and livestock were vital to the isolated Colorado Territory, particularly after it was devastated by fire and flood in 1863 and 1864. With a decrease in production from the mines by this time, coupled by an increase in already high wartime prices, tensions mounted. In the end, the people of the new territory, seeing their future growth checked, took out their frustrations on the most visible human element they saw as an impediment to that growth, the Indians. In the spring of 1864 war broke out between whites and the Southern Cheyennes and Arapahoes arguably when immigrants reported two cases of cattle theft by the Indians; Territorial Governor John Evans sent out provincial troops more to punish the violators than to simply investigate the incidents.[32]

On April 12, at a place called Fremont's Orchard on the South Platte Trail near the modern town of Fort Morgan, Colorado, and again on May 16, along the Smoky Hill, forces of the 1st Colorado Cavalry under the command of Lieutenant Clark Dunn, and soldiers of an independent battery of artillery under Lieutenant George S. Eayre, respectively, engaged the Indians. The later incident was particularly eventful because the conflict started with the killing of an esteemed Cheyenne peace chief, Starving Bear (Lean Bear), who had always prided himself on his peaceful relations with the whites. It is generally believed that Eayre was out to provoke trouble; his men killed Starving Bear when he rode forward to talk with the soldiers.[33]

The troops engaged in these actions were members of volunteer militia regiments organized during the war to protect the territory from both Indians and Confederate invaders. They were under the command of Colonel John M. Chivington of Denver, an ordained Methodist minister. Dubbed "the fighting parson," Chivington had requested a field commission at the outbreak of the Civil War. His flanking movement (as a major) of Sibley's Confederates in March 1862 at the Battle of La Glorieta Pass near Santa Fe, New Mexico Territory, had elevated him to the status of war hero, and he was made commander of Colorado volunteer regiments. Chivington also had strong political ambitions in what local Denver city fathers optimistically believed would soon be the state of Colorado. Along with Territorial Governor John Evans and others, the government gave high priority to Indian removal, a condition the territorial leaders viewed tantamount to admission to statehood. William N. Byers, the founder and publisher of the territory's first newspaper, the *Rocky Mountain News*, editorialized for "a few months of active extermination against the red devils."[34]

These "boosters" of civilization were successful in swaying public opinion toward a policy of severely punishing the plains tribes. This opinion intensified when white settlers brought into Denver and put on public display the mutilated bodies of the Ward Hungate family, homesteaders presumably killed by Indians only thirty miles east of town. When this event was compounded by stories of the Sioux outbreak of 1862 in Minnesota, hysteria spread through Denver as retaliation by the Indians for the killing of Starving Bear begot further retaliation by the whites. Evans authorized the recruitment of the 3rd Colorado Volunteers from among the local population of Denver and Boulder. Many of these recruits held the general attitudes of most whites in Colorado Territory in 1864; that is, they were avowed Indian haters who either held personal grudges for murdered family or friends, or figured they had been hurt in some manner because of Indian depredations.[35]

In any event, according to their particular code of right versus wrong these men felt completely justified in their beliefs. There was little stigma attached to the killing of Indians. Besides, public opinion supported their actions. In little over a month, this militia fought three separate engagements with the Cheyennes, burned four Indian villages, and killed a number of Cheyenne people, including the peace chief Starving Bear.[36]

Then on September 28, at Camp Weld near Denver, Governor Evans, Colonel Chivington, and several others held council with seven peace chiefs and respected leaders of the Cheyennes and Arapahoes, including Black Kettle and the Dog Soldier Bull Bear. Evans gave the chiefs a conflicting set of instructions, which some of them, particularly Black Kettle, took to mean that they could live at peace with the whites near Old Fort Lyon (Fort Wise). In 1864 Bull Bear was the recognized leader of the Dog Soldiers; he was also the brother of the slain Starving Bear. Still he sought peace and even offered to help the whites fight against the Sioux. "I am with you and the troops to fight all those who have no ears to listen to what you say," Bull Bear said to Evans. "I have never harmed a white man. I am pushing for something good . . . I have given my word to fight with the whites. My brother died in trying to keep peace with the whites. I am willing to die in the same way, and expect to do so."[37]

But in response, and with military, public, and journalistic support solidly behind him, Chivington's troops attacked the village of Black Kettle in the early morning light of November 29. Chivington returned home a hero, and most Coloradoans were long in learning the truth. The volunteers killed mostly women and children at Sand Creek, and they scalped and horribly mutilated most of the bodies. The whites were unable to relate to the Indians in anything other than the definition of "an eye for an eye." To them the Cheyennes were savages, perhaps the murderers of their relatives. They considered the Indians just another brutal element of the totally uncivilized environment they were trying to conquer and, as such, viewed them in a fundamental religious sense as a pestilence in the land.

Many of them saw the Indians as culturally unfit, not the equals of civilized human beings. The whites viewed their own roles as civilizing agents to be part of a great destiny manifest to them from the Almighty. Consequently, many whites condoned wanton killing for the same reason they destroyed dangerous wild beasts without hesitation should they roam too close to the settlements and family homesteads. As with the hunting of game animals, Chivington's avengers took trophies. Eyewitnesses who turned against Chivington at two subsequent investigations gave affadavits describing in gruesome detail how the volunteers wantonly murdered infants, scalped women, and cut off their "private parts," which they displayed on sticks or "stretched . . . over the horns of their saddles" or used to make "tobacco pouches."[38]

The Sand Creek Massacre ignited a fury in the Dog Soldiers' camps. In 1865 they joined in a series of raids of revenge with other Cheyennes, Arapahoes, and Sioux and spread a reign of pillage in Colorado and Kansas as far east as Clay County, not far from the modern town of Manhattan, Kansas.[39] On two separate occasions the Indians raided and burned the freight station of Julesburg, Colorado Territory, on the South Platte, killing approximately forty whites. Preying on freighters, they successfully blockaded Denver. From that time forward, the Dog Soldiers swore never to surrender their hunting grounds in the Republican Valley. Thus they refused even to send representatives to the peace talks that got under way in August 1865 at the mouth of the Little Arkansas River.[40]

The Sand Creek Massacre convinced many in Washington, including President Andrew Johnson, that the government should inaugurate something more humane than a brutal military solution to the "Indian problem." Those favoring a peaceful, civilian-coordinated policy were Secretary of the Interior Orville H. Browning, Nathaniel G. Taylor, who was head of the Indian Bureau, and two members of the Senate committee on Indian affairs, James R. Doolittle and John B. Henderson.[41] In the summer of 1865, Doolittle along with associates from both houses of Congress set out for Denver to get the peace talks moving.

Operating under the official sanction of a joint congressional committee examining "the conditions of the Indian tribes," Colorado territorial governor John Evans greeted the committee in July. In the very Denver theater where Cheyenne scalps had been displayed after Sand Creek, Governor Evans, likely aware of what would be the reaction of his constituency, proudly introduced Doolittle to a capacity audience. Looking very much like the distinguished U.S. senator that he was, Doolittle gave a speech calling for reform in dealing with Indians. To illustrate a point, Doolittle posed the question to the crowd of whether the Indians should be placed on reservations and humanely taught to support themselves within the white culture or simply and efficiently be exterminated at considerable government expense. To Doolittle's surprise, "there suddenly arose," he recalled, "such a shout as is never heard unless upon some battle field; — a shout almost loud enough to raise the roof of the Opera House. — 'Exterminate them! Exterminate them!' "[42]

Doolittle's rebuff by the citizens of Denver illustrates the polarization over Indian policy that many westerners and easterners had reached by the late 1860s. Still, the reservation system offered to the government the only acceptable basis for a sound policy. The remaining question was who would carry out the task of assimilating the Indians. As far as Doolittle and his associates were concerned, the military possessed neither the talent nor the inclination for such functions. This belief justified retaining the Indian Bureau within the Department of the Interior.[43] For the time being, Doolittle's position on the matter prevailed. On October 14, 1865, Black Kettle and a few other Cheyenne and Arapahoe peace chiefs, representing only eighty lodges, affixed their marks to the Treaty of the Little Arkansas. Other tribes of the southern plains, the Comanches and Kiowas, concluded a similar treaty. Accordingly, the chiefs agreed to give up their Colorado hunting grounds and to accept a reservation located partially in the Indian Territory (Oklahoma) and partially in Kansas. Although they could range over their former lands on the annual buffalo hunts, they agreed not to disturb the immigrant roads, towns, and forts of the white people. The government agreed to pay annuities to the Indians for forty years.[44]

Although the peace chiefs told the whites they could not speak for those warriors who did not attend the peace talks, and that they could not exercise authority over the decisions of the warrior societies (especially the Dog Soldiers), the agreement on the Little Arkansas River brought a few months of tenuous peace. At the urging of the aging trader William Bent, a lifelong friend of the Indians, other chiefs signed the treaty in 1866. Agent to the Cheyennes and Arapahoes, Edward Wansear Wynkoop felt confident that he had persuaded some of the Dog Soldiers to cease their raids altogether that summer. In the end, however, the new treaty, negotiated at President Johnson's insistence in the wake of the Sand Creek Massacre, solved nothing because the new reservations never materialized. The control of the Texas legislature over its lands nullified the agreement with the Comanches and Kiowas, and the state of Kansas refused to allow a new reservation within its borders. Congress, more concerned with asserting its position with Reconstruction in the defeated South, let the matter slide for two years.[45]

This was the state of affairs when on July 28, 1866, Congress attempted to remedy the other policy disaster brought to light by the Sand Creek Massacre, that of trusting military affairs to state and territorial volunteer militias like the Colorado "Bloody Third" composed chiefly of citizens intent on exterminating Indians. Congress authorized four new regiments of regular U.S. Cavalry that day, the 7th through the 10th, who were charged with keeping the peace on the western frontier. During August and September 1866, Fort Riley, Kansas, became a hotbed of activity as recruits and officers of the 7th Cavalry gathered at the regiment's first headquarters, charged with guarding construction of the Union Pacific Eastern Division.

The 7th's commanding officer was Colonel (Brevet Major General) Andrew Jackson Smith of Pennsylvania. Smith had served during the Civil War in various line positions, ending up as commander of the XVI Corps of the Army of the Tennessee. He would see mostly detached duty with the 7th Cavalry, resigning his commission in 1869 to become the postmaster of St. Louis.[46] Instead, the regiment would be commanded in the field by its jaunty, controversial lieutenant colonel, Brevet Major General George Armstrong Custer, the "boy general" from Michigan. Custer had wangled a commission with the 7th after turning down an offer for a lieutenant colonelcy with the newly formed 9th Cavalry, one of the two black regiments organized in 1866 to serve under white officers.[47]

The other black regiment was the 10th Cavalry, formed at Fort Leavenworth, Kansas, also in 1866. Its founder was Colonel (Major General of Volunteers) Benjamin Grierson, an Illinois music teacher who had once led a six-hundred-mile cavalry raid deep into Confederate territory culminating at Baton Rouge, a feat that General Ulysses S. Grant called the war's most brilliant foray. Under Grierson's leadership, the 10th would become a hard-hitting disciplined unit, proud of their nickname shared with the 9th, an analogy reputedly bestowed upon them by the Indians for their hair and their bravery, the "Buffalo Soldiers."[48]

On July 16, 1866, at Fort Leavenworth, a twenty-six-year-old ex-slave by the name of Reuben Waller signed up as a private in the 10th Cavalry. Waller's master had been a Confederate general in the cavalry and Waller had been with him through twenty-nine battles of the Civil War, including the shameful Fort Pillow Massacre of hundreds of black Union troops. After the war, the freedman went to Kansas. Having "a great liking for the cavalry soldiers," he enlisted for service on the Indian frontier. Later Waller learned to read and write, and in 1930 he wrote his memoirs. Prominent in this account was the role he would play on September 25, 1868, when he helped rescue the Forsyth Scouts at Beecher Island.[49]

By August of the next year, Waller and eight companies of the 10th Cavalry joined Custer and the 7th Cavalry in Kansas, west of Fort Harker, protecting railroad construction, manning frontier garrisons, and occasionally pursuing, somewhat futilely, the Cheyenne Dog Soldiers and a few bands of Oglala and Brulé Sioux. The movement of these regiments onto the plains during the summer of 1867 was brought about by joint failures of both the peace advocates in Washington and the army in the West to fulfill the stipulations and promises of the Treaty of the Little Arkansas. For two years after its signing, the Cheyennes and Arapahoes had no home. Without the promised reservations, the Indians roamed freely over their old hunting grounds in the central corridor between the Platte and the Arkansas. Concerned more with the perceived misconduct of President Andrew Johnson than the leaders of the Cheyenne warrior societies, Congress did little to organize the promised new reservations.

True to the predictions of the peace chiefs, the younger warriors, the Dog Soldiers, and others did not respect the promises of a few old men who made their mark on the white man's paper at the mouth of the Little Arkansas. In August a war party of about forty Cheyennes raided a homestead in Jewell County, Kansas, where they gang raped Mrs. John Marling and left her senseless on the prairie.[50] On December 20, 1866, Captain Miles Keogh, Company I, 7th Cavalry, stationed at Fort Wallace,

Kansas, reported that a band of Cheyennes ran off some stock from the post. A similar incident occurred at the Smoky Hill stage station.[51] And a young Dog Soldier named Fox Tail, in a drunken quarrel, killed a Hispanic herder in the employ of William Bent near Fort Zarah.[52]

Overall, however, the central plains remained relatively peaceful during 1866. Despite this relative tranquility, Kansas governor Samuel Crawford urgently wired Lieutenant General William T. Sherman, commander of the Division of the Missouri, appealing for more troops to protect his state's frontier. He was convinced that the Indians were concentrating for a renewed war and preparing all-out attacks to halt railroad construction. Crawford could offer little evidence of his claims. Sherman personally made a tour of western Kansas late in 1866 and found no evidence of Indian hostilities. In a letter to his brother, Senator John Sherman, the general observed that "these [reports of Indian depredations] are all mysterious, and only accountable on the supposition that our people out West are resolved on trouble for the sake of the profit resulting from the military occupation."[53]

Perhaps Crawford, always aggressive in his Indian policy, wanted to force the situation now that the new regiments were ready to re-garrison the plains. Perhaps, too, it is significant that although he was later exonerated by a legislative investigating committee, Crawford was charged with accepting a bribe from the Union Pacific Railroad.[54] In any event, the governor's urgent telegrams apparently did influence Sherman's subordinate, Major General Winfield Scott Hancock, commander of the Department of the Missouri, in his decision to take the field during spring 1867 and awe the tribes with a bombastic demonstration of military potential.[55]

Throughout the winter of 1866–1867 Hancock had remained at his headquarters at Fort Leavenworth, where he chose to believe Governor Crawford's predictions of an Indian war in the spring. By March 1867 he had put together a sizable force of some 1,400 men composed of seven companies of the 37th Infantry commanded by Brevet Major John Rziha; eleven troops of the 7th Cavalry; a battery of the 4th Artillery under Lieutenant Colonel C. C. Parsons; some Delaware Indian scouts; and a few white scouts including William Butler "Wild Bill" Hickok.[56] Accompanying this entourage was the twenty-six-year-old Henry Morton Stanley, a British expatriate whose impeccable appearance belied an illegitimate birth as "John Rowlands" and an early life of squalor and eventual migration to the United States as a ship's cabin boy. Growing up in New Orleans, Stanley joined the Dixie Grays during the Civil War and fought at the Battle of Shiloh in 1862. Captured in battle, he was paroled under the condition that as a foreign-born immigrant he would join a Union regiment as a "galvanized yankee." Quite early in his life Stanley recognized his gift for words. His graphic, eyewitness account of the Battle of Shiloh is as vivid as any to be found in the literature of military combat.[57]

In the spring of 1867 Stanley was employed by the *St. Louis Missouri-Democrat* to "write up" what was happening in Kansas. Although envious journalists would question the truth of Stanley's reporting, his vivid images of the soldiers and Indians during the Hancock expedition in 1867 are arguably the best portrayal of an Indian wars campaign bestowed to history by a journalist. Like DeBenneville Randolph Keim, Stanley viewed Hancock's command as an agent of empire. By the time Stanley's dispatches were published as a book, *My Life and Adventures in America* (1895), his witty, often humorous, prose was laced with the rhetoric of Social Darwinism and the concept of the White Man's Burden. Although Stanley opposed extermination of the plains tribes, he was an outspoken advocate of modernization and progress and saw the military as the best arm of civilization to accomplish that task, even to the extent of favoring the utilization of local militia over troops of the regular army. "[The Indians are] war-bred savages," Stanley said, "who [are] devoted to internecine strife. . . . When the white race appeared, it was the turn of the haughty savages to be dispossessed, and driven back to the West, where, in 1867, we find them cooped up between the Missouri River and the Rocky Mountains."[58]

Stanley's dispatches for the *Missouri-Democrat* so impressed readers back East that other newspapers were soon asking him for similar pieces. At the close of the campaign, James Gordon Bennett, Jr., of the *New York Herald* hired him, replacing him on the military frontier with DeB.

Randolph Keim, and in 1869 commissioned Stanley to travel to the African bush, where he gained fame by finding the renowned Dr. David Livingstone.[59]

Hancock intended to impress not only the Cheyennes and Arapahoes but the Kiowas and Comanches south of the Arkansas as well, and Stanley intended to make the most of it in his reports. Hancock accordingly sent dispatches to the agents for these tribes, Edward W. Wynkoop and Jesse Leavenworth respectively, of his intent to visit the chiefs within their jurisdictions. On April 3, Hancock's long, impressive column departed Fort Harker, which Stanley decided "in summer, when blossoming with flowers, may appear more interesting, but . . . in its present naked state appears like a great wart on the surface of the plain."[60] The colorful line of men with their shiny artillery marched across the Kansas prairie to Fort Zarah, where agent Leavenworth met them, and thence to Fort Larned, where Wynkoop caught up with them on the 7th. Their ultimate destination was a village of Dog Soldiers and an adjacent village of Sioux located west of Fort Larned.[61]

During the march, which would eventually span hundreds of miles, Major General Hancock looked and acted every bit the important soldier that he was. This dashing Pennsylvanian was forty-three when he took the field in 1867. With flowing hair, strong and deep-set eyes, and a cavalier mustache, Hancock was, stated Henry Morton Stanley, "a tall stately figure, in the prime of life [in 1867], with a commanding appearance, [which] excites admiration and respect wherever he goes."[62]

A genuine hero of the Civil War, Hancock and his II Corps of the Army of the Potomac had played crucial roles in that great conflict. Hancock had unleashed General George B. McClellan's advance on the peninsula at Williamsburg in 1862; he helped hold the center along the "Bloody Lane" at Antietam; he rode the storm of the disastrous Federal assault against the heights at Fredericksburg. But his star shone brightest at Gettysburg. On July 1, 1863, he took over the shattered I and XI Corps from John F. Reynolds, who was killed in the opening fighting, and ordered the Federal line anchored on Cemetery Ridge. On July 2, he repulsed General James Longstreet's two divisions under John B. Hood and Lafayette McLaws, preventing them from flanking the Round Tops,

Major General Winfield Scott Hancock. As commander of the II Corps of the Army of the Potomac during the Civil War, Hancock won the accolade "Hancock the Superb" for his tactical genius. As commander against the Cheyenne Dog Soldiers in 1867, however, this general disappointed his admirers. Many of the Cheyennes agreed that his maneuvers around Red Arm Creek (Pawnee Fork) in southwestern Kansas during the spring of that year precipitated the Indian War of 1867–1869. *Courtesy Kansas State Historical Society, Topeka, Kansas.*

and on July 3, his corps drove back the gallant charge of George Pickett against the Federal left center. Arguably Hancock saved the Federal Army, and quite possibly the Union, on each of the three days of the Battle of Gettysburg.[63]

It was on the third day of the battle that a Confederate bullet drove a nail and bits of wood from Hancock's saddle pommel into his thigh. He never fully recovered from the wound, so he crossed the plains in 1867 with a partially impaired leg. After this campaign Hancock was transferred back East, where he ultimately commanded the Department of the East. In 1880 the old soldier received the Democratic nomination for the presidency. Making little or no campaign for the office, in the modern sense, he nevertheless lost the election to James A. Garfield by only 7,023 popular votes. A shift of New York's thirty-five electoral votes would have resulted in the election of Winfield Scott Hancock. His career from the Mexican-American War through the presidential election of 1880 was so impressive that contemporaries as well as modern biographers have dubbed him "Hancock the Superb."[64]

Eighteen sixty-seven, however, was undoubtedly the low point in Hancock's otherwise brilliant military service record. He simply did not understand, nor did he try to understand, Indian ways, even when strategically it would have been to his advantage. The tone of Hancock's order to his forces at the beginning of the march was explicit: "We wish to show them that the Government is ready and able to punish them if they are hostile," he boldly stated. George Bird Grinnell, who later wrote about the Dog Soldiers' side of Hancock's march onto the plains of Kansas, asserted that the general's attitude "clearly shows Hancock's ignorance of things relating to these Indians; that he marched with infantry and a pontoon train in pursuit of mounted Indians shows how little qualified he was for command of such an expedition."[65]

Indeed, the Dog Soldiers seem to have been peacefully disposed when Hancock finally reached the vicinity of their camp and a camp of neighboring Sioux located some thirty-five miles from Fort Larned, Kansas, on a stream the Indians called Red Arm Creek and the whites called the Pawnee Fork.[66] But after Hancock's pugnacious councils with the Indians in April, all-out war came to the central plains.

This officer [Major General Winfield Scott Hancock] is spoiling for a fight. I will kill him in front of his own men and give them something to fight about.

— ROMAN NOSE
Crooked Lance Society, Northern Cheyenne
April 14, 1867

*F*or Roman Nose there was no question that Major General Winfield Scott Hancock was a fool.[1] For several days, as the soldier chief approached the Dog Soldier and Sioux camps on Red Arm Creek (Pawnee Fork), he evidenced an extreme ignorance of Indian ways. It came to a juncture when Hancock finally reached the proximity of the Indian camps and Roman Nose and others rode out to meet him. Roman Nose came up alongside of the soldier chief and boldly glared for several moments into the face of his adversary. After this, Roman Nose struck Hancock lightly in the face, thus counting coup on the esteemed general.[2] The stern soldier chief held no fear for Roman Nose, especially when the Indian women and children might be in danger. Roman Nose felt nothing but contempt for Hancock.

From the beginning of the campaign, Hancock's lack of understanding and seeming disrespect for the ways of the Cheyennes and Sioux would set off a chain of events that, according to the Indians, touched off the war of 1867–1869.[3] Perhaps Hancock was spoiling for a fight. In any event, he felt perfectly justified in insisting that the Cheyennes conform to the white man's ethics and morality. While at Fort Zarah, Hancock believed a rumor that five hundred lodges had gathered on Red Arm Creek with hostile intentions even though agent Wynkoop had refuted the notion as hearsay. Wynkoop nevertheless was successful in persuading Hancock to meet with the principal chiefs of the Dog Soldiers at Fort Larned on April 10.[4]

That spring the Dog Soldiers made camp some thirty-five miles or more from Fort Larned along with Black Shin's Suhtai band of Southern Cheyennes. With them were a few Arapahoes. Together there were about 110 lodges of various Cheyennes, or, as they called themselves, "the People." Next to the Cheyenne camp was a village of about 140 lodges of Southern Oglalas under Bad Wound and the war leader Pawnee Killer. To the northwest, on the Republican, there was a large village of Sioux and Northern Cheyennes under Spotted Tail, Turkey Leg, Swift Bear, Two Strike, Big Mouth, and others. They were in continuous communication with the Dog Soldiers and Sioux on Red Arm Creek.[5] Guides and interpreters F. F. Jones and mixed-blood Ed Guerrier, a cousin of Roman Nose's wife, were sent to the Dog Soldier village to request that the chiefs come to Fort Larned for a talk with Hancock. The chiefs started for the fort at once and both of these guides reported the Dog Soldiers' apparent peaceful disposition.[6]

On April 9, however, a blinding snowstorm swept the Kansas prairie around Fort Larned. The wind blew the snow into impassable drifts, and the cold became so intense that both Indians and soldiers feared for the lives of their horses. Although the chiefs sent runners ahead to tell of their slowed pace to Fort Larned, Hancock viewed the tardiness as a lack of good faith and declared that if the chiefs did not reach the fort by the 12th he would march to their village. Despite the cold, the delegation of Dog Soldier chiefs reached the fort on the night of the 12th. The greatly respected Tall Bull was there as well as Bull Bear, the brother of the slain Starving Bear who had tried to keep the peace with Colorado territorial governor Evans back in 1864. Also in the party were White Horse, Little Robe, and Lean Face, all chiefs, along with a few other headmen. The People admired all of these men.

Originally one of the six Cheyenne soldier societies, the Dog Soldiers had in 1837 started camping separately from the tribe. In that year one of their leaders, Porcupine Bear, murdered another Cheyenne, Little Creek, in a drunken fight. According to custom the tribe "outlawed" him and forced him to camp apart. Many of Porcupine Bear's followers went with him. The society soon broke through old tribal custom and changed itself into a separate division. Members of other warrior societies joined the Dog Soldiers. For a long time other Cheyennes looked upon the Dog Soldiers as outlaws. Eventually, however, their leaders and many of their warriors gained esteem among the People for their bravery and military ability. It was a custom among brave Dog Soldiers to "stake themselves out" with a "dog rope" attached to the warrior and fastened into the ground with a picket pin. Once staked out, the warrior would fight and die in that spot, for others considered him a coward if he pulled up his picket pin. Another warrior, however, might release the brave man by pulling up the pin and driving the wearer of the dog rope from the battlefield by striking him with his quirt.

By the time of the Indian War of 1867–1869, the Dog Soldiers had become friends with the Sioux and Northern Cheyennes. Intermarriage between Sioux and Dog Soldier people was not uncommon. Often, the Dog Soldiers would camp with the Sioux in the Republican Valley, which served as both a favorite hunting location and a transition zone where the northern and southern allies met for camaraderie. Occasionally the Dog Soldiers and their Sioux friends and families camped farther east or south, as they were doing on Red Arm Creek during spring 1867. By the time of Hancock's march to their camps, all the Cheyennes highly respected the Dog Soldiers.[7]

Exhausted from their hard journey to Fort Larned, the Dog Soldier chiefs asked for food. Hancock granted their request and ordered a tent to be erected for the chiefs' use. Meanwhile, soldiers built a huge bonfire near General Hancock's tent, where he and the chiefs would hold the council. Hancock intended to impress the Dog Soldier chiefs with this evening council. He and his officers put on their finest dress uniforms with gold epaulets and tall hats glittering with gold. The appearance of the artillery officers was especially impressive with their scarlet horsehair plumes flowing from the pinnacles of their formal headgear.[8]

With Hancock on one side of the campfire were colonels A. J. Smith and George Armstrong Custer of the 7th Cavalry as well as a score of officers from the other units in the command. On the other side were agent Edward Wynkoop and the Dog Soldier chiefs. Henry M. Stanley was present, and the appearance of the Indians reflected by the firelight so impressed him that he made substantial mention of it in his report. Some of the chiefs were wearing, like Hancock, blue military uniforms with gold epaulets. Others wore "red blankets," Stanley observed, "while their faces were painted and their bodies bedizened in all the glory of the Indian toilette. To the hideous slits in their ears were hanging large rings of brass; they wore armlets of silver, wrist-rings of copper, necklaces of beads of variegated colours, breast ornaments of silver shields, and Johnson silver [peace] medals, and their scalplocks were adorned with a long string of thin silver discs."[9]

Hancock made a long speech that confused the chiefs. He warned them of reprisal should any of the People break the peace. He warned them to tell their warriors to stay away from the Kansas settlements and the railroads because "if you should ever stop one of our railroad trains, and kill the people on it," Hancock said, "you would be exterminated."[10]

Although Hancock intended to impress the chiefs with this great council, his actions had the opposite effect. By holding the council at night, Hancock either wittingly or unwittingly showed disrespect for the ways of the People, whose chiefs always held council in the daylight hours, when the sun could bless the deliberations. More important, however, Hancock insisted that the Indians submit to the white concept of authority and responsibility. "For any depredations committed by any one of this tribe," he told them, "I shall hold the chief . . . responsible." Either Hancock did not know or more likely he did not care to accept the true role of a Cheyenne chief as a chosen peace official, a civil officer who interfaced with enemies and societies outside the tribe and factions within the tribe for the purpose of negotiating mutual peace and domestic tranquility. A chief exercised little formal decisionmaking authority in matters of war; influential men of the warrior societies, small bands, and even individual warriors made these decisions. Stated George Bent, "There was no such office as war chief." Confusing matters further from the Euro-American perspective, peace chiefs seldom exercised absolute authority over all of the warriors of the People and thus could not ensure general compliance with any peace treaty.[11]

Although Hancock returned a small Arapahoe boy who had been captured at Sand Creek, he nevertheless alarmed the chiefs further by announcing that he would march to their village for further council. Hancock apparently made this decision because he thought that the Indians were not adequately awed by his display of military power and partly because Roman Nose had not accompanied the chiefs to the talks at Fort Larned. Although the chiefs tried to explain that Roman Nose was not a chief or even a headman of a warrior society and therefore not entitled to sit in on such a council, Hancock refused to acknowledge or try to understand the Cheyenne perspective of leadership. To him the absence of the renowned warrior was a sign that the desire for peace was not strong among the People and their Sioux allies camped on Red Arm Creek. So annoyed was Hancock by the absence of Roman Nose that he told the chiefs he would begin his march the very next morning. This greatly alarmed the chiefs, who, with visions of another Sand Creek Massacre, feared that many of the Indians, especially the women and children, would flee the village in panic.[12]

But the obvious concern of the Dog Soldier chiefs made no impression on Hancock. He droned on in his speech, both warning and cajoling them to remain at peace. At one point in the deliberations Tall Bull rose to speak. He told the soldier chief that the Dog Soldiers wanted peace. "Whenever you want to go to the Smoky Hill," he said, "you can do so. When we come on the road your young men must not shoot us. We are willing to be friends with the whites."[13] After that the council broke up. The chiefs returned to their village concerned about what would happen if Hancock marched upon it looking for Roman Nose.

The next morning, April 13, the column moved out toward the Dog Soldier and Sioux camps. The People sent out their "wolves," stealthful scouts, to keep a secretive eye on the soldiers. As the column approached, some twenty miles out from Fort Larned, the Indians set the prairie grass on fire so that the soldiers would have to camp some distance from the villages. Before Hancock stopped for the night, however, a delegation of Indians, both Dog Soldiers and Sioux, came out to meet the column. Included were Pawnee Killer, White Horse, and several other chiefs. They assured General Hancock that the Indians would remain in the villages.

They offered to stay in the soldier camp and told Hancock that more chiefs of both tribes would come out to Hancock's tent at nine o'clock the next morning. When the appointed hour came and runners rode out to Hancock's tent to tell him that the chiefs were on their way but were delayed, Hancock waited a short time longer and then ordered the column to continue their march toward the villages. He told Bull Bear that he would make camp within sight of the villages and council could be held there in his tent that night.[14]

At the villages many of the Indians, especially the women, grew more fearful. No one understood the true intentions of soldier chief Hancock. His behavior had been conflicting, and the chiefs who had held council with him did not trust him. Many believed another Sand Creek Massacre was at hand. Roman Nose listened intently to the stories the chiefs told about the council at Fort Larned. Believing that Hancock's intentions were hostile, Roman Nose made up his mind what he would do. He would kill Major General Winfield Scott Hancock. Bull Bear, a close friend of Roman Nose's, begged him not to do so for fear that the soldiers would retaliate and massacre the women and children. Roman Nose held Bull Bear in high respect, so he calmed down after their talk. It was then that Bull Bear rode out to meet Hancock and tell him that the chiefs were coming to meet the soldiers. Then the chiefs, accompanied by three hundred warriors, left the village to discover Hancock's true intentions.[15]

They came in sight of the soldier column about midday. The chiefs and headmen quickly deployed their warriors into a battle line that stretched across the prairie for over a mile between the troopers and the Indian village. The chiefs sent runners to the rear to relay any news of an attack back to the villages. The Dog Soldier fighting men impressed the whites, dressed as they were in their finest clothing, with their lances trimmed in bright red trade cloth, and accented by their distinctive conical raven-feathered war bonnets. Headmen galloped back and forth in front of their braves, telling them to hold fast and die like warriors should the soldiers, who outnumbered them four to one, attack their position.[16]

Hancock deployed his men, supported by artillery, to face the Indians over the one-mile front. The 7th Cavalry at a gallop formed on the right flank. Officers shouted the order down the line to draw sabers, and the bright blades flashed from their scabbards into the sunlight. There before them in "full battle array," noted Lieutenant Colonel George Armstrong Custer, "were the representatives of civilized and barbarous warfare . . . one of the finest and most imposing military displays, prepared according to the art of Indian war, which it has ever been my lot to behold."[17]

Roman Nose must have been a striking figure in Custer's eyes as he dashed back and forth on his war-horse. Tall and athletic by the standards of his people, Roman Nose wore an officer's uniform with gold epaulets. On his head he wore a sacred war bonnet for his protection in battle that was made years previous by his friend Ice. Alarmed by Roman Nose's display, Bull Bear left the soldier ranks and rode back to the Indian line to reassure the People that Hancock had peaceful intentions. Some of the chiefs requested that Bull Bear speak to Roman Nose and prevent him from killing the soldier chief, as he had previously boasted he would. The great warrior was still parading around the front of the line with the white flag. "This officer is spoiling for a fight," Roman Nose announced. "I will kill him in front of his own men and give them something to fight about."[18]

Then agent Edward Wynkoop and interpreter Ed Guerrier galloped forward to put the Indians at ease. At Hancock's request they brought Roman Nose and the chiefs forward to meet Hancock, Smith, Custer, and other officers midway between the lines. The aged White Head was so nervous that he shook hands with all the officers, hoping to conciliate them, while Roman Nose, who told Guerrier that he intended to kill Hancock, rode up alongside the general and began staring at him in wonderment. The two sat on their horses side by side, each man considering the other, in a scene that epitomized an ultimate contrast of cultures. It was then that Roman Nose counted coup on Major General Winfield Scott Hancock.[19]

It is doubtful that Roman Nose knew much of Hancock's reputation in the Civil War. If he did he probably did not care. After the campaign, the Indians thought so little of the future presidential candidate that they referred to him simply as "the officer who burned the villages on Red Arm Creek."[20] But it is fairly certain that Hancock knew something of the past deeds of Roman Nose, the warrior who would play such a vivid role in the early stages of the Indian War of 1867–1869, especially the Battle of Beecher Island. According to George Bent, "Roman Nose was the most famous Cheyenne warrior of his day."[21] He was probably in his mid-forties at this time, having been born during the halcyon days of the fur trade.[22] As a boy he had been called Sautie (the Bat), but when he became a warrior he took the name Woqini (Hook Nose), which the whites interpreted to mean Roman Nose.[23]

Roman Nose was a northerner (Northern Cheyenne) who belonged to the Crooked Lance Society, also known as the Elkhorn Scrapers or Bone Scrapers. Highly religious, he believed fully in the power of the Medicine Arrows and the sacred Buffalo Hat, objects of such importance to the Cheyennes that they could determine the ongoing fate of the People.[24] A quiet and modest man among his own people, he had continually refused seats among the chiefs of his tribe and among the headmen of his warrior society.[25]

Since early childhood, Roman Nose had prepared to become a warrior. Among a people whose chief occupation was war, he learned the oral tradition of the great battles and the things that brought glory to the warrior, for glory in battle was the way of the People. Glory brought approbation of the elders, and praise by his public was the highest reward a Cheyenne warrior could know. From earliest youth, this future warrior of the People developed a love of fighting. Of course, seeking glory inevitably led to a concept of bravery that warriors measured in degrees of risk. Despite that the practice of counting coup was conceptually benign, it often resulted in the annihilation of a war party or a disproportionate number of warrior deaths on the battlefield that, by the values of other cultures, were unnecessary.[26]

Such warriors needed the spiritual inspiration and protection provided by sacred amulets and charms. So it was about 1860 that Roman Nose sought out his friend Ice (who would later take the name White Bull) to make him such a protective charm.[27] Years previous, during a storm, Ice had a vision of Thunder. In this vision Thunder wore a sacred war bonnet and carried a gun and a saber. When questioned about this by Roman Nose, Ice revealed that Thunder had years ago instructed him in this vision to construct such a war bonnet. Ice then agreed to make the war bonnet for Roman Nose. Ice used nothing manufactured by the white man in making the war bonnet. He used clay, ground stones, and pulverized bones of great animals to make the paint.

Ice made the crown from buffalo hide, and at the front, close to the forehead, he attached a single buffalo horn. Immediately behind the horn he fastened a hawk skin representing the being Ice had seen in his vision carrying a gun and a saber. Two long tails of eagle feathers trailed behind the headpiece, the feathers on the right side being red, the feathers on the left side being white. Tied to the crown were the skins of a barn swallow, a bat, and a kingfisher. The barn swallow flies close to the ground, and the bat darts up and down and is impossible to hit. When a person shoots at the wearer, the real person is not actually within the gun sights. The real person is close to the ground like the barn swallow or darting high up in the air like the bat. The bat also flies at night, giving the wearer protection in battle at that time, and the kingfisher closed up bullet holes in the body because when the kingfisher dives into the water, the water closes over it. The sacred war bonnet made Roman Nose invulnerable in combat.[28]

But Ice warned Roman Nose: "After I have finished this, and you put it on your head, you must never shake hands with anyone. If you do so, you will certainly be killed. If you get into any fight, try to imitate the call of the bird you wear on your head — the kingfisher."[29] Ice warned Roman Nose that he also would be killed if he ate food that had been taken from a dish with a metal implement.[30] Roman Nose had complete faith in his war bonnet, and he wore it into battle on many occasions afterward.

He wore the sacred war bonnet in July 1865, when the Cheyennes and Sioux avenged the massacre at Sand Creek with raids of revenge along the Platte Road. The Indians attacked a wagon train of the 11th Kansas Cavalry during the Red Buttes fight, one of the engagements in the complex of actions near the old Platte Bridge in south-central Wyoming. During the fighting, Left Hand, Roman Nose's brother, was killed. Roman Nose rode up on his war-horse and announced that he was going to "empty the soldier guns."[31]

Roman Nose and his companions raced their horses around the wagons, drawing the enemy fire. Then the warriors mounted a charge at the wagons. The soldiers killed several of the fighting men, but not a single bullet touched Roman Nose. Twenty-two men of the 11th Kansas Cavalry lay dead about the wagons after the charge, and, according to Cheyenne historian Father Peter John Powell, in a rage the warriors treated the bodies of the soldiers the same way that the Colorado volunteers had treated the bodies of the People at Sand Creek. They scalped every one of the troopers and hacked some of their corpses to pieces, scattering their body parts over the prairie. They turned the faces of the dead men to the earth, as was the Cheyenne custom to do to their enemies, and then they shot arrows into the bodies and pinned each corpse to the ground with a lance. In one last gesture of contempt for the whites, the warriors threw away the scalps of their victims.[32]

During the first week of the following September, Roman Nose was involved in a fight in the Powder River country with some troops of General P. E. Conner, who had been sent onto the northern plains to suppress the raids of revenge. Again the troopers had been pinned down when Roman Nose rode up to the fight wearing his famous war bonnet, its long eagle-feathered tails trailing over the flanks of his white war-pony. Quickly he organized some warriors into a battle line for a charge. Roman Nose shouted a war cry and the Cheyennes rushed the troopers. Nearing the smoking guns, Roman Nose wheeled his horse around and rode straight down the soldier line, which drew their fire. But not a bullet touched him, even though the soldiers had shot at him from only twenty yards away down the entire line of defense. Three times Roman Nose rode up and down the soldier line until they shot his horse out from under him. Roman Nose catapulted to the ground but quickly picked himself up and calmly walked away from the fallen pony, his back arrogantly turned to the soldiers, the power of his war bonnet still protecting him from the soldier bullets.[33]

The white soldiers outgunned the Indians in this fight, and the Indians' charges were little more than demonstrations of horsemanship and courage in the face of the enemy. They killed few soldiers. Nevertheless, Roman Nose's great ride solidified his reputation as the greatest of warriors, one who was protected by Ice's medicine. This engagement was thereafter known among the People as "Roman Nose's Fight."[34]

During the winter of 1865–1866, Black Shin's Suhtai band of Southern Cheyennes remained in the north, pitting antelope near the Little Missouri River. Roman Nose was with them. As a northerner, he was not a party to, nor had any interest whatsoever in, the Treaty of the Little Arkansas, which had been signed during fall 1865. Only when he came south in the spring of 1866 did the provisions of that treaty begin to affect him.[35] On August 14 of that year, a number of Cheyenne chiefs, including the great peace chief Black Kettle, met with agent Wynkoop at Fort Ellsworth, Kansas. It was Wynkoop's intention to bring about compliance with the new treaty and to persuade additional chiefs to sign it. Cheyenne emissaries from Black Shin's band attended the conference and Roman Nose came with them. Although Black Kettle and others were quite willing to turn over lands along the Republican and Smoky Hill, Tall Bull, Bull Bear, White Horse, and their Dog Soldiers remained adamant about retaining this rich buffalo country that they loved so much.

Roman Nose left the conference filled with hatred. Although he was a Crooked Lance, he held deep respect for the Dog Soldiers, especially Bull Bear, and he pledged to help them hold on to their Republican Valley lands. From that time forward Roman Nose remained in the south, camped among Black Shin's Suhtai and the Dog Soldiers. In August 1866 he led a war party to Fort Wallace and several of the stations along the Smoky Hill stage road, where he told the Wells Fargo employees to be out of the country in fifteen days. When Lieutenant A. E. Bates at Fort Wallace sent scout William Comstock among the Cheyennes to see what he could find out about all this, Comstock reported that the warriors told him that as soon as the Sun Dance ended the whites had better be out of the country or they would close the Smoky Hill Road.

The Dog Soldier chiefs tried to keep their young men under control that winter, seeking a peaceful coexistence with the whites while simultaneously trying to hold on to their lands in the central corridor. But others, including Roman Nose, proved to be more militant in their demands upon the whites along the Smoky Hill. The ambiguous provision of the Treaty of the Little Arkansas, which allowed the Indians to hunt between the Arkansas and the Platte yet required them to stay away from the Smoky Hill Road, inevitably fostered misunderstanding and resultant tensions.

Then Fox Tail, the young Dog Soldier, murdered the Hispanic herder, and the Indians ran off the livestock from Fort Wallace and again at Smoky Hill Station. These incidents along with the threats of Roman Nose and other warriors and the determination of the Dog Soldiers to hold on to their country constituted the events that so alarmed Major General Winfield Scott Hancock during the winter of 1866–1867. When Hancock received word of the Fetterman Fight in the north (near Fort Phil Kearny in present-day Wyoming) on December 21, it is likely that he became alarmed over the possibility of similar all-out war with the Indians camped in Kansas during the spring.[36]

So on April 14, 1867, Roman Nose and Hancock faced each other between the lines on Red Arm Creek, each calculating the other's next move. The standoff did not go unnoticed by *Harper's* artist Theodore Davis, who noted that Roman Nose was indeed a fine specimen of a warrior, standing "six feet in height and finely formed," armed with a carbine, four revolvers, and a strung bow held in his left hand.[37] Then Roman Nose made up his mind what to do. He turned to his old friend Bull Bear and told him to ride back to the Indian lines because he now was going to kill Hancock. Bull Bear grabbed the reins of Roman Nose's pony and led him away from the general. Bull Bear reminded Roman Nose of the women and children and begged him for their sakes not to kill Hancock. Roman Nose thought this over and, out of respect for his friend Bull Bear, agreed. The pair then rode back to where Hancock was waiting. Hancock addressed Roman Nose through interpreter Ed Guerrier and asked him why he had not attended the council at Fort Larned.[38]

"My horses are poor," Roman Nose replied, "and every man that comes to me tells me a different tale about your intentions."[39]

Hancock then asked if the Cheyennes wanted peace or war and Roman Nose replied: "We don't want war; if we did, we would not come so close to your big guns."[40]

With that Hancock abruptly broke off the council, stating that it was too windy to talk there and that he would move closer to the Dog Soldier village so that the cavalry horses could graze (the Indians had burned the prairie near the present soldier camp). There he would set up his tent and continue the council. This alarmed the chiefs even more because they knew they would not be able to hold back the women and children. Indeed, panic spread throughout the camps on Red Arm Creek. When Hancock reached within one-half mile of the Indian villages, the women and children fled. Hancock then sent for the chiefs again. Bull Bear, Tall Bull, Grey Beard, Medicine Wolf, and White Horse came immediately, accompanied by Roman Nose. Hancock was disturbed that the women and children had left the camps and told the Indians that he thought it looked like an act of treachery.[41]

"Are not women and children more timid than men?" Roman Nose replied. "The Cheyenne warriors are not afraid, but have you ever heard of Sand Creek? Your soldiers look just like those who butchered the women and children there."[42]

Hancock then demanded that the chiefs send runners to bring them back, and when the chiefs told him their horses were in poor condition, Hancock gave them two of his own fresh mounts. The chiefs returned to their village accompanied by Ed Guerrier, whom Hancock had instructed to report back every two hours regarding the Indians' actions. So convinced were the chiefs that Hancock wanted a fight that they prepared all the warriors in the village to leave that night. Mixed-blood Guerrier purposefully delayed his reports to Hancock to give his old friends time to depart. When he finally did send his message to Hancock, the general ordered Custer and the 7th Cavalry to surround the Dog Soldier village on the morning of the 15th, but by early light it was obvious that the chiefs and warriors too had all fled.[43] The People left behind a few of their brethren, including the elderly mother of White Horse and an aged Sioux couple. The old man had recently broken his knees and his wife had refused to leave him. Also in the village was a small girl whom the men of the 7th Cavalry described as feebleminded. It soon became apparent that the girl had recently been raped, ostensibly by some troopers who had slipped away into the Dog Soldier camp after the People had departed. She was found by Custer and his surgeon, Dr. I. T. Coates, cowering in terror beneath a buffalo robe in one of the abandoned lodges.[44]

As soon as Hancock received word that the People had evacuated the village, he dispatched Custer and the 7th Cavalry to pursue them. Custer's orders were to bring the Indians back unless they showed intent to fight, in which case he was to accommodate them. As far as the People were concerned, Custer's pursuit clearly showed Hancock's hostile intent. For many, including Roman Nose, war seemed inevitable, even though the chiefs tried to keep the young warriors at peace a while longer.[45]

But an event was to take place on April 15 that would tip this delicate balance in favor of war. While the Indians from the Dog Soldier camp on Red Arm Creek headed toward refuge in the Republican River country, a group of Sioux from the north, who were either from Spotted Tail's camp or were some of Red Cloud's warriors from the Powder River country seeking to escape that war by coming south, struck the Smoky Hill route. They hit three stage stations in succession. They did the most damage at Lookout Station, where the warriors burned the buildings, ran off the stock, and killed three station attendants, ripping out their intestines, burning their bodies, and leaving the mangled and charred corpses behind for the white people to find.[46] Meanwhile, the escaping Indians from the villages on Red Arm Creek ran off some horses from a work party of the Union Pacific Eastern Division Railroad. As they fled toward the Republican, the warriors broke up into smaller and smaller groups, leaving a bewildering number of faint trails and thus enabling them to easily elude the inexperienced Custer.[47]

On the night of April 16, Custer reached Downer's Station and sent two messages to Hancock reporting that stage company employees had knowledge of small parties of Indians crossing the road on their way north during the previous twenty-four hours. The civilians assumed that these Indians had committed depredations along the road. When Hancock received this report he issued orders to burn the abandoned Dog Soldier and Sioux lodges as a lesson to the Indians.[48] On April 18 Custer rode the thirty-five miles to Lookout Station, where he discovered the burned bodies of the stage station employees. He sent a third message to Hancock that made it clear that neither he nor his Delaware scouts had found any evidence of what tribe committed the depredations. But the message came too late.[49]

On the morning of April 19, Hancock's men carried out his instructions. Altogether they torched 250 lodges along with more than nine hundred buffalo robes and other provisions that the Dog Soldiers and Sioux had left behind when they fled.[50] The dry lodgepoles caught fire like kindling. The fire consumed the surrounding prairie grass as well as a nearby grove of cottonwood trees. The acrid stench of burning hide filled the nostrils of the soldiers, and billows of black smoke engulfed the sky from the smoldering piles of buffalo robes. Fanned by the relentless prairie wind, everything in the vicinity of the abandoned villages caught fire. Smoke could be seen for miles across the unbroken horizon as the lodges burned to ashes. For Roman Nose, many of the Dog Soldiers, and their Sioux allies, Major General Winfield Scott Hancock had stirred up a hornet's nest on Red Arm Creek. Revenge was mandatory. War had come to the central plains.[51]

The most cruel crimes and deeds committed in all history were the crimes the Indians practiced in their warfare . . .

— MRS. OLIVE A. CLARK
Homesteader in the Solomon Valley
1868

On April 9, 1867, the very day that Tall Bull, Bull Bear, and the other Dog Soldier chiefs rode through a spring snowstorm to meet with Major General Winfield Scott Hancock at Fort Larned, a small party of Cheyennes descended upon the newly established White Rock Creek settlement in Jewell County, Kansas. They first appeared at the door of Mrs. Sutzer, a widow who was homesteading alone with a small child. Recently she had taken in a boarder, a neighboring homesteader named Erastus Bartlett. Bartlett was busy splitting rails near the creek when the Indians came into the house and demanded food. Mrs. Sutzer prepared a meal while secretly sending her little son across the creek to the neighboring homestead of Nicholas Ward to warn his family of the Indians' presence.

Returning home for dinner, Bartlett met the warriors as he passed around the corner of the house. After they brutally tomahawked him, the Indians seized Bartlett's own knife and plunged it deep into his throat, where it remained until his body was eventually discovered by neighbors. Apparently when the Indians killed Bartlett Mrs. Sutzer started to run, but she only made it thirty yards from the door of her house. The warriors easily caught her and bashed in her skull with a rock. The Cheyennes then proceeded across the creek to the Ward homestead, where again they demanded dinner. They chatted innocently enough with Mr. Ward while they consumed their meal.

Then one of the warriors calmly loaded his gun and asked Ward in English if "he thought it would kill a buffalo." Ward replied that he thought it would. At that moment the warrior leveled the weapon at Ward's breast and pulled the trigger. Ward dropped dead, shot through the heart. The two children in the house, Ward's adopted son and Mrs. Sutzer's boy, started to run, but the Indians chased them down. The warriors shot the Sutzer boy, killing him instantly, but they only managed to wound the little Ward child, though they left him for dead.

Later the injured boy struggled back to the house under the cover of night to procure some blankets. In the dark he stumbled over the body of his murdered father. The little boy returned to a creek, where the next morning some claim hunters rescued him. The Indians had captured the boy's mother, who was described as a tall prepossessing young woman of twenty-two. Two months after the incident, some troopers of the 10th Cavalry saw a young woman fitting Mrs. Ward's description wandering alone on the Saline River. When she saw the black soldiers, she ran in terror into the timber. Fearing she was a decoy for the Indians, the troopers did not pursue. Despite extensive efforts to locate her that were made by her neighbors and her relatives in southern Illinois, Mrs. Ward was never seen again.[1] In spite of the energies exerted by the peace chiefs, the intrusion of Major General Winfield Scott Hancock's force into western Kansas during spring 1867 inspired a number of young warriors, Dog Soldiers and other Cheyennes, Sioux and Arapahoes, to try to drive the hated white trespassers from the central corridor.[2]

Although the Cheyennes, Arapahoes, and Sioux who chose the path of war in 1867 concentrated their efforts on railroad workers and the Wells Fargo stage stations along the Smoky Hill and Platte River roads, homesteaders living on isolated claims in western Kansas nevertheless huddled in fear of a sudden visit from those whom the newspapers called "Lo the poor Indian" and whom the homesteaders themselves overwhelmingly referred to as "the savages." Some of the settlers had good reason to be afraid. In August 1867, J. W. McConnell was breaking sod on his claim in Rooks County, Kansas, when a single Indian attacked him. Later he joined a group of settlers who were hiding from a larger group of warriors. From one hundred yards away McConnell yelled out at the Indians, "Are you Pawnee?"

"No," came a reply from one of the Indians.

"Otoe, Cheyenne, Arapahoe?" McConnell shouted.

"No."

"Then," McConnell screamed, "what the hell are you?" whereupon the leader of the band muttered something in his native language and the group moved on.[3]

Eighteen sixty-seven became the worst year in Kansas history for raids on whites by Indians. Overall, the Indians killed an estimated 128 people during that year.[4] But despite a new treaty signed at Medicine Lodge, Kansas, in October, in terms of individual acts of brutality committed against civilian homesteaders the year 1868 may have been even worse. Some of the warriors, annoyed by the slow response of the government to issue guns and provisions in accordance with the new treaty, joined with others who always had sworn never to relinquish lands between the Arkansas and the Platte. By the summer of that year, a large war party, principally Dog Soldiers and other Cheyennes from the villages of Bull Bear, Medicine Arrows, Black Kettle, and Little Rock, along with twenty Sioux and four Arapahoes, swept like a summer whirlwind through the Saline and Solomon valleys, killing, raping, and pillaging. Among their war leaders were Red Nose, Tall Wolf, and Porcupine Bear.[5] By autumn some seventy-nine western Kansas settlers were dead.[6]

On August 12 the Indians slashed through the settlements on Asher and Spillman creeks. Mrs. Olive A. Clark, who lived in a sod dugout with her family in the Solomon Valley near the newly established town of Minneapolis, Kansas, in Ottawa County, remembered the terror when neighbors reported Indians near her home. "Everyone was in great haste," she wrote, "to get [their] families safely out of danger. . . . The Indians had taken advantage of a time when the soldiers were on a buffalo hunt [to] begin their depredations. . . . Although we escaped the savages our property did not. Our dugout was destroyed and the edition [*sic*] burned. The lumber [for a house] which father had hauled from Junction City and piled in a neat pile by the dugout was also burned. The windlass was broken and the pieces thrown in the well, the cow ran off and the mare and colt were stolen."[7]

The settlers' instinct was to congregate in some predetermined spot, a nearby town if one existed, for mutual protection. Edwin C. Hardy recollected vividly the manner in which settlers in Ottawa County "fled indiscriminately" in a desperate attempt to reach safety. "We all hid in ravines until dark that night," he remembered, "then tried to find our way to Minneapolis, but lost our way and wandered about in a circle. Later we scattered into two different parties, we could hear each other, as we wandered around in the night, but [we] were afraid to get together. There were twenty or more in each party, but there were only two men, one gun and no ammunition in our group."[8]

Mrs. Clark's father had gone to the nearby settlement on Asher Creek to help protect the Gates family when the Dog Soldiers descended on the homesteaders. They visited every house they came to and killed or ran off the settlers and then destroyed all the property they could not carry away.[9] On Spillman Creek thirty warriors gang raped Mrs. Shaw and her sister Mrs. Foster "until long after they had become senseless." Near the present town of Beloit, in Mitchell County, the Indians captured two small girls from the Bell homestead but left them on the prairie when troops in pursuit from Fort Harker came close to overtaking them.[10]

Up on White Rock Creek, Gordon Winbigler, his neighbor Adam Rosenburg, and a number of other settlers were cutting hay when a body of mounted warriors surprised them. All fled to a nearby camp that they had established for such an occasion. All of them made it with the exception of Winbigler, who stopped long enough to try and recover his hat, which had fallen off along the way. As he did so, a single warrior overtook him and thrust a lance into his neck, severing instantly the farmer's jugular vein.[11]

On August 13, some of the warriors moved into adjacent Cloud County, where they appeared at the White homestead on Granny (or Granite, later named White's) Creek. A distant neighbor, Frank Lawrence, took to the trail with a posse of other settlers to pursue the raiders. He described what happened at the White homestead:

[The Indians] robbed the house and tore the eldest daughter [eighteen-year-old Sarah] from the arms of her screaming, half-crazed mother, bound her upon a horse and carried her into a captivity which I consider an earthly hell.

In the struggle between the Indians and the mother and younger children, the one to take her, the other to save her, [Sarah White's] clothes were nearly torn off her — she having on nothing but a linsey shirt, and thus helpless, bare headed, and bare footed she was taken across the prairie in the broiling sun. Old Mr. White was making hay on the prairie some four miles off. When found, Mrs. White was wandering over the prairie, carrying the youngest child and two or three crying behind her, hunting her husband, little knowing, poor soul, that he lay slowly bleeding to death, shot by another of the party of the same band, because he tried to persuade them not to take his horses, which they had seized.

Word came to me that night of the outrage just as I had retired to bed, after a hard day's work. I saddled a horse and by riding nearly all night I arrived at the place about daylight and found thirty-five men ready to take the trail; we followed it that day and the next when a majority of the party gave it up — being out of food.[12]

Two months later, on October 13 (shortly after the Beecher Island fight), a small group of warriors, either Sioux or Cheyenne, once again struck the Solomon Valley ten miles northwest of Minneapolis, in Ottawa County, killing at least four persons.[13] On that day James S. Morgan, a veteran of the 2nd Colorado Volunteer Cavalry during the Civil War, was in his field husking corn some two miles from his house when he heard shooting from a nearby farm. His twenty-four-year-old wife, Anna Belle, was at home in the cabin. The newlyweds had only been married for one month.

Ordinarily Morgan was in the habit of taking his gun with him when he left home. But today he had not done so because it was a damp, foggy day and he had reasoned that it would be difficult for the Indians to use their bows because wet bowstrings lose tension when they expand from the moisture. Morgan hadn't figured that the Indians had acquired guns. Just before noon a small group of warriors approached him. One of the Indians then shot Morgan in the hip. The shot frightened Morgan's horses, causing them to run off. That saved James Morgan's life. The Indians went after the team, which allowed Morgan to hobble off through his standing corn to hide in the willows beside a stream. The Indians followed drops of his blood toward the stream and then went away. Morgan was found alive near his cornfield by some men looking for victims of the raid.[14]

Morgan's bride, Anna Belle, however, feared the worst for her husband when she saw one of his horses enter the yard of their homestead. Instinctively she grabbed a revolver, jumped on the horse, and rode out to the field where her husband had been working. Spotting the Indians, she became so frightened that she froze in terror. Finally gaining her senses, she spurred her horse and tried to make her escape. But a warrior easily overtook her; he rode up alongside her and struck her with his war club. After tying her so she could not struggle, the Indians bound her to her own horse and rode away.[15]

About the same time that the Indians captured Anna Belle Morgan, another party of Indians, possibly a combined group of Cheyennes, Arapahoes, and Kiowas, captured Mrs. Clara Blinn in an attack on a freighter's wagon train along the road to Santa Fe, somewhere between Fort Dodge, Kansas, and Fort Lyon, Colorado. The warriors wounded her husband in the attack. Clara Blinn had with her a small two-year-old son, Willie. By November, she was in a Southern Cheyenne camp located northwest of the Wichita Mountains in the Indian Territory (Oklahoma). On November 17, a trader named Cheyenne Jack went to the village and came back with a letter from Clara Blinn to any interested party in the outside world. Her words were articulate but desperate:

> Kind Friend: Whoever you may be . . .
> Do all you can for me; write to the Peace Commissioners to make peace this fall. For our sakes do all you can, and God will bless you. If you can let me hear from you again let me know what you think about it. Write my father, send him this. Goodby [sic].
>
> (Signed) Mrs. R. F. Blinn
>
> I am as well as can be expected, but my baby is very weak.[16]

By November 27, Clara Blinn and her baby were in the Southern Cheyenne village of Black Kettle on the Washita River. Instead of sending the peacemakers that day, Major General Philip Sheridan sent Lieutenant Colonel George A. Custer and the 7th Cavalry. As a climax to Sheridan's winter campaign to punish the Cheyennes for their depredations of 1867–1868, Custer's troops surprised the village at dawn, killing about one hundred warriors and men, including the peace chief Black Kettle. Arguably the Battle of the Washita was not a massacre on the scale of Sand Creek. Nevertheless, the troopers killed a number of women and children during the engagement.

But not all of those who died were Indian people. While inspecting the battleground, some officers discovered the mutilated and frozen remains of a white woman and her baby. Members of the 19th Kansas Volunteers identified them as Mrs. Clara Blinn and her child, Willie. During the attack, some of the angry Cheyennes tomahawked Clara Blinn and then tore her baby from her arms and "dashed its brains out against a tree." The young woman's body was clothed only in an old blanket, with one undergarment of buckskin. On her feet were a pair of lady's stockings and a worn pair of Cheyenne moccasins.[17]

In March 1869, Custer and the 7th Cavalry along with the 19th Kansas learned that the Cheyennes were holding Sarah White and Anna Belle Morgan in the village of Medicine Arrows (Stone Forehead) on a tributary of the Red River of the South along the Texas–Indian Territory border. Fearing that an attack might result in the death of the two women, as had befallen Clara Blinn at Washita, Custer decided to negotiate with the Cheyennes. But Custer held the trump card. Surrounding the village, the lieutenant colonel of the 7th Cavalry took hostage two chiefs, Dull Knife and Big Head, and a warrior the soldiers called "Bummer," who had come out to parley. Custer then threatened to hang the Indians if the captive women were not released within two days. On the fourth day (March 15), with the hangman's ropes ready, a party of Cheyennes brought the two women to the soldiers. Custer instructed the men of the 19th Kansas to receive their state's women. "How each bronzed and weather-beaten soldier struggled to keep down the lump that *would* rise in his throat," observed one member of the 19th Kansas, as the women passed through the lines. "Such a scene paid [a reward to] us for many a hard, weary day's tramp."[18]

"Two lines were formed as they passed between," noted another soldier, "and it surely was a pitiful sight to behold . . . they all dismounted and the larger woman led by Col. Moore and the other by Maj. Jones passed down the lines. The larger one [Anna Belle Morgan] appeared to be 50 years old, although she was less than 25. She was stooped, pale and haggard, looking as if she had been compelled to do more than she was able. She was quite tall, with light hair that was bleached on top until it was dirty brown from exposure. Her clothes were made of three or four kinds of material, pieces of tents and blankets, all worn out and sewed together with strings. . . . The younger one [Sarah White] was . . . pretty much the same. The Indians did not even allow them a blanket to cover their ragged clothing."[19]

Arthur Brewster, Anna Belle Morgan's brother, was present at the rescue. "Oh sister," he cried as he was reunited with his loved one, "how you must suffer."[20] The women told of trying to escape and of being beaten. Although reports held that both women were pregnant at the time of their rescue, there is evidence that only Anna Belle Morgan gave birth, soon after reunion with her husband. Neighbors hoped she had become pregnant before her capture by the Indians, but such was not the case.

Mrs. Olive A. Clark of the Solomon Valley knew Anna Belle Morgan from having worked for the Morgans after Anna Belle's release. Writing for the Kansas State Historical Society, Mrs. Clark tactfully guarded the honor of her friend while nevertheless allowing her readers insight into how captivity among the Cheyennes offended the Victorian sensibilities of nineteenth-century women like Anna Belle Morgan. "I do not remember of Mrs. Morgan ever saying anything about her life with [the Cheyennes]," she remembered. "I believe she thought it a terrible disgrace and any reference to it only added to the infamy." Anna Belle Morgan herself, who generally refused to give anything of her story to reporters and writers, once commented to her friend Emily Haines Harrison that although the Indian man she lived with was generally kind to her, she regarded her experience as a horrible one that she never quite got over. "After I came back," she said, "the road seemed rough, and I often wished they had never found me."[21] A few months after Custer's forces recovered her from the Indians, she gave birth to a baby boy. In the summer of 1870 Mrs. Olive A. Clark "took particular notice of the child. He was a strong, healthy little fellow," she remembered, "and certainly resembled the Indians both in features and disposition."[22]

Anna Belle's brother Arthur likewise considered his sister's captivity a moral disgrace. He "requested his sister to give into his keeping this little boy after he had attained a certain age," Mrs. Clark remembered, "so that he could take him and go to the haunts of the Indians, and shoot and kill all savages sighted as long as both or either lived and thus gain a partial revenge for the crime committed."[23] Brewster never got his chance. The little mixed-blood boy the Morgans had named "Ira" died when he was about two years old.[24] Anna Belle Morgan and her husband lived for many years on their claim and raised three children who lived to maturity. But she may never have emotionally reconciled the strain of her ordeal. "Mrs. Morgan's story is a pitiful one," said Emily Haines Harrison. Although Sarah White sold her story to interested writers, "Mrs. Morgan [continually] refused to do [so]. . . . She considered it a disgrace."[25]

Although Anna Belle may merely have suffered from senility or Alzheimer's disease, she was nevertheless pronounced insane by a physician around the turn of the century and died June 11, 1902, at the age of fifty-eight in the Home for the Feeble Minded in Topeka, Kansas. Sarah White became a schoolteacher in Clyde, Kansas, and lived a long life. She married H. C. Brooks of Clyde and the couple raised seven children. In later life, while living at the house of her son in Concordia, Kansas, she filed suit against the state to gain compensation for her ordeal at the hands of the Cheyennes.[26]

In contemporary revisionist histories, which are concerned with correcting the stereotypes of Indian "savagery," the argument has been advanced that settlers' fears, especially the fears of women, were unrealistic.[27] Certainly, to generalize about specific episodes such as the captivity of Anna Belle Morgan and Sarah White, or the murder of Clara Blinn and her child, as being typical of pioneer life on the Great Plains Indian frontier is misleading and false. There were acts of kindness as well as acts of true "savagery" committed by both white and Indian. But to minimize the *perceived* fear of one culture to correct a stereotype of another culture merely inverts the relationship. In fact, real or imagined, there was a *fear* of Indian attack among settlers on the central and southern plains frontier from 1867 to 1869. Even though most settlers in western Kansas and eastern Colorado did not die at the hands of Indian raiders, just as most settlers did not die from nonhuman threats such as tornadoes or rattle-snake bites, there were enough of each of these disasters to keep home-steaders' fears kindled, however unrealistic those fears might have been overall.

When these individual episodes of cruelty did occur, however, they legitimized the terror and panic displayed by settlers. Similarly, although soldiers did not always massacre Indian women and children, there were enough episodes like Sand Creek to legitimize the feelings of panic exhibited by Indian noncombatants when a military force like Hancock's approached a village for the purpose of a parley or when Custer's troops surrounded the camp of Medicine Arrows in order to secure the release of Anna Belle Morgan and Sarah White. When it came to *perceptions* of each other's hostile intentions, valid exhibitions of fear developed into recognizable behavior patterns displayed by both Indians and whites.

Current historical interpretations, however, often minimize this re-ality for the broader purposes of portraying Indians as the complex human beings that they truly are. Often these interpretations draw from the diaries of overland pioneers who were not at that time in the Cheyenne country to possess the Indians' land but merely to pass through it on a journey elsewhere. "Evidence minimizing western fear of Indians as a Victorian stereotype," wrote historian Craig Miner, "has drawn extensively on travel accounts. It was a different experience to watch Indians from the safety of a wagon train in the midst of an armed group or from a railroad car than from an isolated farmstead about to be attacked. . . . As danger increased, so did fear." By 1867 and 1868, social conditions had changed. The whites came then to usurp and possess the plains, pushing the Indian out. When one remembers that 1867 and 1868 were the worst years in Kansas history for white deaths at the hands of Indians, Miner's words ring true: "As danger increased, so did intolerance and stereotyping."[28]

Certainly cultural relativism meant nothing to the majority of pioneers, for no lands on the American frontier of 1867–1868 were more
coveted by young farming families starting out in life than the rich soil of
Kansas. It simply did not matter to them that the Cheyenne Dog Soldiers
claimed the country before the homesteaders. The biblical references to
making the land fruitful were justification enough for these simple rural
people to try to inherit the land from a society that, in the estimation of
the agriculturalists, had no right to possess it because they refused to make
it productive.

Some were willing to share the land with the Indian through the
reservation system at least for a while, but some were not, unless, perhaps,
the Indians took up farming and adopted the elements of the white man's
civilization. Some Indians were willing to coexist with whites within the
framework of this arrangement, yet many warriors refused to tolerate the
presence of whites in their former lands, which had been ceded by the
peace chiefs without their individual consent. The uncompromising ones
in both cultures produced much of the true brutality on the frontier. And
that brutality was real enough from 1867 to 1869 to cause genuine
concern.

Much of the fear that caused the Indians to try to drive out the white
newcomers was the result of the attempt to segregate the tribes north of
the Platte and south of the Arkansas. Although the Indians retained the
right by the Treaty of the Little Arkansas (1865) to hunt the buffalo in
the central corridor between those rivers, the new Treaty of Medicine
Lodge (1867) required the southern tribes to hunt no farther north than
the Arkansas. All Kansas lands were ceded. Consequently, buffalo concentrated in the central corridor, away from treaty lands and reservations,
to escape hunting pressure from the tribesmen.[29]

When white farmers began to take up homesteads in western Kansas
in 1867, they began to benefit more than the Indians from hunting these
concentrated herds of buffalo. Eventually groups of neighbors and even
entire settlements organized large communal hunts to fill winter larders.
By 1868 "it was great sport, as well as means to furnish meat for the larder,
to hunt the buffalo," Mrs. Olive A. Clark remembered.

The men would organize, mount their horses and sally forth in small bands on these hunts and kill enough to supply their respective families for some time. All animals killed on the hunt would be butchered where they fell, the meat cut and loaded in the "follow-up wagon," which would always be found trailing the hunt. . . . The carcasses would be left on the prairie where the animals fell, and I have seen the prairie white with their bones, bleaching in the sun, which were mute evidence of the great slaughter waged against the buffalo.[30]

For many of the tribesmen this economic displacement was too much for them to bear.

Typically the laissez-faire philosophy of the federal government meant that few of the Kansas settlers received much aid or compensation for the depredations of 1867–1868, although individual settlers made efforts to obtain help. Mary A. Bickerdyke, a widow from Salina, Kansas, known as "Mother Bickerdyke" for her various philanthrophic activities, secured from General Sherman rations for one thousand persons for a period of four weeks during the autumn of 1868. With the help of Kansas senator S. C. Pomeroy, she secured additional rations from the Department of War for five hundred people over a ten-month period. General O. O. Howard, the Freedman's Bureau chief, gave Mother Bickerdyke five hundred blankets to distribute to needy Kansas settlers.[31]

For reasons like these, probably a substantial majority of western Kansas settlers favored a military solution to the "Indian problem" of 1867–1869. They agreed with the army, and the press, that protection of settlers would be more effective if the government concerned itself less with trying to extend the "olive branch," as advocated by the Indian Bureau, and discontinued spreading budget appropriations between the two agencies, instead taking up the "sword." "It is my opinion," emphasized Mrs. Olive A. Clark, "that many . . . unfortunate pioneer men and women, would have had a much pleasenter [sic] life, that would have had a happier ending than was the case, had there been proper protection along the [Solomon] valley. . . . The soldiers," she claimed, "were nearly always a few hours too late to check the savages before damage was done."[32]

When the military did succeed, however, its officers often became heroes to the pioneers for many years to come. Writing in 1914 to a member of the 19th Kansas Volunteers who helped rescue her from Medicine Arrows' village in 1869, Sarah White, then Sarah Brooks, left no doubt about her feelings toward the controversial Lieutenant Colonel George Armstrong Custer. "I shall always think of you men and Grand old Custars [*sic*] as the grandest and best of heros," she remembered. "Yes the memory of that day will always be in my mind and the reverence for Dead Custar [*sic*] and all the men that was with him will always be with me as long as my life lasts."[33]

Samuel J. Crawford, governor of Kansas in 1867 and 1868, mirrored well the anti-Indian sentiments of his constituency. Elected in 1865 at age twenty-nine, Crawford became the state's youngest governor as well as one of its most popular.[34] Tall and gaunt, Crawford was often a firebrand in his remonstrations about the Indians in his state. He had reason to be. Because he was an ardent booster of settlement into the western half of the state, more settlers died at the hands of the plains tribes in Kansas during the last two years of his administration than in all other years of the state's history.[35] Crawford opposed all treaty making with Indians. He wrote to Washington in 1867, with the support of most voters in the state as well as the Kansas legislature, recommending that Congress be memorialized to transfer the Indian Bureau to the War Department.

Blaming the Indian traders for much of the bloodshed in Kansas, Crawford secured legislation prohibiting the sale of liquor in the unorganized portion of the state.[36] Of the "Blue Ribbon" Peace Commission charged with extending the olive branch to the Indians at the time of the Medicine Lodge Treaty, Crawford thought its actions were based on "a maudlin sentimentality in the East, derived from Cooper's novels and impressed upon the [War] Department by ignorant but well-meaning humanitarians."[37]

Overall, Samuel J. Crawford reacted to the turmoil in Kansas as would any modern governor in times of disaster. A new raid would usually bring either himself or the adjutant general to the scene. After assessing the damage, Crawford would then appeal for federal assistance. Often he would organize a local militia to cope with the situation while requesting that companies of the regular army be transferred to the Kansas frontier. If he judged the forthcoming manpower insufficient, he would offer to raise a regiment of volunteers for the state's defense, a situation that the Indian Bureau and the War Department always feared would unleash a host of recruits bent on exterminating the Indians, thus making it almost impossible for the regular army to uphold current treaties. But the state of Kansas in 1868 was still so young that the government lacked sufficient resources to provide for a large militia force.[38]

During the raids of 1867, however, Sherman permitted Crawford to organize the 18th Kansas Volunteers. Four companies of cavalry were recruited in two weeks at Fort Harker. Two of the companies participated in a fight with the Indians on August 21 and 22 known as the Battle of Prairie Dog Creek (Beaver Creek). With the coming of winter the regiment was disbanded in favor of the new Peace Commission. By then cholera, which spread through western Kansas in the summer and autumn of 1867, had taken more of a toll than the Indians had. By November, about 10 percent of the 18th Kansas had lost their lives from various causes.[39]

But with the renewed killing of 1868, Crawford was at it again. On August 22, he sent off a letter to President Johnson asking for more troops. "If the Government cannot protect its own citizens," he sarcastically told the president, "let the fact be made known, that the people may endeavor to protect themselves, or if volunteers are needed we will furnish . . . all that may be necessary to insure a permanent and lasting peace. The Peace Commission is a mockery and their policy a disgrace to the nation. I trust, therefore, that you will keep the Commissioners at home, and stop issuing arms, ammunition and supplies to hostile Indians while they are robbing, murdering and outraging a defenseless people."[40]

The central government, however, was not yet ready to grant Crawford's request. Instead, Major General Philip Sheridan authorized the formation of the Forsyth Scouts under regular army control. But after the Battle of Beecher Island, Governor Crawford finally got his way. In October he authorized the organization of the 19th Kansas Volunteer Cavalry. Response to the call was tremendous. In little over three weeks,

Major General Philip Sheridan. As Hancock's replacement as commander of the Department of the Missouri, Sheridan authorized the formation of the Forsyth Scouts to protect settlers in western Kansas. By October 1868 he would abandon the idea of utilizing an independent "ranger unit" in favor of an all-out war of attrition during the winter months by concentrating troops of cavalry to attack Indian villages. *Courtesy Kansas State Historical Society, Topeka, Kansas.*

twelve full companies (about thirteen hundred men) had been recruited, and the 19th Kansas marched out with Custer and the 7th Cavalry toward the Washita as one wing of Sheridan's winter campaign. At the head of the new regiment was "Colonel" Samuel J. Crawford, who resigned the governorship to lead his Kansas recruits against the Indians, who he felt were the root cause of all his official woes.[41]

In Colorado Territory, at the western end of the Smoky Hill route, although settlers did not suffer as heavily from Indian depredations as their western Kansas neighbors, there was still fear and panic in late summer 1868. By August about two hundred Arapahoes, close allies of the Dog Soldiers who had been camped on Red Arm Creek, began raiding and stealing stock along the eastern slope of the Colorado Rockies. The appointed territorial governor, A. Cameron Hunt, was in the mountains with a tourist party headed by vice-presidential candidate Schuyler Colfax when the raids commenced. Consequently, Hunt dumped the "problem" in the lap of Acting Governor Frank Hall.

Immediately Hall called upon communities to organize militia units for their own protection. In twenty minutes, Georgetown raised a company of "fifty mountain boys, good & true. To arms! To arms!" bugled the headlines of the Pueblo *Colorado Chieftain*, its exterminationist rhetoric not unlike that printed in the territory's yellow newspapers shortly before the Sand Creek Massacre. "The red fiends are again on the warpath. . . . Whole families are being murdered and being scalped by these devils incarnate."[42] Similar militia companies were raised elsewhere. On one occasion, a war party of Arapahoes came into Colorado City, looked over the town's military preparedness, and promptly announced that they were after their traditional enemies, the Utes.

When the bodies of Mrs. Henrietta Dieterman and her five-year-old son, killed by the Arapahoes, were brought into Denver on August 28, however, panic similar to the hysteria of 1864 before Sand Creek, when the mutilated bodies of the Ward Hungate family were displayed to the public, seized the frontier city. Acting Governor Frank Hall, who just happened to be passing by at the very time some citizens were displaying the Dietermans' bodies, was suddenly grabbed by a mob and thrust into an express wagon whereupon he was "invited" to explain what he proposed to do about the situation.[43] Like Crawford in Topeka, Hall in late summer 1868 sent off a series of frantic messages to both Sheridan and Sherman at the headquarters of the military Department of the Missouri and the Division of the Missouri respectively. He reported that the Arapahoes were killing settlers and destroying ranches "in all directions." He told Sheridan that Indians had almost surrounded Colorado and that the Wells Fargo freighters upon whom the city of Denver depended for supplies had to fight their way into the territory daily. Finally Sherman authorized Hall to raise militia. He also gave Colorado a company of the 7th Cavalry currently at Fort Reynolds but scheduled to be transferred to Fort Dodge.[44]

But Hall lacked the efficient machinery that Crawford had perfected in Kansas for quickly raising militia. Based only locally, most companies could not communicate effectively and thus were unable to coordinate their activities. As with some of the Kansas volunteers, a number of the Colorado recruits signed up to "exterminate" Indians. When Frank Hall inquired about the qualifications of a militia commander in Pueblo, the reply came that "he was in Baxter's company at Sand Creek. He is a good man to fight Indians." As far as the acting governor was concerned, the response was sufficient endorsement to approve the appointment.

By mid-September the scare in Colorado calmed down and the territorial government avoided the undesirable task of issuing inflationary scrip to supply the militia, a situation that would only have added to the ongoing economic slump in Colorado during 1868. About the only meaningful act Hall initiated was to send a scout out from Denver in September to find Major George A. Forsyth and his command, who at the time were riding toward their fateful encounter with Roman Nose and Tall Bull at Beecher Island. Hall wished to offer to Forsyth the services of some of Colorado's militia companies. The scout never found Forsyth on the Arickaree, however. The only thing he did find was the Honorable Roscoe Conkling, the stalwart Republican party leader from New York who had been one of Governor Hunt's "distinguished" vacationers that summer and was now returning home across the plains with his entourage accompanied by a heavy guard. "All of which is very nice," the scout commented wryly, "for these eastern men that are afraid of loosing [sic] their hair."[45]

But during the warfare of 1867–1869, mostly Kansans, not Coloradoans, would actually engage the Indians on the central plains frontier.
These men considered themselves "defenders" of home and community.
Consequently, there was rarely a shortage of volunteers when the state
government called for militia. The regular army on the frontier usually
faced a dilemma with how to employ these volunteer troops, who often-
times wanted nothing more than to kill as many Indians as possible in as
short a time as possible. Because commanders feared a repeat of the Sand
Creek Massacre, allowing such units to act independently was usually out
of the question.

Nevertheless, it was almost impossible to keep besieged settlers from
trying to organize and defend themselves, especially with the regular army
spread so thinly across the plains and the civil governors pressuring the
high command and even the president for swift and immediate action. In
August 1868, Major General Philip Sheridan, having replaced Hancock
as commander of the Department of the Missouri, compromised by
authorizing the formation of a highly mobile strike force composed of fifty
"first class hardy frontiersmen" from the Kansas settlements to be enlisted
at Fort Hays and Fort Harker. These men, however, would not form an
independent "state" militia company but would instead technically be
mustered as scouts in the army's quartermaster's department and operate
directly under regular army officers Major George A. Forsyth and First
Lieutenant Frederick H. Beecher.[46]

As could be expected, a substantial number of the men who enlisted
in the Forsyth Scouts lived in Lincoln, Ottawa, Mitchell, Cloud, and
Jewell counties, not far from the Indians' deadline at Waconda Springs,
and near the settlements where most of the raids during 1867 and 1868
had occurred. All of these counties, with the exception of Ottawa, had
been organized in 1867 and thus represented the frontier line in the
Smoky Hill country close to the ninety-eighth meridian in those years.
Eager to drive the Indians further west so that homesteaders could
prove-up their homesteads without interruption, these men were anxious
to join the new experimental "ranger unit" that Sheridan authorized.
From Lincoln County near the future towns of Beverly, Lincoln, and
Tescott, came Chalmers Smith, a Civil War veteran who had settled there

in 1866. Neighbor James ("Jack") Peate, son of a New York Methodist preacher, had run away to the Kansas frontier in 1865 to "fight Indians." At age eighteen, he already had gained experience as a scout. George Greene, another recruit, settled in 1866. His sixteen-year-old wife, "who could ride and shoot as well as he," was reputedly the first white woman settler in Lincoln County. From Ottawa County came Howard Morton, son of a Plymouth, Massachusetts, shipbuilder; he was formerly a captain in the 30th Massachusetts Volunteers during the Civil War.[47]

From along the banks of the Saline River came Louis Farley and his son Hutch. Young Eli Ziegler, also from the Saline Valley, already had a reputation as being the "best shot" in Lincoln County.[48] Frank Harrington, who lived nearby, was also a New Yorker and was a veteran of an Illinois regiment during the Civil War; he signed up eagerly.[49] From Jewell County, the scene of some of the bloodiest raids, came thirty-six-year-old farmer Fletcher Vilott of Limestone Township.[50] Although these men would not be able to prevent the depredations committed in October, they would, on September 17, 1868, at the Battle of Beecher Island, as members of the Forsyth Scouts, get the chance to avenge the grievances of their neighbors who suffered at the hands of the Indians in 1867 and during the summer of 1868.

Hancock's War and the Battle of Prairie Dog Creek

If any man thinks there is no war with, or danger from, the Indians, let him make a trip from Wallace to Harker and then he will realize it.

— UNIDENTIFIED SCOUT, 7TH U.S. CAVALRY
Summer 1867

At almost every turn, the Indians frustrated the soldiers of the regular army who were detailed to protect homesteaders, freighters, and railroad workers on the central plains frontier during summer 1867. Beginning in May, and continuing through the warm months, the Indians struck hard both along the Smoky Hill route and the Platte River Road. At any given time, Sioux, various bands of Cheyennes, Kiowas, as well as Arapahoes raided along the central corridor between Fort Harker and Denver. But most of the attacks came at the hands of the angry Dog Soldiers in retribution for Hancock's burning their village on Red Arm Creek.[1]

Homesteaders were not the only ones to suffer the wrath of the plains warriors. Wells Fargo stage stations, railroad construction sites, military patrols, and even forts were all fair game. Returning eventually to his headquarters at Fort Leavenworth, Major General Winfield Scott Hancock left much of the active campaigning that summer to companies of the 7th and 10th cavalries. At any given time there were scarcely enough troops in the field in the critical location to successfully combat the large numbers of warriors they encountered. Commanders even kept troopers from the field to help aid and feed the settlers who had abandoned their homes and sought the safety of the military posts.[2]

After initially reporting the depredations that the Indians had committed along the Smoky Hill route after Hancock broke up the Dog Soldier and Sioux villages on Red Arm Creek, Custer found himself immobilized for a month at Fort Hays waiting for necessary shipments of forage, food, and other supplies. Morale suffered terribly and desertions became frequent. Although reports of Indian depredations came in, there was little Custer could do until he received his supplies and until the prairie grass was sufficiently high for his horses to forage.[3]

Custer and six companies of the 7th Cavalry finally marched from Fort Hays on June 1. In an effort to mitigate the fears of Colorado territorial governor A. Cameron Hunt that the war was about to spread up the South Platte Trail toward Denver, Sherman ordered Custer to proceed up the Platte to Fort McPherson, Nebraska, near present-day North Platte and thence west to Fort Sedgwick (Old Julesburg), Colorado Territory. There he would receive further instructions from Lieutenant General William T. Sherman, the division commander himself.[4] The only signs of the Indians that the men of the 7th Cavalry saw on the march to Fort McPherson were the austere ruins of several abandoned and burned-out homesteads and ranches, several with crude wooden crosses on the property bearing the hastily carved inscription "Unknown — Killed by the Indians."[5]

While waiting for orders from Sherman, the 7th Cavalry camped near Fort McPherson in the vicinity of the Jack Morrow Ranch, where in early June they were unexpectedly visited by the Oglala headman, Pawnee Killer, Turkey Legs, a Northern Cheyenne who frequently camped with the Sioux, and the Dog Soldiers.[6] Informing Custer that he wanted nothing to do with the Cheyennes, whom he referred to as "bad Indians," Pawnee Killer told Custer that he would be happy to bring in his band to Fort McPherson. Soon after this parley Sherman arrived in person at Fort McPherson and ordered Custer to move the 7th to the Republican Valley and scout the headwaters of that river for the Indians who had escaped the village on Red Arm Creek. Custer would then move west to Fort Sedgwick for supplies.[7]

Custer moved out on June 15 and a few days later made camp on the Republican near present-day Benkleman, Nebraska, just north of the

Kansas state line. On June 23, he ordered Lieutenant W. W. Cooke with forty-eight troopers and sixteen wagons to move out to Fort Wallace to replenish supplies while simultaneously dispatching Major Joel Elliot to Fort Sedgwick with messages for Sherman. The next morning a party of warriors swept down on Custer's reduced force while they were still encamped and tried to stampede the soldiers' horses. They failed in the attempt but wounded a picket in the attack. The Indians retired to a nearby hill, where they remained in clear view of the soldiers, flashing signals to other warriors with mirrors. Soon Custer's men found themselves surrounded. Custer wisely decided to use his Osage scouts to parley with the Indians. He sent out a scout named Gay to arrange a meeting between the lines.

A small detachment of Indians moved down to talk with Gay and it was then revealed that the leader of the party was none other than Pawnee Killer. The war leader agreed to meet with Custer. The conference came to nothing, as the commander of the 7th Cavalry spotted Indians creeping down the ravines toward the parley. Fearing treachery, Custer quickly returned to camp, where he ordered the entire command to mount their horses and pursue the Indians.

The warriors broke off from their positions on the hillsides and in the ravines surrounding the soldier's camp but still easily eluded Custer's pursuit, breaking into smaller and smaller bands, leaving faint trails that eventually could not be followed. Returning to camp, the weary command again spotted Indians. Custer ordered Captain Louis Hamilton, a grandson of Alexander Hamilton who would be killed a year later at the Washita, to pursue the Indians. The warriors easily decoyed Hamilton's troopers by keeping just out of rifle range. Hamilton kept up the chase for eight miles. When the Indians split up, Hamilton divided his command. Soon he and twenty-five men found themselves surrounded by a party twice their size. Hamilton ordered his troopers to dismount and form a circle around the horses. He fought off the ensuing attack with ease and without casualties. The Indians sustained two killed and a number wounded.[8] Hamilton returned to camp safely after having inflicted the first and last casualties that the troopers of Custer's expedition would impose and half the total casualties of Hancock's spring campaign.[9]

On July 6 Custer eventually returned to the safety of the South Platte at Riverside Station, some forty miles west of Fort Sedgwick in Colorado Territory, having been pushed to the limit by the Indians. There he wired Sherman. *Missouri-Democrat* correspondent Henry M. Stanley had been there before Custer arrived. While Custer was down on the Republican the Indians were raiding up on the Platte. "Between Bishop's Ranch and Junction Cut Off, eighty miles from Denver, there are no less than ninety-three graves," Stanley reported on June 25, "twenty-seven of which contain the bodies of settlers killed within the last six weeks. Dead bodies," he claimed, "have been seen floating down the Platte."[10]

To Custer's amazement, the reply came back from Sherman that the Indians had shifted their activities back south to the Smoky Hill route. Suspecting that they were being reinforced by warriors from south of the Arkansas River, Sherman had dispatched Second Lieutenant Lyman S. Kidder, 2nd Cavalry, and ten troopers from Fort Sedgwick to Custer's camp on the Republican with orders for the 7th to move back to Fort Wallace. It is possible that the two commands passed near each other about June 30 without realizing it. Because Kidder had not been heard from, Custer began to fear for his safety.

So once again the 7th Cavalry turned south, hoping that Kidder had done likewise and reached the safety of Fort Wallace. Indians swarmed over the country between the South Platte and the Smoky Hill. Dissatisfaction mounted among the troopers of the 7th Cavalry. Thirty-four deserted while still on the Platte, slipping away in parties of two and three. A half-day march prompted ten more "snowbirds" to head west to the comparative serenity of the Colorado gold camps. Angered by this desertion, Custer ordered Major Joel Elliot to pursue these last deserters and shoot to kill if they faced resistance. Some of the deserters were on foot and Elliot easily caught up with them. He had to shoot three of the men, wounding one of them fatally.

That night some of the men alerted the officers of yet another plot to desert en masse. As a result of a concerted watch, however, the night passed without incident. Custer then moved quickly southward toward Fort Wallace, wearing out his men's horses on the march. Soon the command picked up Kidder's trail, which had turned toward Fort Wallace after Kidder had found Custer's abandoned camp on the Republican. A little farther along, they encountered a dead cavalry horse; buzzards circled in the distance, and Custer feared the worst.[11]

His dread was justified. Buffalo were plentiful in the Republican Valley that summer and the Indians had hunting parties out pursuing them along the forks of Beaver Creek. Shortly after Kidder and his troop turned toward Fort Wallace (probably July 2 or 3), a hunting party of Sioux and twelve Cheyennes struck them. The Sioux were members of Pawnee Killer's band. The Cheyennes, including some Dog Soldiers, were under the leadership of Howling Wolf, Tobacco, and Big Head. The Sioux hunters first discovered Kidder's pitifully small troop and brought the news to their Cheyenne friends. "Hurry and gather your horses, all you Cheyenne men," one of them purportedly shouted. "Soldiers with pack mules are coming." Kidder's little command never had a chance. Seeing the Indians approach, the lieutenant ordered his men to dismount and take refuge in a nearby ravine along the bank of the South Fork of Beaver Creek in present-day Sherman County, Kansas. The Cheyennes and then the Sioux rushed up and surrounded them. Soon it was over. Kidder, all ten troopers, and a Sioux scout named Red Bead lay dead.[12]

Custer found them on July 12. The awful stench in the little valley led the 7th Cavalry right to the ghastly scene. "A sight met our gaze which even at this remote day makes my very blood curdle," Custer remembered. "Lying in irregular order, and within a very limited circle, were the mangled bodies of poor Kidder and his party, yet so brutally hacked and disfigured as to be beyond recognition save as human beings. Every individual of the party had been scalped and his skull broken — the latter done by some weapon, probably a tomahawk — except the Sioux chief Red Bead, whose scalp had simply been removed from his head and then thrown down by his side. . . . The sinews of the arms and legs had been cut away, the noses of every man hacked off, and the features otherwise defaced so that it would have been scarcely possible for even a relative to recognize a single one of the unfortunate victims. . . . Each body was pierced by from twenty to fifty arrows, and the arrows were found as the

Fort Wallace, Kansas, in 1867. Troops from Fort Wallace, which was established in 1866 on the bank of the Smoky Hill River, were supposed to protect the Smoky Hill route as well as construction of the Union Pacific Eastern Division. Because this area was often garrisoned with minimal forces of infantry, the effort was usually futile — the Indians raided express stations near the fort almost at will. *Courtesy Kansas State Historical Society, Topeka, Kansas.*

savage demons had left them, bristling in the bodies."[13] Custer ordered the pitiful remains to be buried in a mass grave there on the Kansas prairie where the troopers had fallen.

Moving on to Fort Wallace, Custer found that Asiatic cholera had broken out along the Smoky Hill route. Fearing that the disease was also present at Fort Riley, where his wife was quartered, Custer left Fort Wallace abruptly on July 18 with a handpicked escort of seventy-five troopers and Captain Hamilton. They made the ride of 156 miles to Fort Hays in fifty-five hours, fighting off Indians along the way at Downer's Station on the Union Pacific Eastern Division; two troopers were killed in the process. Custer rode on to Fort Harker. There he reported to his district commander, Colonel A. J. Smith, and arranged for badly needed supplies to be sent to Fort Wallace. Then he went on to see his wife at Fort Riley.

Shortly thereafter, Custer was arrested for absence without leave, for needless abuse of his animals during the campaign, and for unnecessary cruelty to the deserters of his command. He was made the scapegoat for the army's failures on the central plains during the summer of 1867. Tried by court-martial at Fort Leavenworth, Custer was sentenced to suspension from rank, command, and pay for one year. Thus the Hancock-Custer campaign, which had begun as a bravado display of military power, ended in shambles. Far from stopping the raids and forcing the Indians back to their reservations, the campaign had the opposite effect. The overland routes, many now thought, were unsafe for travel or railroad construction.[14]

Although much excellent scholarship has been exercised recounting Custer's frustrating march up and down the central plains during June and July 1867 in futile pursuit of the Sioux, Dog Soldiers, and other Cheyenne bands, the Indian raids along the Smoky Hill route during the same period and the response of the Kansas state government have received but scant attention in many modern histories. While Custer was otherwise occupied around the Platte and the Republican, ostensibly protecting the Colorado frontier, the Indians made life miserable for both civilians and soldiers in western Kansas. Between May 22 and June 24, railroad construction of the Union Pacific Eastern Division was all but halted. On June 16, while on an inspection tour of the Smoky Hill route, Major General Winfield Scott Hancock declared that every station along the road for 170 miles on either side of Fort Wallace had been attacked by the Indians at least four times.[15]

During May and June the Indians concentrated a number of raids in the vicinity of that remote outpost on the shortgrass prairie of extreme western Kansas. Major A. R. Calhoun described Fort Wallace in 1867 "as being beautifully located on the north fork of the Smoky Hill River." He wrote that its buildings "were being erected of a beautiful pink-colored magnesian limestone which can be cut with a saw and plane, and hardens on exposure."[16] The officer largely responsible for supervising the construction of the post at that time was twenty-seven-year-old First Lieutenant Frederick H. Beecher, who within a year would cast his lot with the Forsyth Scouts and give up his life in the battle that would afterward bear his name.

Beecher was the nephew of the outspoken New England abolitionist clergyman, Henry Ward Beecher. Partially lamed at Gettysburg in 1863 by a Confederate artillery shell that shattered his knee while he was serving as a lieutenant in the 16th Maine, Beecher's military career seemed over. But in 1865 he received a commission in the regular army as second lieutenant in the 3rd U.S. Infantry and was promoted to first lieutenant in 1866. A graduate of Bowdoin, Beecher served as post adjutant and then quartermaster of Fort Wallace in 1867. It was during the raids around that post that Beecher got his baptism of fire against the warriors of the central plains.[17]

On May 27, Company I of the 7th Cavalry under Captain Miles Keogh skirmished with Indians near Pond Creek Station, just west of the fort, where a number of livestock had been run off. On June 4, a war party attempted to steal horses from Fort Wallace itself. On June 11 and 15, Indians and soldiers from Fort Wallace fought engagements at Big Timbers, about twenty miles west of the post. Also on the 15th, warriors attacked a Wells Fargo stagecoach between Big Timbers and Goose Creek Station. During the month of June, lookouts spotted Indian fires every night north of the fort. After Custer's three hundred troopers of the 7th Cavalry moved north from Fort Hays for the Platte on June 1, the Kansas forts became depleted. Only about fifty effectives remained to defend Fort Wallace. Among them was First Lieutenant Frederick H. Beecher.

On June 21, between two hundred and three hundred Dog Soldiers and other Cheyennes once again ran off the stock at Pond Creek Station and then turned the next day on Fort Wallace itself. A handful of soldiers, including Beecher, left the fort to drive off the warriors. The engagement lasted for an hour and a half. The Indians killed two soldiers and wounded two others in the engagement. That same day, the Indians attacked a party of men quarrying limestone within sight of the fort. They killed a contractor named Pat McCarty and one other worker in the attack. By June 24, Fort Wallace was in a virtual state of siege.[18]

Two days later, on June 26, the Dog Soldiers and Sioux struck yet again at Pond Creek Station. Captain Albert Barnitz, who had just reported for duty at Fort Wallace two days previous, took Company G of the 7th Cavalry out to thrash them. The Indians withdrew to the brow of a hill two miles from the fort. Barnitz ordered the charge at a gallop, but to his utter amazement the Dog Soldiers formed into a line and, imitating the whites' style of fighting, countercharged the troopers in the manner of a squadron of cavalry. It was a sight that Captain Barnitz would

First Lieutenant Frederick H. Beecher. Nephew of abolitionist Henry Ward Beecher, Frederick H. Beecher was introduced to Indian warfare while stationed at Fort Wallace in 1867 as a member of the 3rd Infantry. In 1868 Sheridan would name Beecher as second in command of the newly organized Forsyth Scouts. *Courtesy Kansas State Historical Society, Topeka, Kansas.*

not soon forget. "They turned suddenly upon my line," he remembered, "and came literally *sailing* in, uttering their peculiar Hi! — Hi! — Hi! and terminating it with a war-whoop — their ponies, gaily decked with feathers and scalp-locks, tossing their proud little heads high in the air, and looking from side to side, as their riders poured in a rapid fire from their repeating arms, or sending their keen arrows with fearful accuracy and force."[19] (It is doubtful that the Indians possessed repeating arms.)

The fighting was desperate and at close quarters. The Dog Soldiers gave tremendous exhibitions of riding; whenever a warrior was shot from his horse, two companions would ride forward in the midst of the fighting, pick up their fallen comrade, and carry him back to safety.[20] Captain Barnitz, in a letter to Jennie, his bride of only four months, described the scene that took place when several of the warriors recognized him as the soldiers' commander. "One Indian dashed toward me, as I rode from the centre to the left," he wrote, "and fired several shots at me over his pony's head, and then when opposite me turned, and rode parallel with me, on my right side, lying lengthwise on his pony, and firing from under his pony's neck, his left arm being thrown over the pony's neck, and grasping his rifle! The shots came *very* close!"[21]

Although Corporal Prentice G. Harris thought he identified Roman Nose in this fight, Roman Nose was actually at the time miles away in the Dog Soldier camp on Beaver Creek. The warrior in question was actually a Sioux riding a fine gray horse. The man was quite conspicuous in the battle, dashing into the midst of the fighting on his powerful war-pony. As he was about to spear a prostrate soldier, Corporal Harris rode up and slashed the warrior with his saber. The Sioux turned on Harris but the corporal instantly placed the muzzle of his Spencer on the warrior's chest and fired. With blood flowing from the wound, the Indian fell forward on his horse.[22]

A powerful warrior, either a Dog Soldier named Big Moccasin or a man named Long Chin who had lost a son in an earlier fight with whites,[23] literally picked up a wounded bugler, Charles Clark, and stripped him of his clothes as he rode along. The warrior then mashed Clark's head with his war club and threw the body under his horse's feet. "The body of Sergeant Frederick Wyllyams was also fearfully mutilated," exclaimed a

Harper's Weekly reporter. "His scalp was taken, two balls pierced his brain, and his right brow was cut open with a hatchet," the reporter continued. "His nose was severed and his throat gashed. His body was opened and his heart laid bare. The legs were cut to the bone and the arms hacked with knives." An engraving copied from a photograph of Wyllyams's body accompanied the *Weekly* article, undoubtedly designed to shock eastern readers and garner sympathy for the "military solution" on the frontier.[24]

The Indians, with overwhelming numbers, drove Barnitz's men back to Fort Wallace with the loss of seven men killed, several wounded, and half the horses captured or killed. Then the Indians rode out toward the Republican, where they attacked the 7th Cavalry supply train under Lieutenant W. W. Cooke, which was returning from Fort Wallace to Custer's camp on the Republican. Relief for the beleaguered post came on July 13 when Custer straggled in, after having buried Kidder's men, with what remained, after desertions, of companies A, D, E, H, K, and M of the 7th Cavalry; their significant campaigning was over for the year.[25]

Early in July, Sherman made a personal inspection of the Kansas frontier and concluded that heavy rains more than Indians were the cause of delayed railroad construction. The unprofitability of the Wells Fargo stage line to Denver, Sherman concluded, had as much to do with the company's cessation of services that summer as with the Cheyennes and Sioux. Suspecting that the people of Kansas were exaggerating the Indian danger to gain more expensive protection, Sherman was nevertheless convinced, after much indecision, to allow Governor Samuel J. Crawford to authorize the enlistment of the 18th Kansas Volunteer Cavalry to assist in the protection of the Smoky Hill route and the construction of the Union Pacific Eastern Division. Sherman further augmented this militia with nine companies of the 10th U.S. Cavalry (the "Buffalo Soldiers"), which moved into defensive positions along the Smoky Hill route and the Santa Fe Trail.[26]

On July 15, four companies of the 18th Kansas, under Major Horace L. Moore of Lawrence, reported for service at Fort Harker. Almost immediately the command became demoralized when Asiatic cholera broke out at the fort. Every company lost men, and Company C lost thirteen in two weeks. As with Custer's regulars, desertion spread through the ranks of the volunteers.[27] The disease had not yet subsided when the troops moved out to Fort Hays. By August 1, meanwhile, the Indians had resumed their raids along the Smoky Hill route with several night assaults on black soldiers (mostly members of the 38th U.S. Infantry) who were guarding the railroad construction along the route. Officers stationed these men in adobe bunkers and entrenchments along the line west of Fort Hays. One observer wondered if the white officers had stationed these small groups of black soldiers there "as bait for the Indians."[28]

In response, Captain Brevet Lieutenant Colonel Henry C. Corbin, the commandant at Fort Hays, ordered out the 38th Infantry and Company F of the 10th Cavalry under Captain (Brevet Major) George A. Armes to find the raiders. Armes's cavalry broke off and camped near the site of a contractor's camp, where the Indians killed seven workers on August 1. On August 2, a party of about seventy-five or eighty Cheyenne warriors hit Armes's command as they scouted along the Saline River. Company F dismounted and fought on foot as the Indians surrounded the thirty-four troopers. For six hours under the broiling sun the soldiers fought off their attackers until their ammunition ran low. Then the troopers mounted and fought their way through the Indian lines. For the next fifteen miles the warriors pursued the soldiers before the Cheyennes broke off the engagement. Captain Armes claimed that his command killed six Indians. Armes himself took a bullet in the hip, and Sergeant William Christy from Pennsylvania was shot in the head and killed, the first battle death of a "Buffalo Soldier" in the 10th Cavalry.[29]

Later in the month, Captain Armes, who had sufficiently recovered from his wound to resume command, proposed taking Company F of the 10th Cavalry, along with two companies of the 18th Kansas, to break up a large concentration of Indians he believed to be camped on the Solomon River. Meanwhile, Major Moore, with the remaining companies of the 18th Kansas, would scout the same stream. If they located the Indians, he reasoned, the commands could combine and engage the warriors. One of the scouts for the 18th Kansas on this campaign was a rather ordinary-looking young man from Topeka named Allison J. Pliley. At twenty-three, Pliley was already a veteran campaigner. He had been on the plains since he was seventeen, driving ox teams and hauling flour to Denver, gaining experience with both Indians and the country along the Smoky Hill route. During the Civil War he had enlisted in Company F, 15th Kansas Cavalry. During Major General Sterling Price's raid into western Missouri in 1864, Pliley's company distinguished themselves when they participated in a charge that drove Brigadier General Joseph Shelby's Confederate brigade from the field during the Battle of Westport.

When the 18th Kansas marched in August 1867, Pliley took a detachment to scout an area of recent attacks on a party of buffalo hunters who were supplying meat to a railroad construction gang along the breaks of the Saline. After he picked up an Indian trail, Pliley surprised a small party of Arapahoes, all of whom fled except for "one fellow who was bolder and better mounted than the rest," Pliley remembered nostalgically years later from the comfort of his home in Kansas City. "I let him think he was gaining upon me until I got him far enough away, and then I began to circle around him Indian fashion, and presently he began the same tactics, and out there on the prairie we fought it out, circling about at full speed, all the time drawing closer and shooting to kill. After a few shots the Arapahoe reeled from his horse and fell to the ground. I rode to him, and dismounting, took off him a medal about three inches in diameter which he wore around his neck. On one side it had the head of Lincoln and on the other a representation of an Indian village. That was all I had time to take, as the rest of the band hearing the firing were hastening to the rescue."[30]

On the night of the 21st, Pliley scouted the breaks along Prairie Dog Creek in what today is Phillips County in extreme northwestern Kansas. The Dog Soldiers had their "wolves" out watching every move of the invaders. "It was a beautiful night," Pliley remembered, "and all went well until we got near the banks of the Prairie Dog, in the after part of the night. Then I saw signal arrows going up, the object of which I well knew."[31] After reporting back to the command, Armes ordered Lieutenant John W. Price of the 18th Kansas to take the supply train with sixty-five men and camp out of harm's way along the banks of the Prairie Dog some five miles from the command. Pliley was then sent out on another scout. Meanwhile, Captain George B. Jenness of the 18th Kansas had succeeded in getting lost while scouting the same region. Pliley caught up with Jenness the next day at Price's camp, and together, their combined forces totaling only twenty-nine troopers, they left the wagon train and proceeded to move out to locate Armes. They didn't make it that day. As Jenness's group stopped to water their horses along a tributary of Prairie Dog Creek, Pliley rode out and looked over the field with his glasses. To his horror he spotted a half-mile away "a band of at least 300 Indians coming . . . full tilt."[32]

Jenness ordered his men to form a hollow square. The tactic worked for a time and the command fought its way in the general direction of Captain Armes's command. But the Dog Soldiers were too much for them. Warriors surrounded Jenness's men and waved blankets, making some of the cavalry horses stampede. The Indians forced the troopers to take refuge in a depression on the prairie. During the initial fighting the Dog Soldiers circled around the hollow square and fired at the troopers from under the necks of their war-ponies. In a daring display of horsemanship, a magnificent warrior, who might have been Roman Nose, led a charge. The soldiers stopped it with their seven-shot Spencer carbines. This lone warrior, however, refused to break off; he rode down one man and then on through the square. He escaped to the other side without a scratch even though the whites fired at least fifty shots at him.[33]

Several men were wounded in the fighting, including Pliley, who took two bullets in quick succession in the calf of his right leg. Soon the Indians were reinforced by what Pliley estimated to be an additional four hundred warriors, a band that had only shortly before repulsed Armes's men about the same time that Jenness had been hit. Seeing that they could not reach Armes to their front, Jenness's little command fought their way back over the same ground to a dry canyon that ran down into Prairie Dog Creek. At this point Jenness's force had suffered one killed and fourteen wounded. Fortunately for Jenness, the Indians possessed only old Spring-field and Mississippi rifles; otherwise casualities would undoubtedly have been much higher. During this retreat the Dog Soldiers taunted Jenness's men with insults. One warrior claimed that Armes's command had been massacred and the same was about to happen to them. Another Indian, brandishing on the tip of his spear the scalp of the black trooper who had been killed during the retreat down to the creek, shouted in plain English, "This is the way we will serve you all."[34]

Pliley then advised his commander to turn loose the remaining horses to divert the Indians and thus cover the retreat of the men into the little canyon. The stratagem was successful, as a number of warriors scrambled after the horses before they had gone two hundred feet. "As they rushed [the horses] in a bunch," Pliley recalled, "it was like shooting quail, and before they had time to realize what had happened, we poured several volleys into them."[35] The Indians finally broke off to attack Price's wagon train and darkness ended the fighting for the day. The next morning, however, the Indians appeared again in full force and Pliley made a desperate ride to locate Price's wagon train and some reinforcements for Jenness's crippled command. Pliley found the train surrounded. Soon a group of Indians spotted him and immediately gave chase, "firing a very hail of bullets after me," Pliley said. "My horse fairly flew and as I lay over his side I heard the bullets singing about me like a swarm of bees."[36]

Although Price had problems of his own and could offer no help, Captain Armes and the main command soon appeared and broke through the Indian lines. Armes ordered Captain Edgar A. Barker's company out to form a square around Jenness's men, and the group thus fought their way back to Armes's position. In this fashion the two commands finally reunited by the afternoon of August 22. For the most part Armes and the 18th Kansas, along with Company F of the 10th Cavalry, remained on the defensive for the remainder of the day. Again the warriors taunted the soldiers. Through the clear prairie air came a shout in English: "Come out of that hole you sons of bitches and give us a fair fight." Another warrior yelled out, "We don't want to fight the niggers; we want to fight you white sons of bitches."[37]

Under the cover of darkness Armes moved his force back toward the Solomon River in the direction of Fort Hays. But he found himself surrounded again on August 23. It wasn't until that night that the Indians withdrew sufficiently for the command to finally reach the safety of Fort Hays. The warriors had driven their enemy from the Dog Soldiers' country. Armes reported that Company F, 10th Cavalry, lost one man killed and thirteen wounded, and Jenness reported two dead and sixteen wounded. Armes claimed to have killed fifty Indians with three times that number wounded. Both officers reported that total Indian strength exceeded eight hundred. Besides Roman Nose, Satanta of the Kiowas was recognized, as was Charley Bent, the mixed-blood son of William Bent. Arapahoes, Kiowas, and Sioux as well as Dog Soldiers and other Cheyennes were supposedly in the fight.[38]

Although Colonel Corbin, the commander at Fort Hays, tried to claim a victory on behalf of Armes and the 10th Cavalry, Major Horace L. Moore, commander of the 18th Kansas, who never made it into the fight, pointed out that the command had been driven from the field and blamed the defeat on Armes, criticizing him for dividing his command on two occasions.[39] In a letter of explanation to Governor Crawford, Moore blasted the regular army officer. Armes's "miserable failure," Moore wrote, "is owing entirely to his having been too anxious for a fight of his own which led him to run away from me and [to] his want of judgement in scattering his command all over the plains."[40] Controversy aside, the black soldiers of the 10th Cavalry fought well alongside the Kansas frontiersmen for a group of raw regular army recruits. A modern scholar of the Buffalo Soldiers wrote that Armes "no longer led a bunch of recruits after August 21, but a company of fighting men."[41]

Nevertheless, the rivalry between the officers of the state militia and the regular army mirrored once again the belief of many that volunteer regiments would ultimately be more effective than those of the regular army in defending their own states and territories. In 1867 neither the state of Kansas nor the regular army could afford such controversy, given their miserable performance from April through August that began with Hancock's disastrous campaign and ended with the Battle of Prairie Dog Creek. During his time on the plains in 1867, war correspondent Henry M. Stanley came to favor the use of the volunteers. "The regular troops can fight the Indians when they get a chance," he said, "but the difficulty with them is to find the Indians."[42] Stanley felt that the volunteer officers were more competent than the regulars and that they had more interest in defending their homelands. Although Stanley did not favor extermination, he concluded that the volunteers knew the ways of the plains warriors better than "men trained at West Point who never saw Indians [and] thousands of eastern soldiers just as inexperienced as themselves [whom the government sent] to catch savages who were always on the gallop."[43]

Congress agreed only halfway with Stanley's assessment. Even before the 18th Kansas took the field they had recognized the failure of the regular army that summer to control the tribesmen of the central and southern plains. But neither was militia the answer in their estimation. Consequently, on July 20 Congress authorized the creation of a "Blue Ribbon" Peace Commission to formulate and conclude new treaties. The Battle of Prairie Dog Creek thus ended offensive operations in the central corridor for 1867, as the troops were recalled from the field during August in favor of extending the olive branch of peace to the plains tribes.

In reality both the volunteers and the regulars lacked sufficient manpower to effectively protect settlers and workers on the overland trails during the summer of 1867. By th summer of 1868, however, Major General Philip Sheridan, who followed Hancock as commander of the Department of the Missouri, would attempt with the creation of the Forsyth Scouts to streamline the army's ability to pursue, after an initial attack, the swift-moving Indian raiders.

So most of the men of the 18th Kansas Volunteer Cavalry went home during the autumn of 1867. The notable exception was Allison J. Pliley, whose fateful journey toward a rendezvous at Beecher Island with many of these same determined warriors of the plains had only begun.

The cause of our troubles is the Powder River road running north, and the Smoky Hill road on the south. In that little space of country between the Smoky Hill and Platte River there is game. That is what we have to live upon. By stopping these roads I know you can get peace.

— PAWNEE KILLER
Autumn 1867

On August 6, 1867, Sleeping Rabbit, who was a Cheyenne warrior and a member of Turkey Legs's band, along with his friends Porcupine, Red Wolf, and others, wrecked a Union Pacific freight train. The incident took place near Plum Creek Station on the Union Pacific main line in central Nebraska, about sixty miles southeast of North Platte. The men, members of a war party led by Spotted Wolf, were returning home following a raid on their old enemies the Pawnees.[1] The three friends agreed that with the coming of the whites, who had burned their villages and destroyed their possessions, the Cheyennes had become impoverished. The railroad carried things that might be of use to the People.[2]

"Now the white people have taken all we had and have made us poor," one of them said, "and we ought to do something. In these big wagons that go on the metal road, there must be things that are valuable — perhaps clothing. If we could throw these wagons off the iron they run on and break them open, we could find out what was in them and could take whatever might be useful to us."[3]

"If we could bend the track up and spread it out the train might fall off," Sleeping Rabbit suggested. "Then we could see what was in the cars."[4]

"Red Wolf and I tried to do this," Porcupine remembered years later before his death in 1929. "[First,] we got a big stick, and just before sundown one day tied it to the rails and sat down to watch and see what would happen. Close by the track we built a big fire. Quite a long time after it got dark we heard a rumbling sound, at first very faint, but constantly growing louder. We said to each other: 'It is coming.' Presently the sound grew loud, and through the darkness we could see a small thing coming with something on it that moved up and down. [It was a handcar carrying six telegraph repairmen.]

"When the men on the car saw the fire and the Indians, they worked harder so as to run by them quickly, but when the car struck the stick, it jumped high into the air. The men on it got up from where they had fallen and ran away, but were soon overtaken and killed.

"On the handcar were two guns, and in handling them the Indians pulled something and the guns broke in two in the middle and the barrels fell down. [These were Spencer carbines, the first breech loaders the warriors had ever seen.] The Indians said: It is a pity these are broken; if they had not been, we should have had two good guns."[5]

When the Cheyennes wrecked the handcar they scalped the men who had been on it. As they examined the guns, they did not notice that one of the telegraph repairmen, an Englishman named William Thompson, was still alive and "playing possum." Thompson's quick thinking saved his life. After the collision threw him and his companions from the handcar, they exchanged a few shots with the Cheyennes, but a mounted warrior rode up, shot Thompson in the arm, and then clubbed him to the ground with his rifle. "He then took out his knife, stabbed me in the neck, and making a twirl round his fingers with my hair," Thompson told reporters in Omaha a couple of days later, "he commenced sawing and hacking away at my scalp. Though the pain was awful, and I felt dizzy and sick, I knew enough to keep quiet. After what seemed to be half an hour, he gave the last finishing cut to the scalp on my left temple, and as it still hung a little, he gave it a jerk. I just thought then that I could have screamed my life out. I can't describe it to you," Thompson said. "It just felt as if [my] whole head was taken right off."[6] The warrior galloped away, but as he did Thompson's scalp fell from his belt. In the darkness of the night Thompson was able to retrieve his scalp and hide until the Indians departed. He had a long painful wait.

It was at this point that the warriors took Sleeping Rabbit's suggestion and pried up the rails with some sort of levers. The Indians then lay down in the grass to see what would happen. Looking east over the level plains, Sleeping Rabbit, Porcupine, Red Wolf, and their companions finally spotted a light on the horizon that they mistook for the morning star and then another light. It was two trains, one following the other. Soon they could hear the steam locomotives puffing along through the night. Several warriors rode up the line and fired on the train but it did no good.

The little wood-burning locomotive puffed and made a loud noise, throwing sparks into the air, going faster and faster until it reached the break in the tracks. It jumped into the air, followed by the trailing wooden boxcars, all of which smashed together and then came crashing down beside the tracks. Quickly the Indians shot the engineer. Then from behind the caboose, carrying a lantern, came the fireman, who the warriors could tell was quite angry by the volume of profanity he uttered. He was killed immediately. The second train backed away. The warriors did not attack it.[7]

The Indians then broke into the boxcars to search for things of value. Dawn's light revealed goods strewn all over the prairie. There were bolts of silk and calico, sacks of flour, sugar, and coffee, boxes of shoes, and other goods. Two barrels of whiskey were located and several warriors broke in the head of the cask and many of the People became very intoxicated. Several young men then had a rollicking good time with the bolts of cloth, galloping their ponies wildly across the prairie with a bolt of calico or silk bounding behind and unrolling in billowing waves while other young men tried to ride over the ribbons of flowing cloth.[8] Around Cheyenne campfires on cold winter nights for many years to come, the men had a good laugh whenever this story was told.[9]

A warrior named Wolf Tooth had no use for the calico and silk. He said he preferred his buckskins even though he had seen other men's squaws make beautiful shirts from the fine bright cloth. Instead Wolf Tooth and his friend Big Foot went back to the caboose to see what they could find. They came back with some lunches that had been prepared for the train crew. There was bread, some "sweet stuff," and bacon. They put it in a bucket and took it home with them. Later Wolf Tooth told a joke of his own around the campfires — that he was the first one of the People to eat the white man's food.[10]

Finally the Cheyennes took hot coals from the firebox of the locomotive and shoveled them into the wooden boxcars, setting them ablaze. The bodies of the train and handcar crews where thrown into the pyre. Missing was William Thompson, but the Indians apparently did not notice it. Then the Indians packed as many goods as they could carry on their ponies and departed toward the Dog Soldier camps on the Republican River.[11] Meanwhile, Thompson had managed to crawl away, and he finally found refuge at Willow Island Station. By this time news of the raid on the train had been telegraphed all along the line.[12] Within a few days another westbound freight appeared at Plum Creek Station. When the boxcars were opened, out came Major Frank North and his celebrated Pawnee Scouts.[13] They had traveled 120 miles to Plum Creek Station. The scouts crossed the Platte River and lay in wait. Shortly Turkey Legs's band of Cheyennes returned with packhorses and some women and children to recover more valuables from the wreck.[14]

Turkey Legs's band had only about one hundred warriors, who were armed mostly with bows and lances. Major North had armed his blue-uniformed Pawnees with seven-shot Spencers and Colt revolvers. As the Pawnees slowly advanced, the Cheyenne warriors, along with some Sioux who were with them, gave a yell and charged their old enemies. With the first volleys from their repeating carbines the Pawnees killed seven of the Cheyennes and Sioux. Then they drove them back several miles across the prairie, capturing many of their ponies and taking prisoner a Cheyenne boy and a woman. The woman escaped the same day on an island in the Platte and made her way back to the People. Her friends gave her the new name of Island Woman because of her heroic feat.[15]

The news of the wrecking of the train had spread through the central plains like a prairie fire. On August 8, an eastbound freight brought back to Omaha the charred remains of the train crew. A huge crowd was on hand that included correspondent Henry M. Stanley. For those who "wished to pay the last sad tribute to murdered friends," Stanley reported, a small box was opened and there, surrounded by cotton, "lay a charred [human] trunk about two feet in length, resembling a half-burnt log of the same size."[16]

Also on the train, and very much alive, was William Thompson, carrying in a pail of water his scalp, which, according to Stanley, appeared to be about "nine inches in length and four in width, somewhat resembling a drowned rat as it floated, curled up, on the water."[17] Dr. R. C. Moore of Omaha tried to sew Thompson's scalp back onto his head but the surgery failed. Thompson eventually returned to England, where he had his scalp tanned. He mailed it back to Dr. Moore, who donated it to the Omaha Public Library, where as late as 1961 it was still on display.[18]

Although railroad workers such as William Thompson knew well the dangers from Indians, passengers traveling in comparative comfort aboard the lavish Pullman cars had quite different perceptions. Historian John Stilgoe has argued that the "built environment" of nineteenth-century American railroads created a unique subculture aboard the nation's passenger cars. This subculture represented a world unto its own no matter where the express passed — it was a world of urban civilization encapsulized in the heart of the primitive wilderness.[19] Passengers rarely left this world, no matter how wild the lands they passed through. In essence the railroad represented a thin ribbon of self-contained fashionable middle-class culture, whose participants traveled, if only fleetingly, for hundreds of miles through a bizarre untamed landscape. Outside the windows of the cars was the frontier, a surreal museum for the amusement of the passengers, who remained safe from its alleged dangers in their surroundings of oak veneer and plush velvet.

This almost ironic contrast created what historian Craig Miner has described in his insightful study of western Kansas, *West of Wichita*, as a situation where white Americans viewed the West through a "cultural screen or secondary environment such as the one Stilgoe suggests was created by railroads." Indians, Miner argued, were viewed "through this kind of cultural (ethnocentric) lens." Efficient transportation brought settlers and ostensibly created new markets. The taming of the wilderness was sure to come quickly in its wake. Miner asserted that the predominant attitude of nineteenth-century white Americans was that "Indians were in the way of something whose time had come." That something was white Judeo-Christian civilization, and the steam locomotive not only symbolized the movement but spearheaded it to the extent that Miner has called the institution of the western railroad the "Steel Nile."[20]

Even before the Union Pacific Eastern Division changed its name to Kansas Pacific and spiked its last rail into Denver, or before the Union Pacific linked up with Leland Stanford's Central Pacific at Promontory Point, Utah, enthusiastic middle-class whites were taking nonstop excursions through the central corridor to the end of the track and back again to sample the "wild West" casually and in comfort, with minimal risk. In August 1868, a party of two hundred "ladies and gentlemen" left Topeka for just such a trip across the plains of Kansas. On board for their enjoyment were delicacies consisting of "Ice Cream, Lemonade, Cherry Cobbler, Mint Julips, wines, etc."

As the train passed through Ellsworth just past the ninety-eighth meridian where the new line of counties had been organized in 1867, an excursionist named John H. Putnam expressed his adventuresome mood, safely detached of course, in a letter he was writing on board the train. "We are now, in the West," Putnam declared. "Here is — life." Later the party stopped at Hays City, where they were met by William Butler "Wild Bill" Hickok, who tantalized the ladies with stories of hundreds of Cheyennes camped nearby. Some of the Indians finally appeared and several of the amused giggling ladies "wondered if they would like some scalps of foreign hair."[21]

Certainly Major General Winfield Scott Hancock believed the railroad to be an instrument of civilization. In a talk he gave to passengers on a Union Pacific Eastern Division excursion train, shortly after he had burned the Dog Soldier and Sioux villages on Red Arm Creek, Hancock expressed the sentiment that the mere presence of the railroad would immediately transform the wilderness. In respect to the recent death and scalping of a soldier near Fort Harker, Hancock said, "This will never occur again. This great railroad brings civilization with it, so that when the Rocky Mountains are reached, the wild Indian and the buffalo will have passed away."[22]

Scholars continue to disagree about the effects of western railroads. In terms of profitability, much of the railroad building on the frontier during the late 1860s and 1870s was indeed only developmental and possibly premature. Its psychological effects, however, may have been quite more profound for a majority of Americans, including the plains Indians. For men like Sleeping Rabbit, Porcupine, and Red Wolf, the railroad was no mere curiosity. It represented "valuable things," the increasing affluence of the white man at the expense of the Indian. There is little doubt that construction of both the Union Pacific and Union Pacific Eastern Division railroads across the central plains aggravated the Indian War of 1867–1869.

In later years the old warriors admitted that they would have tried to wreck many more trains at this time but did not because soldiers heavily guarded the lines after the Plum Creek raid. For some, however, the danger was still worth the effort. An unidentified warrior, either Cheyenne or Arapahoe, sometime after the Plum Creek incident tried to lasso a locomotive. Apparently the diminutive 4-4-0 wood burner seemed tame enough to the warrior at the time, but it jerked him off his horse and dragged him over the prairie for some distance before he let go.[23]

On the Union Pacific main line the Pawnee Scouts helped protect the Platte Road. On the Union Pacific Eastern Division the 7th and 10th cavalries drew much of the duty. Accustomed to seeing scores of Oregon- and California-bound pioneers traveling the Platte Road in covered wagons, the plains tribes objected more to the Union Pacific Eastern Division. The whites were building that road through the rich buffalo country along the Smoky Hill route near favored camping grounds, where northern and southern bands annually joined the Dog Soldiers to hunt, tell stories, and renew old friendships. Although warriors harassed track crews and workers on both lines, they were especially tough on the Union Pacific Eastern Division. In addition to the attacks on the express stations and forts near the rails, track crews working out on the lonely prairie also suffered the wrath of the tribesmen. On August 1, 1867, thirty Cheyennes killed and scalped an entire party of unarmed railroad workers west of Fossil Creek Station (present-day Russell), Kansas.[24]

On September 19, two contractors named Thomas Parks and Charles Saffel, along with an unnamed black cavalryman, left the guarded security of the main Union Pacific Eastern Division work crew. A rescue party later found their two bodies. Saffel's body lay in the usual manner, scalped, with the face to the earth and the mutilated body bristling with arrows. Parks's body, however, was discovered by the rescuers with the scalp intact. The Indians had laid out his watch, wedding ring, and new Henry rifle beside his body along with a blue mackinaw blanket. Perhaps the Indians had honored Parks for putting up a stiff fight. Rescuers found the soldier severely wounded but still alive.[25]

In another incident, a young railroad contractor and his wife from Ohio, who lived in a dugout along the railroad, suffered the wrath of the Indians in a bizarre way. One night an arrow came through a knothole in their door and killed the husband. His wife went insane and began riding around the prairie wearing a black habit. She became something of a local legend around Hays, Kansas, where she was known as the "Wild Huntress of the Plains."[26] Finally, on May 28, 1869, a party of Dog Soldiers led by Tall Bull tore up the tracks and derailed a Kansas Pacific passenger train near Fossil Creek Station. Although the Indians did little physical damage, they rudely shattered the myth of an "insulated environment" of western travel by their deeds.[27]

Some relief for workers could be found in the end-of-track towns, where the companies quartered their construction crews. During the summer warfare of 1867, Ellsworth, Kansas, protected by Fort Harker, was the end of the track for the Union Pacific Eastern Division. By July of the next year, Sheridan, Kansas (now a ghost town), which was protected by Fort Wallace, some 394 miles from Kansas City, became end of track. Named in honor of Major General Philip Sheridan, who reputedly dined in the first sod house on the site, Sheridan was the usual rough-and-tumble "hell on wheels" that characterized all end-of-track towns.[28] Crude gambling houses, saloons, and dance halls proliferated. Shootings were frequent: twenty-six new graves were dug in the town's crude cemetery by the end of the first winter.[29]

One visitor found Sheridan to be a lively, stirring place. "The customs and ways of the town," he said, "are rather free and easy, of a high pressure order, and there is but little danger of the citizens dying from ennui. Whiskey, tents, gamblers, roughs, and 'soiled doves' are multiplying at an astonishing rate and things are lively indeed."[30] Another said that "human life there is at a discount. The scum of creation have there congregated and assumed control of municipal and social affairs. Gamblers, pick-pockets, thieves, prostitutes and representatives of every other class of the world's people, who are ranked among the vicious, have taken possession of the town and now reign supreme."[31]

As headquarters for the men who built the final extension of the railroad into Denver, Sheridan enjoyed a bit longer life than most temporary end-of-track towns. When the Union Pacific Eastern Division ran out of funds for a time in 1868, it appeared that the town might become well established. Stages to Santa Fe departed from nearby Pond Creek Station. Silver from the mines at Georgetown, Colorado, passed through Sheridan on its way to Newark, New Jersey. Flour from Pueblo and Trinidad came through on transit to eastern markets. In a single day in 1868, five carloads of freight bound for Santa Fe were unloaded at Sheridan.[32]

The town was also under constant threat from the Indians. When DeB. Randolph Keim came through in 1868, he described Sheridan the day he arrived as being "in a state of siege. Several days before," Keim said, "a large war party of savages had appeared up on two buttes near the town and opened fire upon the inhabitants. Everybody rushed to arms, and for the larger part of the day a spirited fusilade [sic] was kept up. The people of the place at once organized a regular corps of defenders, and detachments were on the watch day and night."[33] Troops from Fort Wallace were kept constantly busy watching out for the nearby service town.

One of the freighters who helped supply the end-of-track towns in 1867 and 1868 was a young Hungarian Jewish immigrant from a comfortable upper middle class home in the city of New York. His name was Sigmund Shlesinger. A merchant in Leavenworth, Kansas, engaged him when he was age sixteen, and, over his father's objections, Shlesinger went west with a spirit of adventure to live with his new employer and see the vanishing frontier. Soon "Sig," as he liked his friends to call him, drifted westward with the throngs, lured by prospects of work hauling supplies to the end-of-track towns and all the towns in between along the Smoky Hill route.

In addition to hauling freight, the boy found work of various kinds in these ephemeral frontier communities. He was a barkeeper in a tent liquor store, a waiter in a tent hotel, and a clerk in a makeshift grocery. He shoveled for the railroad and cooked for a group of teamsters. He night herded mules for contractors and quarried stone. Once the Cheyennes chased him without incident. On another occasion, the teenager peddled newspapers among the soldiers of the 7th and 10th cavalries, as well as railroad employees. Lieutenant Colonel George Armstrong Custer was one of his customers, as was William Butler "Wild Bill" Hickok, who Shlesinger recalled "was one of the finest gentlemen I met on the plains."

The impressionable youth became enthralled with frontier Kansas and its people. He had his first taste of buffalo meat after watching William F. "Buffalo Bill" Cody bring down a buffalo bull on the prairie. The hunting party slaughtered the beast on the spot and ceremoniously gave Sig a portion to eat alfresco. By late summer 1868, the lad was entirely out of funds, "living on hardtack and coffee most of the time, going from camp to camp looking for something to turn up, but no chance for employment came." Too proud to tell his father about his unlucky financial situation, Sig eventually found his way to Fort Hays and a new opportunity. About this time Major George A. Forsyth was employing his company of scouts and, over the objections of many of the older men, Shlesinger finally joined their ranks and rode with them to the Arickaree and a meeting with Roman Nose. At seventeen he was the youngest member of the Forsyth Scouts. At the Battle of Beecher Island, Sig Shlesinger would play a significant role, leaving to posterity one of the most vivid and complete recollections of that engagement.[34]

As a nineteenth-century New Yorker, Sig Shlesinger certainly believed in a destiny of progress. As a railroad employee he had ample opportunity to see that destiny being fulfilled. Despite Indian raids, both railroad lines marched erratically westward during the summer of 1867. By autumn, as the Union Pacific engulfed Nebraska, and the Union Pacific Eastern Division approached the one-hundredth meridian in western Kansas, it became urgent, as far as the government was concerned,

Sigmund Shlesinger. A Jewish immigrant from New York City, Sigmund Shlesinger worked at odd jobs close to the construction of the Union Pacific Eastern Division near Sheridan, Kansas. As the youngest member of the Forsyth Scouts, this teenager would leave one of the most vivid and complete personal reminiscences of the Battle of Beecher Island. *Courtesy Kansas State Historical Society, Topeka, Kansas.*

to remove once and for all the tribesmen roving freely within the central corridor between the railroad lines.

The roads became a primary concern of both the whites and the Indians during the ensuing talks in October at Medicine Lodge, Kansas. Because of a nearly five-hundred-page report compiled by the Congressional Joint Special Committee on the Indian Tribes, on July 20, 1867, Congress decided once again to extend the olive branch of peace to the plains tribes. On that day it created a "Blue Ribbon" Peace Commission. Some impressive figures were members of the new Commission: N. G. Taylor, Commissioner of Indian Affairs; John B. Henderson, chairman of the Senate Commission on Indian Affairs; John B. Sanborn of Minnesota; Samuel F. Tappan of Colorado Territory, who had presided over an official investigation of the Sand Creek Massacre; and three general officers of the army who were appointed by the president.

Andrew Johnson selected Lieutenant General W. T. Sherman and Brigadier Generals William S. Harney and Alfred Terry.[35] These delegates were charged with the task of bringing together the chiefs and headmen of the plains tribes and making peace with them. The commission had three major objectives: to remove the "causes" of the Indian wars; to make safe the frontier settlements and the construction work on the Pacific railroads; and, most far-reaching, to formulate a plan for eventually civilizing the Indians by assimilating them into the white culture.[36]

Meeting in St. Louis on August 6, the commissioners quickly agreed that the tribesmen must be removed from around the great roads and placed on reservations. In pursuance of this objective, Sherman notified his commanders within the Division of the Missouri to cease offensive military operations pending the outcome of negotiations.[37] The commission met first in September at Fort Laramie with representatives of the northern plains tribes. Some of the chiefs and headmen, particularly Pawnee Killer, spoke freely of their displeasure with construction of the Union Pacific Eastern Division along the Smoky Hill route.

Since many of the Northern Cheyennes were absent from the talks, the council broke up without accomplishing anything other than agreeing to meet again the following spring. The commission returned to Omaha, where General Sherman learned that his presence was required in Washington, D.C. Brevet Major General C. C. Augur replaced him on the commission.[38]

While Thomas Murphy, chief of the Indian Bureau's central superintendency, was in Omaha, he informed the commission that some five thousand members of the southern plains tribes were gathering on Medicine Lodge Creek in southern Kansas, about eighty miles south of the Arkansas. Murphy requested the commissioners to meet him at Fort Larned so that he might formally escort them to the impending council. According to mixed-blood George Bent, Jesse Leavenworth, who was the agent for the Comanches and Kiowas, was largely responsible for assembling the tribesmen. Accordingly, Leavenworth sent a messenger named Salvatore, a Hispanic, with a letter from Leavenworth to the peace chiefs to meet him at Fort Larned for a talk.

At this time George Bent lived mostly with his mother's people, the Southern Cheyennes, and had recently been on a raid at Cimarron Crossing. Salvatore remained in Black Kettle's camp for several days, but none of the People could read Leavenworth's letter until Bent returned from the raid and read it out loud. "After I read the letter," Bent remembered, "Black Kettle said he would go in to see Colonel Leavenworth and asked me to go along with him. To this I consented. The chief then sent a crier through the camp saying the village would move [the] next day."[39]

On October 11, the commission marched from Fort Larned escorted by a two-mile-long cavalcade that included five hundred troopers of the 7th Cavalry under Major Joel Elliot, a large press corps, as well as a host of curious onlookers. With the escort were nearly one hundred wagons filled with presents for the Indians.[40] When the column arrived at Medicine Lodge Creek, nearly five thousand Indians awaited them. Henry M. Stanley was present and vividly described the scene. "Thousands of ponies covered the adjacent hills," he wrote, "while in the valley grazed the cattle. . . . All [the] camps were pitched so as to form a circle, in the centre of which sported the boys and girls, and little papooses in a complete state of nudity.

"Quite a multitude of olive-skinned warriors . . . young bucks, papooses, damsels, and squaws, from the different villages, hurried up to see the commissioners. . . . When we arrived at the camp the Indians were engaged in the important ceremony of 'making medicine.' Shields of tanned buffalo hides were slung on poles facing the sun, with the [objective] of propitiating it."[41]

The commission gave presents to the Indians of clothing, utensils, cloth, and tobacco. The tribesmen returned the commissioners' hospitality by hosting a great feast of cold fat dog. Stanley remembered a similar repast with Spotted Tail's band. "In the centre of [our] circle were three dogs," he wrote, "the hair merely scorched, which had been roasted entire, intestines and all. Over this Indian delicacy was poured the gravy, dog's grease. The dripping had been collected in bone dishes. . . . If we might judge by the oily streaks about the capacious mouths of the chiefs, and the pleasure which sparkled in their eyes, we should pronounce dog meat delicious."[42] N. G. Taylor, commissioner of Indian Affairs, was a barrel of a man and became the object of humor among some of the Indians at the feast. One young chief came up to Taylor and, while gently stroking his arm, softly murmured in English, "Heap big damn son of a bitch."[43]

During these early festivities on Medicine Lodge Creek, Roman Nose reputedly was in camp, although he evidently did not take an active part in the subsequent council, and he did not sign the treaty because he was not a chief. In all likelihood he would have refused to sign anyway. According to Stanley, Roman Nose and ten warriors charged into the camp with the intent of killing the Cheyenne agent Edward Wynkoop for informing Major General Winfield Scott Hancock, back in April, the location of the Dog Soldier camp on Red Arm Creek, which Hancock subsequently burned.[44] George Bent denied Stanley's allegations, however, claiming that Roman Nose stayed at the camp for two days whereupon he had a talk with superintendent Murphy and agent Wynkoop and then left for the Cheyenne camp on the Cimarron, where other headmen were later persuaded to come in and join the great council.[45]

Plains scout Allison J. Pliley was present and could not help but be impressed by the dominating countenance of the great warrior of the Crooked Lance Society. "Roman Nose was the finest specimen of manhood I ever saw," Pliley remembered. "There was a natural impressiveness and dignity about him such as I have never seen in any other man. He was graceful even in the way he wore his blanket. I heard him make a speech [in the camp on Medicine Lodge Creek] which was both eloquent and forceful. I remember particularly his reference to what has been said about the 'Great Father at Washington.'

" 'The Great Spirit is my father, the earth is my mother, and some day I will lay myself down on her bosom still fighting the white man.'

"He made good [on his prophecy], for I saw him killed at the fight at Beecher Island just about a year later, and no Indian could desire a more dramatic finish than he got."[46]

The main council finally got under way on October 19. Old Jesse Chisholm was originally solicited as one of the interpreters for the Comanches and Kiowas but did not take an active role in the council because of a severe illness, possibly cholera.[47] John Smith, whose mixed-blood son Jack had been murdered by Chivington's militiamen at Sand Creek, along with George and Charley Bent and Ed Guerrier, interpreted for the Cheyennes and Arapahoes.[48] The commissioners, soldiers, and Indians came to the council dressed in fine clothing. So did Mrs. Margaret Adams, who also interpreted for the Arapahoes. Henry M. Stanley found himself somewhat enchanted with her. "This woman came dressed in a crimson petticoat, black cloth cloak, and a small coquettish velvet hat, decorated with a white ostrich feather," he remembered. "She . . . speaks fluently the English, Kiowa, and Arapahoe languages."[49] Many of the chiefs from all the southern tribes made speeches. Particular references were made by the commissioners to clearing the central corridor for white settlement and the completion of the Pacific railroads.

During the council the peace chief Black Kettle worked ceaselessly to get the more recalcitrant Cheyennes, especially the Dog Soldiers, to come in from the village on the Cimarron. Although some of his own people made threats against him, Black Kettle finally succeeded and treaties with the Cheyennes and Arapahoes were concluded on October 28. The commission concluded separate treaties with the other tribes.[50] The Cheyennes and Arapahoes agreed to relinquish their former claims in return for a grant of about 4.3 million acres in Indian Territory (Oklahoma). The government was to provide the Indians with food, clothing, and necessary equipment. A resident agent would be assigned to the reservation. The government was to provide the reservation with schoolteachers, physicians, carpenters, blacksmiths, farmers, and other persons. The tribesmen could still hunt buffalo but only south of the Arkansas. In turn, the Cheyennes and Arapahoes promised not to oppose construction of the railroads, to keep the peace, and to stay away from the overland stage routes.[51]

For once the Dog Soldier chiefs initially agreed to the treaty provisions. Signing for the Cheyennes besides Black Kettle were Bull Bear, Tall Bull, Gray Head, Little Rock, and Little Robe. Little Raven, Yellow Bear, and Storm signed the treaty for the Arapahoes. The commissioners wanted Roman Nose to sign the treaty and asked the chiefs why he was absent from the council. The chiefs informed the commissioners that the great warrior was in the village on the Cimarron suffering from a slight sickness and that as a non-chief he did not have the authority to sign the treaty.[52]

In a sense the Treaties of Medicine Lodge were the most important and far reaching ever concluded with the plains tribes, for they marked the beginning of a new era in Indian-government relations. For the first time, the federal government demonstrated a concerted intent ultimately to confine the tribes on restricted reservations where efforts would be made to acculturate the Indians into white society.[53] But in actuality the treaties would not end the conflict on the central and southern plains. Official action on the treaties by the Reconstruction-minded Congress was painfully slow.

Consequently, the promised annuities did not appear on the reservations by the summer of 1868, the time of year when young men were likely to go out raiding. The warriors grew restless and the chiefs began to doubt the promises made at Medicine Lodge. Finally, in June, Tall Bull led a large war party of Dog Soldiers on a raid against their old enemies the Kaws, who were camped near the town of Council Grove, Kansas. The citizens of the little town became greatly alarmed when they looked out of their houses and shops and saw some three hundred angry Dog Soldiers riding down the main street of Council Grove toward the Kaw village. As a result of this somewhat farcical raid, Commissioner of Indian Affairs N. G. Taylor instructed superintendent Thomas Murphy to tell agent

Edward Wynkoop not to issue promised guns and ammunition for the
Cheyennes when the annuity goods finally arrived.[54]

Upon hearing this, dissatisfaction among the Cheyennes intensified
to the breaking point. Consequently Commissioner Taylor changed his
mind. On June 23, 1868, he instructed Wynkoop to use his own discretion
in issuing annuity goods to the Cheyennes.[55] Officials dispersed the
annuities and Wynkoop was certain that peace had been maintained.
Little did he know that at that very time a large war party of Dog Soldiers
and other Cheyennes was moving north to attack the Pawnees. A number
of the more aggressive warriors among the People who rode with this band
urged their comrades instead to attack the Kansas settlements. Although
some voiced opposition to this plan, a majority of the war party turned
south and swept through the Saline and Solomon valleys like a whirlwind,
killing about fifteen persons and raping five women. The famous Saline-
Solomon raid of August 1868 marked the point of no return for the Dog
Soldiers.[56]

Historians of the Indian Wars frequently have used the Treaties of
Medicine Lodge as a convenient division between warfare on the central
and southern plains in 1867 and renewed bloodshed in 1868. In doing so,
they sometimes present the impression of two separate conflicts. This
division, however, is meaningful only from the Euro-American point of
view. In essence the Treaties of Medicine Lodge formalized the unmistak-
able intention of the whites to dominate totally the Great Plains and
everything on them. The construction of the two Union Pacific railroads
served as both practical and cultural icons to the cult of progress so
characteristc of America's budding Gilded Age. Consequently, the Indians would enter a new and conclusive phase of their struggle with the
whites, this time not for land alone but for the retention of their cultural
identity and even for their very survival.[57]

But in 1868, the whites had not yet defeated the Indians of the plains.
Few of the Indians could identify with anything other than the old
nomadic ways. It was a time when the government had to be both delicate
in its relations and punctual in fulfilling its promises if the Indians were
to make the difficult transition to another way of life successfully. Any

delay in annuities, any dispute over the largely one-sided issues delineated in the Treaties of Medicine Lodge were likely to lead to dissatisfaction and renewed attempts by the warrior societies to restore the old balances.

By the summer of 1868, raiding resumed fairly on schedule, almost as if there had been no treaty at all. The normal winter respite when the ponies were in poor condition was nothing out of the ordinary. The raid into the Saline and Solomon valleys showed that the winter's tranquility was not evidence that the Treaties of Medicine Lodge would bring a lasting peace. In 1868, the war that had erupted after Hancock burned the villages on Red Arm Creek simply continued. During that year it intensified and entered a terrible conclusive stage characterized by the bitterest of racial hatred on both sides. George Bent asserted that for the People, the Treaties of Medicine Lodge "marked the beginning of the end of the Cheyenne as a free and Independent warrior and hunter, and eventually changed his old range from Saskatchewan to Mexico, to the narrow confines of a reservation in Oklahoma."[58]

The Trail to the Arickaree   6

It was expected that the command would fight the Indians, and I meant
it should do so.

— MAJOR GEORGE A. FORSYTH

I feel like we are marching right into the jaws of hell.

— SCOUT JACK STILLWELL
Republican Valley
circa September 16, 1868

On September 7, 1867, First Lieutenant Frederick H. Beecher
stepped off a Smoky Hill stagecoach in Denver. With him were thirteen
sacks of mail. The coach had arrived safely from Fort Wallace without
incident from the Indians. All seemed calm for the moment on the central
plains. During the time of his brief stay in Denver, Beecher could little
have realized how a change in overall command in the Department of
the Missouri would affect his future.[1] In Major General Winfield Scott
Hancock, President Andrew Johnson had found the supporter he needed
to head up the 5th military district in the Reconstruction South. Major
General Philip Sheridan, the previous commander, had supported too
enthusiastically the "radical" Reconstruction policies of the Republican
party–dominated Congress and thus had run afoul of the president, who
was fighting not only to uphold Lincoln's liberal policies toward the
defeated Confederacy but to save his very political life as well. As
commander in chief of the armed forces, Johnson used what little power
had not been stripped from his office on July 31, 1867, to remove Sheridan
from command of the 5th district. He replaced him with Hancock.

Phil Sheridan was banished to the frontier when Johnson reassigned him as commander of the Department of the Missouri. Sheridan arrived at Fort Leavenworth on February 29, 1868, to take charge of the department.[2] In 1867 "Little Phil" was one of the nation's most celebrated Civil War heroes and its premier cavalry officer. From 1867 until he assumed overall command of the U.S. Army in November 1883, this short, fiery, and controversial general would direct the greatest Indian campaigns of the nineteenth century. He would arguably become "the nation's preeminent western soldier," stated his biographer, Paul Andrew Hutton, "commanding a large frontier region for a longer period of time than any other officer in the history of the Republic."[3]

Sheridan already had experienced the frontier before the war, and there is no question where he stood regarding Indians. As in most other matters, "Little Phil" was curt and succinct. "The Indian is a lazy, idle vagabond," he wrote in 1868, "He never labors, and has no profession except that of arms, to which he is raised from a child; a scalp is constantly dangled before his eyes, and the highest honor he can aspire to is to possess one taken by himself."[4]

But Sheridan was an obedient soldier, and when he took command of the Department of the Missouri he became determined to enforce the articles of the Treaty of Medicine Lodge. In 1868, within the District of the Upper Arkansas (a subdivision of the Department of the Missouri, which comprised the ceded Cheyenne and Arapahoe lands in the central corridor), Sheridan had only a force of about two hundred cavalry and about fourteen hundred infantry, mostly raw recruits. Within the entire Department of the Missouri there were only six thousand effectives.[5]

So long as the Peace Commission held favor with Congress, it was apparent to Sheridan that regular troop numbers would not increase. Indeed, budget cuts for the military seemed imminent. Given the geographical size of the department's area of responsibility, neither Sheridan nor his divisional commander, Lieutenant General William T. Sherman, agreed with Congress on the issue of cost cutting. Writing to an old friend, Sherman lamented the situation. "Very few men appreciate the vast extent of these territories," he wrote, "and when I travel days & weeks & months and then see on the map how little I have traveled, as compared with the whole, I feel almost in despair at ever bringing all that country into any sort of order or subjugation."[6]

Soon after Sheridan's arrival in the department, he made an inspection tour of western Kansas, where he found many of the warriors defiant and contemptuous of the Treaty of Medicine Lodge. The Indians' recalcitrance came as no surprise to military men already stationed on the Kansas frontier. Captain Albert Barnitz of the 7th Cavalry asserted that the Cheyennes "had *no idea* that they are giving up, or that they have ever given up the country which they claim as their own — the country north of the Arkansas. The treaty all amounts to nothing, and we will certainly have another war sooner or later with the Cheyennes."[7] At Fort Larned, Cheyenne Chief Stone Calf informed Sheridan: "Let your soldiers grow long hair, so that we can have some honor in killing them."[8]

To help cope with the immediate situation, Sheridan developed an intelligence system to keep him informed of the Indians' plans and moves. For this purpose Sheridan employed a number of civilian scouts. Among them were Richard Parr, Abner "Sharp" Grover, and William "Medicine Bill" Comstock, one of Custer's old favorites during his ill-fated 1867 campaign. The scouts were put under the command of First Lieutenant Frederick H. Beecher, whom Sheridan quickly came to admire despite Beecher's developing relationship with hard liquor.[9]

In August 1868, Beecher and his scouts were camped on Walnut Creek when word was received of the devastating Cheyenne raid through the Saline and Solomon valleys. Although a detachment of the 7th Cavalry under Captain Frederick W. Benteen rode out of Fort Zarah, and in a running fight eventually drove off the raiders, Beecher was determined to smooth over the incident with the Indians. Accordingly, he sent Grover and Comstock into the village of Turkey Legs, which was then located on the headwaters of the Solomon River.

Turkey Legs received the two scouts coldly, however, and ordered them out of the village. Seven young warriors escorted Grover and Comstock safely away from the camp. But once out on the prairie, the escort opened fire on the two whites. They took Grover and Comstock by complete surprise. The Indians killed Comstock instantly, but "Sharp" Grover, although wounded, used Comstock's body as a shield and fought off his attackers until nightfall. He then crawled away and eventually made his escape to the safety of Fort Wallace.[10] "Sharp" Grover would recover from his wounds and a month later he would guide Major George A. Forsyth to the Arickaree.

The Saline-Solomon raids and the shooting of Beecher's scouts renewed the warfare of the previous year on the central plains. Soon roving bands of Dog Soldiers, other Southern Cheyennes, Arapahoes, Northern Cheyennes, and Sioux who were not even party to the Medicine Lodge Treaty thrashed the Kansas and Colorado frontiers. Governor Crawford of Kansas renewed his sensationalized pleas for more troops while Acting Territorial Governor Frank Hall of Colorado appealed to General Sherman, somewhat unconvincingly, that the Indians were striking within twelve miles of Denver.[11] Once again regular troops of the 7th and 10th cavalries tried to pursue the swift-moving warriors through the Republican, Saline, Solomon, and Smoky Hill valleys but had little success. During the month of August alone, the "Buffalo Soldiers" of the 10th Cavalry covered more than a thousand miles without evidence of killing a single Indian.[12]

Faced with the same logistical and tactical predicament that had stymied Hancock and Custer the previous year, Sheridan changed strategy. Already "Little Phil" had moved his headquarters from Fort Leavenworth to Fort Hays, where he could better oversee military operations. From there he planned to use the Union Pacific and Union Pacific Eastern Division when practical to move his troops quickly to the scene of depredations. No major effort would be undertaken by regular troops to pursue, as in the past, small raiding parties along the Smoky Hill route. Instead Sheridan would mass troops and militia for sizable offensives against Indian villages. In that respect he projected the winter campaign. Unfortunately, after making garrison assignments to the forts along the Smoky Hill route, Sheridan had remaining at his disposal only eleven companies, about eight hundred men, for offensive operations.[13]

Despite the shortage of troops, the military viewed the protection of railroad construction as a vital necessity; it became one of Sheridan's foremost priorities. To avoid future controversy over possible military action against "peaceful" Indians, as occurred at Sand Creek and on Red

Arm Creek the previous summer, Sheridan ordered all Indians peacefully disposed to return to the reservation in Indian Territory. Many of the warriors who had not taken part in the recent raids in western Kansas, however, remembering the other times when the whites had asked them to gather under their protection, refused the order.

The failure of the military to check the Indians in 1867 gave the warriors confidence that once again, as they had successfully done with Hancock and Custer, they could best this new "soldier chief" that had been sent against them. Sherman and Sheridan designated most of the Cheyennes and Arapahoes as "hostile," and he considered the Comanches and Kiowas who had remained on the reservation and had not participated in the Kansas raids as "friendly." Complicating matters further was the presence of many northern Indians, subject to a separate treaty and not party to the Medicine Lodge agreement, who were camping within the borders of ceded lands alongside their southern allies.[14]

The ineffectiveness of the regular troops in 1867 and during the recent Saline-Solomon raids led Sheridan to initiate a bold plan of creating a swift-moving "ranger" unit of fifty experienced plainsmen. The commander of the Department of the Missouri hoped that this offensive force could at least keep the Indians on the move, thus preventing them from committing depredations on settlements, stage stations, and railroad construction sites. In order to eliminate bureaucratic red tape over troop quotas, Sheridan had to employ the scouts as members of the quartermaster department. To command this nontraditional strike force, Sheridan turned to his friend Major George Alexander Forsyth.

Although Forsyth was technically a line officer in the 9th Cavalry, since July 28, 1866, he had been serving on Sheridan's staff as secretary of civil affairs and then acting inspector general. Bright, articulate, cheerful, optimistic, and athletic in appearance, Forsyth was in no way timorous regarding combat. He had proven his mettle in the Civil War, rising from the ranks to win a brevet as a brigadier general of volunteers at the age of twenty-seven. Born December 7 or 12, 1837 (the exact day is uncertain), at Muncy, Pennsylvania, and educated at Canandaigua Academy in New York, Forsyth was twenty-four and living in Illinois when the Civil War broke out. He enlisted April 19, 1861, as a private in the Chicago Dragoons and saw action at Cairo, Illinois, in Missouri, and during McClellan's West Virginia campaign before being mustered out of service on August 18, 1861.

One month later he gained an appointment as first lieutenant of the 8th Illinois Cavalry. The 8th Illinois was part of the huge Army of the Potomac. By September 1863 he had risen to the rank of major. As such, George A. Forsyth took part in some of the great battles of the war. He was there during the Peninsula Campaign in 1862, where he received a slight wound after the action at Malvern Hill. Later he fought at Fredericksburg, Chancellorsville, and Beverly Ford, where he received a severe wound while commanding his regiment. The 8th Illinois mustered out in 1864, but Forsyth reenlisted and in March was assigned to staff duty in Washington. But at his own request Major Forsyth obtained the command of four hundred recruits and convalescents reorganized from sixteen different cavalry regiments. His new regiment was with Grant's army at the time of the Battle of the Wilderness. Covering the right wing, Forsyth was in the thick of the fighting at Spottsylvania.

After Forsyth led a raid on Guinea's Station, his command was broken up. It was then that Forsyth first became a staff officer of General Sheridan's. Riding with "Little Phil," he saw action at Hawes' Shop, Cold Harbor, Trevillian Station, the siege of Petersburg, and other engage- ments. Asked to take dispatches through Confederate lines to the head- quarters of the Army of the Potomac, Forsyth and three soldiers commandeered a small rowboat and made their way downriver through the enemy lines, under the cover of darkness, to deliver the dispatches. Other actions quickly followed — Fisher's Hill and Cedar Creek, which won Forsyth a brevet colonelcy.

Forsyth and Captain Joseph O'Keefe were the two cavalry officers chosen to make the famous ride with General Sheridan from Winchester, "twenty miles away." In the final campaign involving the Army of the Potomac, he had a part in the battles of Dinwiddie Courthouse, Five Forks, and Sailor's Creek. He was present at the surrender of Lee's Army of Northern Virginia at Appomattox. These last engagements won him on March 13, 1865, the brevet rank of brigadier general of volunteers. He mustered out of the volunteer service on February 1, 1866. At the time,

Sheridan said of him: "I had so much confidence in his soldierly ability that I on several occasions gave him control of divisions and corps under my command."[15]

By summer, however, Forsyth had joined the regular army as a major, serving once again on Sheridan's staff. In 1868, Forsyth, nicknamed "Sandy" ostensibly to help distinguish him from another of Sheridan's staff officers, Major James Forsyth, came west to the Kansas frontier with "Little Phil." Although Forsyth had no experience fighting Indians, Sheridan continued, as he had done during the war, to council with him on many matters regarding military strategy.[16] In later life Forsyth would write two memoirs, *The Story of the Soldier* (1900) and *Thrilling Days in Army Life* (1902). By then the veteran officer had formulated an opinion on Native Americans.

It is evident that Forsyth pondered the now-stereotyped dichotomy of "noble savage" versus "barbarian," but in the end his Victorian sensibilities came to the fore in his belief in the justness and inevitability of Euro-American cultural hegemony and the doctrine of industrial progress. He also recognized the divergence in thinking about Indians between eastern reformers and western settlers. He sympathized with the latter. "The Western Man," he wrote, "who has lost his horses, had his house burned, or his wife violated or murdered, finds a whole lifetime of hatred and revenge too little to devote to his side of the question. . . . The conception of Indian character is almost impossible to a man who has passed the greater portion of his life surrounded by the influences of a cultivated, refined, and moral society."[17]

There is little doubt that in the summer of 1868 Major George A. Forsyth thirsted for action against the warriors of the central plains. It is likewise evident that, as a staff officer without the highest seniority, it would take some finesse, and perhaps a little special privilege, to obtain a coveted field assignment. While at Fort Harker, Forsyth confronted Sheridan with his desires, and "Little Phil," seeing for some time what had been on the mind of his inspector general, complied. "I have determined to organize a scouting party of fifty men from among the frontiersmen living here on the border," Sheridan said in substance to Forsyth. "There is no law that will permit me to enlist them, and I can only employ

Major (Brevet Brigadier General) George Alexander "Sandy" Forsyth. Sheridan's trusted aide, Major George A. Forsyth, had been by the side of his fiery commander since the darkest days of the Civil War. With no combat experience against Indians, Forsyth relished the chance in 1868 for a field command, as small as it might be. *Courtesy Kansas State Historical Society, Topeka, Kansas.*

them as scouts through the quartermaster's department. . . . If you care for the command, you can have it and I will give you Lieutenant Fred Beecher of the Third Infantry, for your second in command . . . understand if I had anything better, you should have it."

"I am glad to get this," was Forsyth's reply.[18]

An hour later "Sandy" Forsyth was handed the following order:

> HEADQUARTERS DEPARTMENT OF THE MISSOURI, FORT HARKER,
> August 24, 1868
>
> Brevet Colonel George A. Forsyth, A.A. Inspector-General, Department of the Missouri.
>
> COLONEL, — The general commanding directs that you, without delay, employ fifty (50) first-class hardy frontiersmen, to be used, as scouts against the hostile Indians, to be commanded by yourself, with Lieutenant Beecher, Third Infantry, as your subordinate. You can enter into such articles of agreement with these men as will compel obedience.
>
> I am, sir, very respectfully
> Your obedient servant,
> (Signed) J. SCHUYLER CROSBY
> A.D.C. & A.A. Adjutant General.[19]

In the summer of 1868, Forsyth had little trouble finding men anxious to "settle an old score" with the Indians. The pay was to be $75 per month for men who furnished their own horse and $50 per month for those who did not.[20] In addition to Beecher, Surgeon J. H. Mooers of the army medical department signed on at Fort Hays. An easterner, Mooers commented that he was eager for the opportunity because "he had always wanted to see a real, live, wild Indian."[21] Forsyth selected Abner T. "Sharp" Grover as chief scout. William H. H. McCall, who had won a brevet of brigadier general of Pennsylvania volunteers after the siege of Fort Stedmen at Petersburg, was chosen first sergeant.[22]

Initially, Forsyth was somewhat troubled by the reputation garnered by his second in command, First Lieutenant Frederick H. Beecher. Beecher, it was well known, had acquired a penchant for the bottle. Forsyth wrote Beecher a confidential letter regarding the matter, to which

Dr. J. H. Mooers. A surgeon at Fort Hays, Mooers joined the Forsyth Scouts so he could see up close "a real live wild Indian." The medical officer would get more than he bargained for at the Battle of Beecher Island. *Courtesy Denver Public Library, Denver, Colorado, Western History Department.*

the lieutenant replied, "From today John Barleycorn and I part company forever." Beecher was true to his word, and he and Forsyth became fast friends. "Of the younger men I knew," Forsyth remembered, "none would have been more acceptable to me as second in command."[23]

At Fort Harker, George Washington Oaks, a veteran Indian fighter and member of Carleton's California Volunteers during the Civil War, signed up, as did many of the men from the Saline and Solomon valleys. They briefly called themselves "the Solomon Avengers." Thomas Ranahan signed up after an angry mob of citizens in Ellsworth, Kansas, threatened several of the peace commissioners who were then staying at the McMeakin Hotel following the Saline-Solomon raids in August.[24] Allison J. Pliley enlisted for $50 per month. At Fort Hays, young Sigmund Shlesinger was waiting eagerly to join the scouts because he needed the money. Forsyth had reservations about enlisting a lad of seventeen. "Why boy, you're not old enough," Forsyth was heard to say. "This sort of campaigning calls for experienced frontiersmen. What could you do in an Indian fight?"

Sig assumed a bold front. "I'll do as well as any man in your command," the boy exclaimed. "Besides, I'm out of work, and there's nothing to do here. I can shoot, and I can ride."[25]

"You are too young and inexperienced," Beecher added. "You wouldn't know how to take care of yourself."[26]

Richard Parr, one of Sheridan's primary intelligence scouts, vouched for Shlesinger, however, and Sig himself begged Forsyth so hard that the major finally turned to Beecher and, according to scout George Washington Oaks, replied, "Oh hell, Beecher, sign him up."[27]

"Huh," Shlesinger remembered a "rough mule-skinner" as saying, "he'll be a-hollerin' for his ma at the first sight of a redskin."[28]

The youthful New Yorker swallowed his anger and walked out of the room on air, "filled with enthusiasm over the expected adventure." That afternoon another youth, only about a year older than Shlesinger, approached him and introduced himself as Jack Stillwell. "Have you had any experience in Indian campaigning?" Shlesinger inquired.

"Well, not much," Jack replied, "but I've been knocking around the plains for the last three years, and [I] am pretty well used to roughing it.

I'm glad you are going. You and I are the only kids in the bunch, I understand, and we'll have to stick together."

Shlesinger was glad to find a friend. "I liked his looks," Sig remembered from this substantive conversation he later reconstructed for E. A. Brininstool for inclusion in a book about Indian fighters of the Old West. "We went over to his quarters, and I helped him sew a collar on a buckskin shirt he was going to wear on the expedition." Thus began a friendship that spanned a lifetime.[29]

S. E. "Jack" (later known as "Comanche Jack") Stillwell was indeed a sandy-haired youth in the summer of 1868. Born on the Missouri River near present-day Kansas City, Stillwell had large blue eyes and a face scout Eli Ziegler described as being "smooth as a woman's." At age twelve he reputedly could speak fluent Spanish and handle a gun like a seasoned frontiersman. By age fifteen he was undoubtedly on the plains working as a scout in the Arkansas Valley. When he signed up with the Forsyth Scouts at Fort Harker, he said it was for the purpose of "recovering the white women who were taken prisoners."[30]

At least two Coloradoans joined the Forsyth Scouts. One was Isaac Thayer, originally a Bostonian, who had come west to the Colorado gold rush of 1859. During the Civil War he served with an artillery company in the 1st Colorado Volunteers.[31] Another was John Joseph "Jack" Donovan of Denver.[32] Donovan, along with the ubiquitous Allison J. Pliley, would risk his life at Beecher Island, stealing through the Indian lines to secure help at Fort Wallace for the besieged command on the Arickaree.[33]

There were others, mostly veterans of the Civil War. H. H. Tucker from Ottawa County, Kansas, had been a brevet captain in the 143rd Illinois.[34] John Hurst served three years in the 1st California Volunteers, mostly fighting Apaches on the Arizona–New Mexico frontier.[35] Thomas Alderice, likewise, had joined a Union regiment in Illinois and then had come to Kansas after the war. Perhaps of all the Beecher Island survivors, Alderice would suffer the most from the aftermath of Sheridan's campaigning. In 1869 he would lose his wife and children at the hands of Tall Bull's Dog Soldiers.[36] Charles H. Cormack, as a runaway boy, had served in Missouri during the war and then migrated to the frontier.[37] Little is

Jack Stillwell. At eighteen or nineteen, "Comanche Jack" had been around the plains for a long time. During the Battle of Beecher Island, he would risk his life to bring help from Fort Wallace to rescue the besieged Forsyth Scouts. Stillwell and "Sig" Shlesinger maintained a lifelong friendship beginning in 1868. *Courtesy Kansas State Historical Society, Topeka, Kansas.*

known of the earlier lives of other scouts who figured prominently in or left accounts of the Beecher Island fight — Chauncey B. Whitney, Louis McLoughlin, Thomas B. Murphy (possibly the last surviving member of the scouts, although Cormack also claimed the honor), and Pierre Trudeau ("French Pete"), who, at nearly sixty, was the oldest member of the command in 1868. Most of the scouts left no recollections at all.

On August 29, Sheridan ordered Forsyth to march. Only Forsyth, Beecher, possibly Sergeant McCall, and Surgeon Mooers wore army uniforms; the scouts were clad in civilian garb. Forsyth's objective was to scout Beaver Creek to Fort Wallace and there await further instructions. Forsyth equipped his scouts well. Each carried a seven-shot Spencer repeating rifle, a Colt revolver (army size), and 140 rounds of rifle and 30 rounds of revolver ammunition. The command carried 4,000 extra rounds of ammunition, supplies, and extra rations in a pack train, and each man carried seven days' rations in his haversack.[38]

Forsyth, always eager and optimistic, was glad to be on campaign. "The fresh air of the plains, the clearness of the atmosphere, the herds of buffalo, which scarcely raised their heads . . . as we passed," he reminisced, "the half haze, half vapory mist that marked the line of the Smoky Hill River, and above all, the feeling that civilization was behind us, and the fascination that the danger of campaigning in the enemy's country ever holds for a soldier was before us."[39]

Others did not share Forsyth's almost romantic enthusiasm. "I will never forget the first day's ride," Sig Shlesinger remembered. "I was not familiar to the saddle, and my equipment was all the time where it should not have been. My bridle arm became stiff; my equipment would not remain in any one place, and I was sore and galled. I was too exhausted to eat any supper, while to cap the climax, I was detailed for guard duty . . . no sooner was I directed to my post than I dropped on the ground and fell fast asleep."[40]

The next morning Jack Stillwell reassured his new friend Sig Shlesinger. "You'll get hardened to things in a few days," young Stillwell said.

"As with many groans I clambered awkwardly into my saddle the next morning," Sig remembered.

"Keep a stiff upper lip," Jack told him.[41]

By August 29, both Shlesinger and scout Chauncey B. Whitney had begun diaries that would span the expedition. On August 30, both scouts noted that it rained most of the day.[42]

The command sighted no Indians between Fort Hays and Fort Wallace. No sooner had they reached Fort Wallace on September 5, however, than news was received from Sheridan, Kansas, at the end of the Union Pacific Eastern Division, thirteen miles to the east, that a war party of about twenty-five Indians had attacked a freighter's wagon train, killing two Hispanic teamsters. Immediately, Forsyth started in pursuit. "We arrived at Sheridan and found the ox freight train had been attacked in the western suburbs [of town]," scout Tom Murphy remembered. "The train was scattered and the [dead] oxen and [burned] wagons were all around the scene of action."[43]

Moving northwest from Sheridan, the command picked up a fresh trail on September 14 and followed it into the Republican Valley and thence up the Arickaree Fork of that river. In so doing, the command crossed into Colorado Territory. The scouts "rode out upon a rich and fertile prairie as far as we could see," Tom Murphy remembered, where "the blue stem grass grew as high as a horse." As the little command continued westward the trail became more obvious. "After several miles travel this trail became a beaten path," Murphy claimed, "proving that a large part of the Indians dragging their lodge poles had passed this way."[44]

Eventually the trail grew so big that the men knew that many Indians with their families were in the vicinity and that the command was likely to catch them, "and [with] our company being so small," John Hurst remembered, "we would likely get whipped. We made our anxiety known to Forsyth."[45]

" Some of my men grew apprehensive," Forsyth recalled, "and entered a protest upon our further advance into the Indian country."[46] Stillwell could feel the tension, stating to Beecher, "I feel like we are marching right into the jaws of hell."[47] But Forsyth told the protesters that "the company was out to fight Indians and that [he] was taking all the risks that they were [being exposed to]." Forsyth told them "it was expected that we would hunt these people down . . . at any rate." Forsyth later wrote, "I meant to fight them, and I did not believe that they could annihilate us even if we were not strong enough to whip them."[48] "Furthermore, it was expected that the command would fight the Indians, and I meant it should do so."[49]

Chief scout "Sharp" Grover was concerned, Shlesinger remembered. "We'll have a big fight on our hands, within twenty-four hours," he had said. Once again Jack Stillwell told his friend Sig Shlesinger: "Keep a stiff upper lip."[50] For the second time, some of the men came to Forsyth with their concerns. Stillwell and Louis McLoughlin begged Forsyth to stop advancing and camp in the relative safety of the mostly dry riverbed. "If he [Stillwell] and I had not protested," McLoughlin remembered, "the entire Forsythe [sic] expedition would have ridden into a trap and been massacred the night before the fight on the island began. We knew for two days that we were biting off a chew that we could not get away with, and we urged Forsythe [sic] to give it up, but he went right on."[51] Forsyth replied by asking the men "if they had not enrolled to fight Indians?"[52]

"That ended the discussion," John Hurst later wrote, "but all the same, it did not convince us of the wisdom of the course."[53] George Washington Oaks had a different opinion (in retrospect) of the Indian's numerical superiority. "This didn't faze us," he asserted, "We were looking for a fight, and . . . we sure got one."[54]

On the evening of Wednesday, September 16, Major George A. Forsyth and fifty-one men went into camp on the bank of the Arickaree opposite a small sandbar island situated in the mostly dry riverbed. "There were quite a few willows and plum trees on the island," George Washington Oaks recalled. The island "was about seventy-five yards long by about thirty yards wide. On the downstream end of the island stood a lone cottonwood. Across from the island was a patch of tall grass, just under the bank of the river."[55]

"We unsaddled our horses and picketed them out to graze and built our fires," scout Eli Ziegler remembered. About dusk "we saw a signal [arrow] go up south of us and a little east and then we saw more go up in different directions." Forsyth "put on more guards that night and ordered us to be ready at any moment."[56]

John Hurst and Tom Murphy "cooked some beans" that evening for the men who relieved them on guard duty. Then they "lay down with . . .

saddles for pillows, and our guns at [our] sides, and were soon fast asleep, not knowing the danger that threatened us."[57] Sig Shlesinger noted in his diary: "Seen signal Fire on Hill 3 miles off in evening late."[58]

There is little doubt that everyone in the command knew that many Indians were nearby. The exact location of the warriors' camps, however, was still a mystery. It is also evident that some of the men suspected because of the signal arrows and fires in the distance that the Indians had discovered their relative position. The possibility of attack apparently troubled "Sandy" Forsyth. He later remembered becoming restless in the chill night air of approaching autumn. His mind wandered, contemplating Sheridan's impending winter campaign. "In my wakeful hours of this September night," he wrote, "as I paced the ground to and fro along the river bank in front of the line of my sleeping men, I felt that the coming winter's campaign in the Indian country would result in much hardship outside of actual fighting. I had seen personally to the posting of our sentries, and had given especial instructions not only to hobble the horses, but directed that every scout should be especially careful to see that his horse's lariat was perfectly knotted," and to see that his picket pin "was firmly driven into the ground . . . for I was somewhat apprehensive of an attack at daylight. Several times during the night I rose and visited the sentries, for I was restless, anxious, and wakeful."[59]

Twelve miles away there were three good-sized camps of Brulé Sioux, Northern Arapahoes, Dog Soldiers, and other Cheyennes, who were mostly northerners because a majority of the Southern Cheyennes, with the notable exception of the Dog Soldiers, were at that time south of the Arkansas camping with Black Kettle. Pawnee Killer was there. So was Roman Nose, still living on the central plains with Red Shin's band and helping the Dog Soldiers defend their traditional homelands in the Republican River country. Bull Bear and Tall Bull were present, as was White Horse. They were very much aware of the presence of Forsyth's command somewhere in the general vicinity of their camps. They prepared to seek out the whites at dawn and destroy them.[60] Fortunately for the Forsyth Scouts, topography favored their position. Had they traveled a half-mile farther to make camp, Sig Shlesinger later asserted, "not a mother's son would have escaped alive."[61]

Cheyenne Ledger book drawings. Along with the oral histories collected by George Bent and George Bird Grinnell, the only other significant record of the Dog Soldiers' struggle to suppress white encroachment in western Kansas and eastern Colorado was a collection of drawings recovered from the Summit Springs battlefield in 1869. The Dog Soldier Ledger Book, or Summit Springs Scrapbook, gives modern Americans the only visual record, from the Indian side, of this warrior society's combat engagements with white soldiers during the Indian War of 1867–1869. *Courtesy Colorado Historical Society, Denver, Colorado.*

When we got onto the high ground . . . the Indians were in full view,
and such a picture! All were mounted on their war horses, in war
costume, with feathers and plumes flying, shouting war whoops, their
horses running at full speed. . . . We . . . knew that we would be no match
for that army of red men [out] in the open.

— SCOUT JOHN HURST

The other day something was done that I was told must not be done.
. . . If I go into this fight, I shall certainly be killed.

— ROMAN NOSE
Arickaree Fork of the Republican River
Colorado Territory
September 17, 1868

About two o'clock on the morning of September 17, 1868, scout
John Hurst relieved George Washington Oaks of guard duty along the
bank of the Arickaree. The night had grown cold and the men lay in pairs
under their blankets. Major Forsyth and Lieutenant Beecher lay together,
restless. Before Oaks turned in he warned Hurst to keep an eye on his
horse because he did not think the animal would stand picketed. Just as
the first faint streaks of daylight began breaking over the Colorado prairie,
Oaks was shaken from his slumber by the shouts of one of the men. "A
herd of buffaloes is coming right into camp, boys," Oaks remembered
hearing. A moment later Forsyth's voice rang out: "Indians! Turn out!
Turn out!"[1]

Soon the scouts saw a group of warriors approaching their camp yelling and shouting. Many of them were shaking blankets and making noise in order to stampede the horses. It was a scene young Eli Ziegler never forgot. "I believe I heard the first whoop they gave," he recalled, "but I was so sleepy I thought it was a flock of geese; just then the guards fired. I gave a jump and said to [G. W.] Culver, 'They are here.' As we were all dressed and our revolvers and cartridge boxes all buckled on and our carbines lying by our sides we were ready for action as soon as we raised up. . . . We were so close we could see [the Indians] by the flash of their guns . . . the next thing I saw was a few of our horses going over [a hill] with quite a little band of Indians closed in behind them." Seven of the animals were captured by the warriors.[2]

The Indians came out of the east and stampeded the horses around the north side of the scouts' camp. The horse of George Washington Oaks tore up its picket pin and joined the stampede. Oaks was able to catch hold of the rope, however, but was dragged over the ground before the horse stopped. Several of the scouts scattered throughout the tall buffalo grass along the banks of the river and began to return the Indians' fire.[3] Forsyth ordered his men to "saddle up quickly." As the pink rays of dawn spread into the river valley even more Indians appeared. "Sharp" Grover stood by Forsyth's side and exclaimed in amazement, "Oh heavens . . . look at the Indians."[4]

"The ground seemed to grow them," Forsyth recalled. "They appeared to start out of the very earth."[5] Young Sigmund Shlesinger's perceptions were the same: "They seemed to spring from the ground like Roderick Dhu's Highland Scots. . . . I will frankly admit that I was frightened almost out of my senses. I felt as if I wanted to run somewhere, but every avenue of escape seemed closed." Accordingly the teenager sought out his commander, Major Forsyth, and clung to his side: "I was reassured by his [Forsyth's] coolness and self possession."[6]

A complete withdrawal was impossible. A defensive stand seemed the only alternative. Thomas Murphy and Jack Stillwell suggested to Forsyth that the command move to the island in the middle of the mostly dry riverbed, and Forsyth gave the order to fall back. Forsyth then instructed

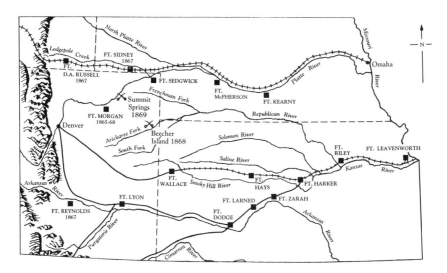

Map of the Republican Valley and the location of the Beecher Island fight. Adapted from Robert Utley, *Frontier Regulars*, University of Nebraska Press.

the men to tie their horses to the bushes around the circle of defense they were to form on the island and entrench as quickly as possible.[7]

The result was anything but an orderly military retreat, despite Forsyth's later claim to the contrary. "There was no regular order preserved at all," John Hurst noted, "but we all made a grand rush for cover like a flock of scared quail and immediately we were pretty well scattered over the island."[8] "Pell-mell, helter-skelter," recalled Eli Ziegler, "every man for himself, with a grand rush over the embankment, across the dry creek bottom, up the bank and the island was gained in less time than it takes to tell it."[9]

In the scramble to the island, Ziegler sought the apparent safety of the far bank. "I tied my horse to a bush," he recalled, "then I looked around to see what spot I would take and I saw George Clarke [sic] and [Louis] Farley and a couple of others running across the river; they got behind a bank on the north side, so I thought that would be a good place to go. As I started the Indians made a charge down through that way so I had to stop. . . . Just then the colonel [many of the scouts called Forsyth by his brevet ranks] saw me and asked me where I was going. I told him I was going across the river where Farley [was]. He said you can come with me, I want you around on this side."[10]

Meanwhile, Indians were creeping through the tall grass and shooting down the scouts' horses, which Forsyth, perhaps foolishly, had ordered tied so closely around the defensive perimeter so hastily formed. "It was unfortunate," Hurst recalled, "that some of our horses were located within the zone of fire near where many of the men were fighting. This brought the men in range of bullets that were intended for the horses."[11]

George Washington Oaks and John Lyden took shelter behind a drooping cottonwood tree but decided the shelter of the horses afforded greater protection. A moment later the cottonwood tree was riddled with bullets.[12] Meanwhile, the men who had reached the north bank, Louis Farley, Frank Harrington, Richard Gantt, Martin Burke, and Tom Murphy, found the hail of bullets so thick that they decided to get back to the island to escape the murderous fire from the Indians. In trying to do so, however, Harrington, Gantt, and Farley received wounds. Only Murphy made it back to the island before nightfall. Although Farley held out throughout the siege of Beecher Island, his wound proved fatal. "In crossing back to the island I sought the shelter of a wounded horse," Murphy related, "when McCall called out, 'Look out Tom, that horse will kick; he isn't dead.' Feeling that a kick from a horse was less to be dreaded than a savage's arrow and bullets, I maintained my position until ammunition at hand was nearly exhausted."[13]

Under fire the scouts used any tools available to dig shallow rifle pits for protection. "We used our tin cups and plates to dig rifle pits in the sand," Murphy noted.[14] "There was nothing but our hands and the knives at our belts with which to work," Sig Shlesinger remembered, "but the soil was soft, loose sand, and the light sod was easy to cut. Kicking with toes and heels, and working with knives and hands, we soon had shallow holes that afforded a slight shelter."[15] "We all went to digging when we could and shooting when we had to," Ziegler remembered. "I moved a little south . . . and got down and tried to dig some, but they [the bullets] kept coming so fast and so close that it did not seem that there was much chance to dig." Soon, however, Ziegler and Jack Donovan worked out a

After entrenching themselves on the island in the Arickaree, the scouts' grueling ordeal with hunger and thirst began. Digging rifle pits with cups and bare hands, the men were able to hold off several massed charges by the Dog Soldiers and their allies. *Courtesy Colorado Historical Society, Denver, Colorado.*

system whereby one of them dug while the other kept up a rapid fire at the Indians.[16]

To a significant degree, the effectiveness of the seven-shot Spencer carbines with which the scouts were armed saw them through the early crisis at Beecher Island. Although Forsyth and others later claimed that the Indians were armed with repeating rifles, it is doubtful, as many of the Indian participants years later denied the claim. Most of the plains Indians in 1868 had never seen a Spencer, although the firearm was available as surplus as early as 1865. As scout John Hurst acknowledged: "Our bullets . . . seemed to daze the Indians. We were armed with Spencer seven-shot repeating rifles, and this was another thing that puzzled our foes, who could not determine how we were able to load and fire so rapidly."[17]

Nevertheless, in the early stages of the battle the Indian marksmen exacted a heavy price from the Forsyth Scouts. Louis Farley, George Clark, and Frank Harrington remained on the north bank of the Arickaree, unable to regain the island until nightfall. Each received wounds. The young schoolteacher Harrington took an arrow, the steel head imbedding partially in the bone above his left eye. Harrington fought on with the arrow protruding from his head. Clark, who lay next to him, tried to remove the shaft but failed. Eventually Harrington received another wound, this time by a bullet fired from the gun of a charging warrior. Miraculously, the bullet struck the butt of the arrowhead protruding from Harrington's head at such an angle that it knocked the arrow from the scout's head. Harrington survived and his wound became one of the favorite stories of the Forsyth Scouts. In reminiscing about the gunshot that may have saved his life, Harrington said: "I do not think the Indian saw me until he was almost upon us. He was mounted and coming from the north and he rode almost over me; we both fired at the same time, and we were so near together I am sure I hit him, and at the same time the arrow fell to the ground."[18]

Back on the island, H. H. Tucker had his left arm broken by a rifle ball and lay down beside John Haley. While trying to tend Tucker's wound, Haley was shot in the hip. Next, Eli Ziegler tried to tie up Tucker's arm but an arrow grazed the upper part of his leg and went on to embed above Tucker's knee. Ziegler pushed the arrow completely through Tucker's leg and bound up both wounds.[19] Howard Morton received a head wound. The bullet passed in back of one of his eyes, destroying the eye, and lodged in the bones of his nose. Morton wrapped a handkerchief around his head and fought on.

Sergeant McCall and scout G. W. Culver were digging a rifle pit when someone shouted: "If you fellows on the outside [of the perimeter] don't get up and shoot, the Indians will be charging us." With this plea both

McCall and Culver jumped up looking for a target. Suddenly McCall heard the report of a rifle. A bullet grazed his neck and then flew on and struck Culver in the head, killing him instantly.[20]

Major George A. Forsyth was wounded early in the fight. He had his hands full disciplining his command during the initial attack. At one point a voice cried out: "Don't let's stay here and be shot down like dogs! Will anyone try for the opposite bank with me?" Forsyth, along with Beecher, quickly had to restore order in the ranks. Forsyth began walking from man to man to reassure them and keep order. But in so doing, Forsyth took a bullet in the forepart of his right thigh, the lead slug ranging upward and tearing flesh. Forsyth lay down in a rifle pit. As Dr. Mooers began tending the wound Forsyth turned over to give an order, exposing his other leg. Instantly a bullet smashed into the leg, crushing the bone midway between his ankle and knee. A short while later Forsyth received a minor scalp wound.[21]

About mid-morning, a force of several hundred warriors massed an organized charge on the scout's position on the island. A half-Sioux half-Cheyenne named Bad Heart led the charge; it was not led by Roman Nose, as "Sharp" Grover claimed and Forsyth later described all too vividly in his published accounts of the battle. The onslaught must have struck terror into the hearts of the less experienced scouts when they saw the charge of the Sioux warriors wearing their bonnets of trailing eagle feathers, which contrasted sharply with the peculiar bonnets of the Dog Soldiers, which were made from raven feathers without a tail. More frightening still were the eerie sounds emanating from the Indian war whistles, constructed from the wing bones of eagles and hung by a beaded cord around the neck of the warrior. The frightening notes made by the whistles protected the wearers from the white men's bullets as they charged the island.[22]

Sig Shlesinger never forgot the charge. "No living thing could withstand such a seething hell of flame and lead," he later wrote. "With wild cries of rage, the onrushing savages . . . passed [us] like a tornado."[23] "I thought we were all going to be killed and scalped," John Hurst remembered, "and I think this belief was quite general with all the men. I heard Forsyth call out and ask if anyone could pray. He said, 'We are beyond all

"Sandy" Forsyth. After the Battle of Beecher Island, Forsyth became a symbol of glory, admired by other aspiring officers of the regular army, including George A. Custer. *Courtesy Kansas State Historical Society, Topeka, Kansas.*

human aid, and if God does not help us there is none for us.'. . . However, nobody volunteered to make a prayer."[24]

"Every trooper [scout] realized that his time had come," Ziegler later remembered, "and a heroic determination was pictured on the countenance of every man to sell his life as dearly as possible. . . . Volley after volley was poured into the charging foe in rapid succession. . . . Soon horses and warriors were mingled in disorganized confusion."[25]

But not every scout conducted himself as valiantly as history would later ascribe to the command as a whole. Scout Martin Burke found himself caught on the bank of the Arickaree during the charge and did not reach the island until later. Taken by surprise by a charging warrior, Burke equally startled the Indian with his unexpected presence on the bank. Partially paralyzed with shock, Burke was able only to point his gun at the warrior and shout "boo." Immediately thereafter Burke began running in panic. Risking a glance over his shoulder, however, he saw that the frightened Indian was retreating just as rapidly in the opposite direction.[26] Another scout, whom Ziegler took notice of during the fight, "was shaking like a man with palsy, and [he] seemed utterly unnerved by the awful predicament we were in. . . . He made a run for the bushes and took no part in the fighting."[27]

John Hurst noted that "a warrior coming from the north [Bad Heart?] almost ran over me on horseback, and would have done so had not his pony shied to one side and the Indian had hard work to keep his seat, insomuch that he had no chance to fire at me. However, I was glad his pony took him away, for had he fallen off it would have meant death to one of us. I shot at him as his pony rushed along, but [I] did not see the Indian fall."[28] Scout Chalmers Smith noted that Lieutenant Beecher seemed to be exhilarated by the action, as if he were on holiday. Smith heard Beecher declare it to be "like shooting sparrows."[29]

With the major exception of Bad Heart, who rode over the island and back again unscathed, at the last second most of the warriors broke off their charge, divided, and rode thunderously to each side of the island. After the fight Louis McLoughlin reflected on the matter. "Two or three times," he later wrote, "if the Indians had kept on a minute or two longer they would have got us, as sometimes we would hardly have a shot left when they broke [around the island]."[30]

As the Indians rode off, Forsyth remembered turning to "Sharp" Grover and calling out, "Can they do better than that, Grover?"

"Man and boy, I have been on the plains for more than thirty years," Grover replied, "and I never saw anything like that before. I think they have done their level best."[31]

Although several of the scouts writing many years later claimed that they took a devastating toll on their attackers, the Indians themselves claimed that no warriors were killed in the first charge. For the scouts, however, the fighting to this point had not been without sacrifices. Already scouts G. W. Culver and William Wilson were dead. Then Dr. Mooers, who according to Forsyth had "been doing splendid service with his rifle," received a fatal wound. The surgeon was in the same rifle pit with Forsyth when a shot penetrated their barricade. "I heard the peculiar thud that tells the breaking of bone by a bullet," Forsyth recalled. "Turning to the doctor, I saw him put his hand to his head, saying, 'I'm hit,' his head at the same time falling forward on the sand. Crawling to him, I pulled his body down into the pit and turned him upon his back, but saw at once that there was no hope. A bullet had entered his forehead just over the eye, and the wound was mortal. He never spoke another rational word, but lingered nearly three days before dying." Occasionally, "he would push his body forward and kick out with his foot, a half-unconscious proceeding on his part that caused me much pain. He could neither see nor hear, and yet he was evidently able in a dim way to reason regarding the situation."[32]

Soon thereafter Lieutenant Frederick H. Beecher rose from his rifle pit and staggered to where Forsyth lay and calmly lay down by the side of his commander. Beecher turned his face down on his arm as he said, simply and calmly, "I have my death wound, General. I am shot in the side, and dying."

"Oh no, Beecher — no!" Forsyth exclaimed. "It can't be as bad as that!"

"Yes. Good-night," Beecher replied.

Beecher Island inspired numerous artists and illustrators, among them Frederic Remington. Much of this work is highly inaccurate. Except for Forsyth, Beecher, and possibly Surgeon Mooers and Sgt. McCall, the scouts did not wear army issue uniforms, as is depicted in this early illustration. *Courtesy Colorado Historical Society, Denver, Colorado.*

In a few moments several of the men heard Beecher murmur, "My poor mother." He then drifted off into semiconsciousness. "At times," Forsyth remembered, "I could hear him talking in a semi-unconscious manner about the fight; but he was never again fully conscious, and at sunset his life went out."[33]

After the first concerted charge, the warriors began circling the island and shooting at the scouts, who were busy deepening their rifle pits. During this time the scouts shot the man whom the Indians claimed was the first warrior killed in the battle, a Cheyenne named Dry Throat. A number of other warriors, however, had their horses shot out from under them.[34]

The scouts could see some of the Indian women watching the battle from a bluff abutting the river valley, ready to strip the corpses of Forsyth and his men for valuables should they be annihilated. That night the scouts heard the chanting of the women from this precipice, which has since come to be called "Squaw Hill."[35]

By this time all the scouts' horses had been shot down. As the last one fell, Forsyth and a number of the scouts distinctly heard a voice from the Indians' line exclaim in good English, "Well, there goes their last damned horse, anyway."[36] Scout Allison J. Pliley noted that "dead . . . horses were scattered in every direction."[37] As the Indians circled the island, Sig Shlesinger was greatly impressed by the warriors' great courage. The Indians, he remembered, displayed "such magnificent horsemanship as I have never seen before or since. Rifle smoke and clouds of dust, shot through with flashes of powder, are ever in my memory when I think of that awful fight."[38] Shlesinger was in a rifle pit with Louis McLoughlin. McLoughlin received a wound and could not return the Indians' fire.

The young greenhorn Sig Shlesinger remembered getting more than he had bargained for when he had joined the Forsyth Scouts back at Fort Hays. "In the south channel of the then dry creek was a tree trunk," he recalled, "floated there by a flood. . . . From this stump came many shots to the annoyance of Lou McLoughlin and myself. I employed my tactics of suddenly going up in the air and firing at the stump. After several shots the sniping from that direction ceased."[39]

At one point during the morning, Forsyth ordered Jack Stillwell along with two or three other men (Pierre Trudeau included) to secure an opposite side (probably the west end) of the island. But instead of remaining on the island, Stillwell and his party crossed the sandy river channel and dug a rifle pit among a stand of tall buffalo grass under a low bluff on the mainland. There they hid themselves from the warriors and in the next few hours did much damage to the Indians who charged over them toward the island.[40] Sometime around midday the Indians once again unleashed a loosely organized charge against the island. During this charge, or shortly before, Stillwell and his companions began to demonstrate the tactical advantage of their concealed but dangerously vulnerable position. A mounted warrior charged the island, shaking his war shield over his head defiantly when he rode almost over Stillwell's rifle pit. He never saw the whites. As he passed them in the high grass a volley rang out and the Indian fell from his horse, shot in the hip, the bullet ranging upward and exiting the top of his back. Stillwell and the other scouts with him hunkered back down in the rifle pit. Thick smoke hung in the air over the tall buffalo grass. No other Indians assaulted their position or fired at them. The scouts on the riverbank had not been discovered.[41]

✳ ✳ ✳

Weasel Bear (Ermine Bear), whose boyhood name had been Scalp, lay paralyzed in the buffalo grass on the bank of the Arickaree where Stillwell and his men had shot him from his war-horse. He was a brave warrior of the People, the brother-in-law of White Horse himself, the renowned Dog Soldier chief. Weasel Bear also had a nephew in the fight, White Thunder (Old Lodge Skins). Soon his family would be looking for him. If several ambitious young warriors in the villages had not been so impatient to win individual glory, Weasel Bear might not have been lying there severely wounded.[42]

When the Indians had first discovered the scouts, they assumed that the whites were coming to attack the villages. To prevent this, the warriors moved stealthfully toward Forsyth's command in order to attack them first. But Forsyth was not aware of the exact location of the villages, only that many Indians were nearby. Consequently, he had gone up on the river and did not know that the villages were below him. Unknowingly, when he changed direction, he actually began moving away from the villages. As a result, the Indians temporarily lost Forsyth's exact position. When nightfall came the chiefs halted the warriors until they could relocate the white scouts in the morning.[43]

Earlier, White Horse and Tall Bull had gone down to the Sioux camp and urged them to join forces with the Dog Soldiers so that the Indians could attack as one force. They did the same with other warriors, Arapahoes and Cheyennes who were camping with the Dog Soldiers and Sioux, asking them to wait so that all might attack together. Criers had been sent through the villages as men painted their faces and put on their finest war clothing. The criers announced that any warrior who tried to slip away and attack the whites separate from the main body would be beaten. The Dog Soldier war leaders meant the threat — the Dog Soldiers were famous on the plains for their organized attacks. When darkness came, the warriors did not stake out their horses, for they were to be ready to move against the scouts when the morning star appeared in the east.[44]

But despite the threat of a beating, eight young men, Starving Elk and Little Hawk, both Cheyennes, and six Sioux, decided to slip away from the other warriors and find the whites first. Just before daybreak on September 17, they had spotted the campfires of the whites. It was they who had stampeded the horses of the Forsyth Scouts. About the same time, the main body of warriors had started off. Their "wolves" had discovered the signal fires of the scouts about the same time as Starving Elk and his companions. "It is the soldiers," they told the chiefs. The Indians then formed a broad front and began their assault on Forsyth's camp from about two miles away, reaching the scene shortly after Starving Elk and his companions stampeded the whites' horses.[45]

By the middle of the day, however, the only great deed that had been done was Bad Heart's ride over the scouts on the island. Bad Heart's ride was not all that awe inspiring to many of the warriors because, like Roman Nose, Bad Heart possessed bullet-proof medicine. Still, years after the fight, Bad Heart's ride remained vivid in the memory of Jack Stillwell, who told George Bent that at the time he thought Bad Heart to be insane. But despite the drama of the feat, the chiefs later admitted disappointment that the Indians had not seized the island first and prevented the scouts from making an effective defensive stand. Now, after the failure of the morning charge, the whites started to inflict casualties on the Indians, including Weasel Bear, brother-in-law of White Horse.

Nineteen-year-old White Thunder, who was Weasel Bear's nephew and White Horse's own son, had indeed seen his uncle fall from his horse, but he could not determine where the shots had come from. He went down to the river to find his uncle. When White Thunder entered the tall grass on the riverbank, he was only about ten feet from Stillwell's rifle pit. When they shot him, the bullet passed through his body and came out at the waist, killing him.[46]

About this time, Two Crows, brother of White Horse and uncle of White Thunder, who was on foot, had his horse shot from under him. White Horse told him, "Your nephew, White Thunder, has been killed. You will do well to get his horse and go into the fight." Two Crows got the horse and joined the second charge on the island. Once again the Spencer repeaters repulsed the Indians' assault; again the warriors split and rode swiftly around both sides of the island. After this charge three warriors crept toward the island, dug rifle pits of their own, and fired into the scouts' entrenchments on the island. But the scouts' marksmanship was too much for them. The scouts shot in the head two of these warriors, Prairie Bear, a Cheyenne, and Little Man, a Northern Arapahoe. The third man, Good Bear, ran away, dodging from side to side to avoid being cut down by the scouts' rifle fire.[47]

Much later in the day, Two Crows, along with some companions, went down toward the river to recover the bodies of Weasel Bear and White Thunder. When they got there they discovered three other Cheyennes who had come to the river for the same purpose. One of these men said to Two Crows: "Be very careful how you creep through the grass, because whenever the soldiers see the grass move they shoot at us, and two or three times they have come near hitting us." Stillwell and his men still lay hidden and undetected.

As Two Crows and the other warriors crept slowly toward their wounded comrades, two shots cut through the buffalo grass in front of them. A warrior named Bear Feathers was grazed in the shoulder. Two Crows, Black Moon, and Cloud Chief continued to creep toward the bodies. Presently two more shots rang out and the bullets whistled in front of them. A bullet hit Two Crows's shield, which was tied to his back, and it nearly turned him over. The other bullet wounded Black Moon in the shoulder.

By this time Two Crows and Cloud Chief were only about ten feet from the bodies of Weasel Bear and White Thunder, dangerously close to Stillwell's rifle pit. Spotted Wolf and Star now crept up toward their companions. After they moved the grass, more shots rang out, and Cloud Chief was wounded in the arm. Star came up behind Two Crows, catching him by the feet. He asked, "How much farther away are they [the bodies]?"

"They are right over there ahead of us, only a little way," Two Crows replied.

Weasel Bear and White Thunder were lying almost side by side, with Weasel Bear slightly ahead of his nephew. When Two Crows reached them he saw that White Thunder was already stiff. They began to drag away White Thunder's body, being careful not to move the grass. Just as they began, however, Star noticed a movement. "Look at Weasel Bear," he said, "he is still breathing."

"Are you still alive, Weasel Bear?" Two Crows asked.

"Yes," came the reply from Weasel Bear. "I am badly wounded; I cannot move."

"Wait," Two Crows told him, "we are trying to get your nephew away from here, and when we get him away, we will come back and try to get you."

Weasel Bear asked, "Is that my brother-in-law?"

"Yes," replied Two Crows.

"I feel all right," Weasel Bear said, "except that I am badly wounded through the hips and cannot move."

"We cannot move White Thunder," Star said. "I will creep quietly back and have them get a rope. In that way we can all get hold and pull him away."

Star secured the rope and passed it up the line of men hiding in the grass to where Two Crows and Spotted Wolf were lying next to White Thunder's body. The two warriors looped the noose of the rope around White Thunder's feet. Two Crows and Spotted Wolf moved to one side as the other men pulled White Thunder away.

Again the grass moved, and shots split the air but did not find their marks. Two Crows and Spotted Wolf lay still in the grass. Soon the rope was passed back to Two Crows and he said to Weasel Bear: "My brother-in-law, we have come for you now."

"That is good," Weasel Bear replied. "I am glad of it. I feel all right except that my legs are paralyzed. I cannot move."

Two Crows looped the rope around Weasel Bear's feet and the men dragged him to safety. But later that night Weasel Bear died. The first day of the Battle of Beecher Island was thus a sad one for White Horse, who had lost his son, White Thunder, and his brother-in-law, Weasel Bear, both shot down by a hidden enemy.[48]

Another dramatic episode of September 17 at Beecher Island was the charge of Yellow Haired Woman. She was about forty-two years old, the widow of a warrior of the People who had been a member of the Crazy Dog Society. Her husband's name was Walking Bear, and he had died the previous year, a victim of an accidental discharge from his own gun. Hoping to join him in death, Yellow Haired Woman rode up to the battlefield on a fine black horse her father had given her for this purpose and joined a group of warriors for the second charge on the island. Yellow Haired Woman rode boldly against the white scouts in their entrenchments. Suddenly a bullet tore through the sleeve of her dress, leaving a clean hole but causing her no harm.

Four times she wheeled around on the big black horse and charged up to the edge of the island. By her fourth assault she temporarily lost some of her nerve. She reined the horse and stopped for a moment. A warrior named Wooden Leg, seeing her courage, shouted out to the other Indians. "What are you men doing?" he asked. "You are letting a woman get the best of you." Yellow Haired Woman completed her fourth charge toward the scouts' position. Then she broke off around the island and rode away, not finding death after all.[49]

Not long after the Indians' first charge failed, runners had been sent back to the village where Roman Nose was staying. The messengers asked Roman Nose to hurry and join the fighting. The great warrior reluctantly mounted his war-pony, a renowned horse among the People, an animal that would dance along with the Cheyennes during their ceremonies, keeping time to the drumbeats with its hooves.[50]

It was late in the day when Roman Nose reached the battlefield. He topped the hill above the Arickaree, went behind it, and dismounted. There two fellow warriors, Tangle Hair and Eagle Feather, joined him. Soon Roman Nose's good friends, the Dog Soldier chiefs Tall Bull and White Horse, came riding up and dismounted by his side. Puzzled as to why Roman Nose had not yet joined the fighting, Eagle Feather said to him: "You have always made it easier for the rest of us in a fight, but now you are staying away. Why don't you look at your men fighting. Some of them have already been killed."[51]

Then another warrior, the aged White Contrary, rode up and said, "Well, here is Roman Nose, the man we depend on, sitting behind this hill. He is the man that makes it easy for his men in any fight." White Contrary then addressed Roman Nose directly. "You do not see your men falling out there?" White Contrary asked. "Two fell just as I came up."

Roman Nose laughed and then admitted: "What the old man says is true."

White Contrary continued. "All those people fighting out there feel that they belong to you," he asserted, "and they will do all that you tell them, and you are here behind this hill."[52]

It was then that Roman Nose told his friends what had happened to him. "At the Sioux camp the other day something was done that I was told must not be done," Roman Nose said. "The bread I ate was taken out of the frying pan with something made of iron. I have been told not to eat anything so treated. This is what keeps me from making a charge. If I go into this fight, I shall certainly be killed."[53]

While Forsyth was marching toward the Indians' camp, Roman Nose had been the guest of the Sioux at their camp for a feast. The woman preparing the food for the occasion used an iron fork to take some fry bread from the pan she was using. Roman Nose had unknowingly eaten some of the fry bread. A Dog Soldier named Eight Horns noticed what the woman had done, and, too late, he pointed it out to Roman Nose. Having already eaten the fry bread, Roman Nose simply told Eight Horns: "That breaks my medicine."[54]

Although Tall Bull, when he heard of the matter, advised Roman Nose to go through with the purification ceremonies that would restore his medicine, the scouts' presence near the villages had been discovered, and there had been no time to complete the lengthy required ritual. Nevertheless, one of the Dog Soldier chiefs asked Roman Nose to lead another charge despite his broken medicine.

The great warrior rose to his feet and moved to where his horse awaited. He unpacked his war bag and began painting his face the holy red, yellow, and black, as Ice had taught him long ago. He had come to the battlefield without war clothes, ostensibly hoping to remain out of the fight, so other warriors gave him leggings, richly beaded moccasins, and possibly a scalp shirt as well. Roman Nose then untied the painted parfleche cylinder that contained Thunder's war bonnet, which had been made for Roman Nose by Ice and had protected him from the white men's bullets in the north at the Red Buttes fight and on the Powder River. He offered the war bonnet to the Cheyenne deities, and to Mother Earth, asking their blessings. Then he placed the war bonnet upon his head, its single buffalo horn protruding from the middle of his forehead. Finally he mounted his war horse. Roman Nose was ready to die.[55]

Because it was late in the day, not as many warriors participated in this third assault. Roman Nose rode to the head of the Indian line and gave the order to charge. Onward toward the island rushed Tall Bull's Dog Soldiers, other warriors of the People, and their Sioux and Arapahoe allies. They went around the bluff and through a small canyon, with Roman Nose in the lead. As in times past, the twin tails of Roman Nose's war bonnet unfurled behind him and flowed in the wind at the front of the charging warriors. As the Indians swiftly approached the island, volleys of gunfire exploded from the scouts' entrenchments, as once again the Spencers spread a hail of bullets into the front of the onrushing warriors. Roman Nose rode speedily over the riverbank. His horse almost trampled Stillwell and his men hidden in their rifle pit amid the tall buffalo grass. Roman Nose never saw them. As he rushed past them on his way toward the island, Stillwell's men fired at him. A single bullet struck Roman Nose in the small of the back above the hips. The other warriors rushed on past him. But once again the hail of lead from the Spencer carbines broke their charge; the Indians split and rode hastily to either side of the island.

Meanwhile, Roman Nose turned his horse around and rode back to the rear. There he dismounted and lay down upon the earth. Soon Bull Bear and White Horse rode up to him. Roman Nose told the chiefs he had been shot by scouts hiding on the riverbank. Stillwell's presence had finally been discovered. But Roman Nose clung to life. Later some of the Indian women came up to look after the wounded and took Roman Nose back to the camp.[56]

The fulfillment of Ice's warning with the shooting of Roman Nose ended the assaults on the island for the day. During the late afternoon the Indians tried to recover their dead and wounded. As with the recovery of Weasel Bear and White Thunder that afternoon, the scouts continuously sniped at the Indian rescuers. Late in the day, up on the hill behind the river and from a considerable distance, a bullet struck a Dog Soldier named Killed by a Bull, who was helping carry off the body of Dry Throat. Killed by a Bull dropped to the earth, according to the Indians, and was the last warrior to be fatally shot in the Battle of Beecher Island.[57]

At about the same time of the day, toward sunset of September 17, the lives of two men of war flickered and went out. Each carried with him the courage of his convictions and the assurance afforded by the norms of his culture that he was right and that he had died fighting for a just cause. Because the fighting had immobilized Forsyth's command, the scouts buried First Lieutenant Frederick H. Beecher and the other whites killed on the island, which would forever bear Beecher's name. The Cheyennes ceremoniously buried Roman Nose on a traditional scaffold in the Republican Valley about September 21. According to oral tradition, Medicine Woman, in later life the wife of Porcupine Bull, helped Roman Nose's wife bring up the lodgepoles and erect the burial scaffold. She wrapped Roman Nose's body in a shroud consisting of a richly decorated buffalo robe, and his followers laid him upon the scaffold. Thunder's war bonnet was on his head in death as it had been in life during his battles to defend the lands of the People.[58]

With the deaths of Frederick H. Beecher and Roman Nose, the terrible first day of fighting on the Arickaree came to an end.

The Scouts' War   8

My God! Have you deserted us?

> – SCOUT CHAUNCEY B. WHITNEY
> *Beecher Island*
> *September 24, 1868*

The Forsyth Scouts suffered heavy casualties during the first day of fighting at Beecher Island. "Considering the fact that my command, including myself, only numbered fifty-[two] men," Forsyth wrote, "the outlook was somewhat dismal. Lieutenant Beecher, Surgeon Mooers, and scouts Chalmers Smith and Wilson were dead or dying [Smith survived]; scouts Louis Farley and Bernard Day were mortally wounded [Day's fate is unknown]; scouts O'Donnell, Davis, Tucker, Gantt, Clarke, Armstrong, Morton, and Violett [*sic*] severely [wounded], and scouts Harrington, Davenport, Haley, McLaughlin, Hudson Farley, McCall, and two others [in addition to Forsyth himself] slightly wounded."[1]

In addition, the scouts had used up most of their rations. They abandoned most of their medical supplies in favor of loading extra ammunition on the pack mules during the rush for the island, and their physician was mortally wounded. Fort Wallace was over one hundred miles away and the Indians still greatly outnumbered the command and essentially had the scouts' position surrounded. But in other ways the scouts were more fortunate. Water was readily available by digging in the sand of the island. So at the suggestion of Martin Burke the scouts dug a makeshift well. During the evening of the 17th the men deepened the rifle pits, connected them with a system of trenches, and reinforced their position with saddles, packs, dead horses, and dead mules. They dug a pit especially for the care of the wounded. Finally, the men cut chunks of flesh from the dead horses and buried them in the sand to use later as food.[2]

But in the long run the scouts' only hope rested on reinforcements coming from Fort Wallace. That possibility could only be realized if one or two of the scouts risked their lives to make the long journey through the Indian lines to the fort. "Sharp" Grover warned the men that the Indians would tighten their cordon around the scouts' position and would be watching for any man who tried to leave the island. Nevertheless, Forsyth had no shortage of volunteers. "Colonel," Jack Stillwell said, "if I can get someone to go with me, I'll take the risk." Pierre Trudeau spoke up, "I'll go with you Jack." Immediately, the wounded Forsyth wrote out an urgent dispatch for Colonel Henry Bankhead, the commander at Fort Wallace.[3]

About midnight Stillwell and Trudeau began their dangerous journey. "Jack was the best imitator of an Indian that I ever saw," Eli Ziegler remembered. "They fixed themselves up as Indians the best they could and took off their boots and tied on some rags and blankets on their feet so that if the Indians saw their tracks next day they would think it some of their own party and not follow them [and kill them] before they got to the fort. . . . At a late hour they gave us their hand and crawled out," walking backward so that the Indians would not discover tracks coming *from* the island.[4] Young Sigmund Shlesinger worried that he would never again see alive his new friend Jack Stillwell. "We listened for some time," Shlesinger reminisced regarding Stillwell and Trudeau's exodus from the island, "fully expecting every moment to hear the warwhoop which would announce their discovery and capture, but not a sound followed their departure."[5]

Later that evening, after bidding his friend a farewell, Sig Shlesinger began to feel the first pangs of hunger. He remembered some "wild plums," which he had gathered the previous day and stowed away in his saddlebags. "I got out of my hole," Shlesinger remembered, "and creeping on hands and knees to the spot where my dead horse lay, [I] began feeling around in the darkness. I came in contact with something cold, and upon examination found it was Scout Wilson's [dead] pallid hand. . . . The shivers chased up and down my back, but I got to my horse and tugged until I secured the saddlebags containing the plums."[6] "On my way back to my hole I passed [the rifle pit] where Doctor Mooers lay wounded, moaning piteously. I put a plum in his mouth, and I [with George Washington Oaks] saw it between his teeth next morning."[7]

Despite fatigue, there was little sleep that night for many of the Forsyth Scouts. "All night long," Sandy Forsyth remembered, "we could hear the Indians . . . their camp resounded with the beats of drums and the death-wail of the mourners."[8] Before trying to sleep, Chauncey B. Whitney and Sigmund Shlesinger scribbled in their diaries brief accounts of the day's action. Late that night a wakeful George Washington Oaks heard Forsyth talking to his chief scout, "Sharp" Grover. The conversation, Oaks concluded, was about the fate of Stillwell and Trudeau. "I think I can sleep," he heard Forsyth say. "I believe they got through."

"Yes," Grover replied, "I think so too." Then Oaks heard Grover make a statement as if he were talking to himself. "It's a hundred miles to Wallace," Grover mumbled, "maybe they'll have to crawl a big part of the way."[9]

✳ ✳ ✳

The first light of dawn on September 18 found Jack Stillwell and Pierre Trudeau on the South Fork of the Republican River and, to their dismay, close to the Indian camps. They hid during the daylight in a low ravine along the river, well hidden by an overgrowth of coarse prairie grass and sunflowers. All day long the two scouts observed warriors riding toward the village. When darkness came, they crossed the river and made their way southeast without incident.[10]

During the day of the 19th the scouts again hid themselves under the high banks of a stream and inside the decayed and dried carcass of a buffalo that had died the previous winter. That night they made good progress. The morning of the 20th found them on the treeless Kansas prairie, where the only hiding place they could find was a dry buffalo wallow. Sometime during the day a large party of Indians stopped within one hundred feet of the wallow. At almost the same time that the Indians rode up, a large rattlesnake came wriggling to the spot where the scouts lay hidden. To shoot the snake would mean sudden discovery from the nearby warriors. The two scouts lay perfectly still and waited.

At this point one of Jack Stillwell's bad habits saved his and Trudeau's lives. Jack chewed tobacco. As the rattlesnake drew closer, the young Kansan let fly with a large spit. Whether by sheer luck or through many hours of practice, the dose of tobacco juice hit the snake directly in the face. Alarmed for a moment, the snake finally veered off and beat a retreat from the buffalo wallow. A few minutes later the warriors rode off, never knowing the little life-and-death drama that had been acted out in the nearby buffalo wallow. That night the elderly Trudeau all but broke down from the ordeal. Jack Stillwell encouraged the old man to muster all his strength, as they surely were close to Fort Wallace. Stillwell helped Trudeau along as best he could during their travels of September 21. To Jack's great joy, the two weary scouts finally saw in the distance the faint ribbon of road that was the Smoky Hill stage route.[11]

✳ ✳ ✳

On the morning of September 18 a group of warriors made a weak charge on the island. The scouts easily repulsed them.[12] Later, Sig Shlesinger noticed the Indians raising a white flag. But the scouts feared that this tactic was merely a ploy to get close to the island in order to assess the remaining strength of the command. The whites poured a volley into the flag bearers and the warriors came no closer.[13] John Hurst did not even mention the assault that morning; instead he remembered the action of the 18th as being "confined to desultory firing by the Indian sharpshooters."[14]

But Eli Ziegler vividly remembered the attack. "They did come early," he reminisced, "just before the sun rose. It seemed to me there were just as many and as bad as the first day and the squaws took their places on the hills just the same as the day before. Our orders were about the same, 'Hold your fire till they get close, but don't let them ride over us.' We were in a good deal better position and could all be together which gave us a better show than we had had the day before." Eventually the Indians "stopped fighting and put up a white flag, but most of us were too old to be scalped alive that way and we showed no signs of a white flag so that did not last long with them. [Their sharpshooters] soon commenced again and poured in [volleys of gunfire] on us as hard as ever the rest of the day."[15]

Forsyth remembered that "at daylight [the Indians] again took up the fight from their former position in ambush, but as we were now fully protected, they did us no particular harm. It was now apparent that they meant to starve us out, for they made no further attempts to attack us openly."[16]

Despite the scouts' precarious situation, a few of them found time to take notice of humorous events. During the second day's sniping, George Washington Oaks remembered lying in his rifle pit, "talking to [Martin] Burke, when an arrow came whizzing out of the sky and struck me in the hip. You ought to have heard Burke," he later reminisced. " 'Haw! Haw! Haw! Lookit Oaks with a Cheyenne arrow stuck in his hind end.' I'm not given much to swearing but that's one time I came pretty near shooting that goddam Irishman. But Burke was alright," Oaks admitted, "he grabbed the shaft and slowly worked it out. If left too long the blood-soaked sinew [holding the arrowhead to the shaft] would loosen so badly that when the shaft was pulled out the arrowhead would stay."[17]

Sig Shlesinger later told how he and Jim Lane had come face to face with a pack mule that was badly wounded with arrows. "Jim Lane, my neighbor [in the rifle pits] decided to kill him," Shlesinger remembered. "Upon being shot, he fell and lay between us. He served the double purpose as a barricade and food. Two or three days later when Jim was cutting meat off the mule he must have cut deeper than he intended, for he cut an intestine and received its full contents over himself, nearly filling his pit! This was one of the humorous incidents, but of course not to poor Jim, judging from the blue streaks in the air around him."[18]

That night two more scouts, Allison J. Pliley and Chauncey B. Whitney, tried to make it through the Indian lines in case Stillwell and Trudeau had not succeeded. They could not get through, however, as that night the Indians closed off every avenue of escape. Soon the two men returned to camp. "The third day [September 19] was a repetition of the second," John Hurst remembered, "very little firing, but close watching on the part of the Indians. After dark Colonel Forsyth again called for volunteers, and Jack Donovan and A. J. Pliley started out, with directions to come back straight across the country [rather than taking Custer's longer route of the previous year along the Republican River, which Stillwell and Trudeau were using] with soldiers and an ambulance and medical supplies, together with plenty of food."[19] The next morning Chauncey B. Whitney noted in his diary, "It rained all night steady, and everybody was wet and cold."[20]

❋ ❋ ❋

Pliley and Donovan made it safely through the Indian lines. "After changing our boots for a pair of moccasins, which we had taken off two dead Indians, in order to make as light a trail as possible," Pliley remembered, "and after filling our pockets with tainted horse meat, we bid a silent 'so-long' to our comrades and started to crawl down along the north side of the island, stopping frequently to let a party of Indians who had surrounded the island pass by. After getting outside of their lines, we straightened up, and taking our course by the north star started on our long, weary walk, and we soon found we had made a mistake by putting on the moccasins."[21]

"The prickly pear [cactus thorns] penetrated the wet leather like needles," Donovan recalled. "Before we had covered ten miles our feet were like pincushions and began to swell. From that time on the trip was like a nightmare."[22] "We had to tear up our shirts and tie up our injured feet," Pliley later told a reporter from Olathe, Kansas. "We traveled by night and hid in buffalo wallows by day. We suffered for water and lived on rotten horse flesh with which we had filled our pockets before leaving camp."[23]

Soon the two scouts came upon one of the camps of the Indians. Detection seemed imminent. But "Pliley here proved his genius," Donovan remembered. "He waited until one of the sentries had reached the end of his beat and shot him dead. But we did not pass over his body. The shot alarmed the whole village and every Indian who was able to run started for the point at which it had been heard. We kept back of the line and ran in the direction of the village. It was through . . . the village that we escaped to take up the wilderness trail for Fort Wallace, more than one hundred miles away."[24]

The Coloradoan Jack Donovan knew the Republican River country fairly well and, consequently, the two scouts did not have to follow the creeks and trails. Instead they cut cross-country, toward Fort Wallace.[25] The next day the men hid in a buffalo wallow, "lying there all day in the hot sun," Pliley remembered, "without water, eating that rotten horse meat in order to keep up strength. . . . About three o'clock in the afternoon our attention was drawn to a party of twenty-five Indians coming toward us; ten minutes more and they would be upon us. We placed our guns where we could get them easily and prepared for the closing acts of our lives. When they got to within a quarter of a mile of us they halted, and after a short consultation they bore off to the northwest and past [sic] us without seeing us. Jack, who was always light hearted in danger, commenced singing *Oh, for a thousand tongues to sing.* After dark we again took up our weary walk, footsore and almost famished for water. About twelve o'clock that night we struck the south fork of the Republican. After spending an hour drinking and bathing our sore, swollen feet, we hurried on our mission. It appeared that every hour added more thorns in our feet and more pain from those that were already in them, until it seemed impossible to go on, but the thoughts of our comrades who depended upon us spurred us on.

"When we started from the island we laid our course to hit the Smoky Hill stage [route] north of Cheyenne Wells and on the fourth night out [September 22] at three o'clock we struck the road." Soon the two scouts spotted the sod buildings of a ranch.[26]

✳ ✳ ✳

"While the scouts were making their way to Fort Wallace," John Hurst remembered, "we who were left on the island were having a serious time. The Indians gave up the siege after the fifth day [September 21], and on the sixth day [September 22], some of the men were prompted to advise saving the lives of those who were uninjured by striking out for the fort and leaving the wounded to their fate, thinking none of the volunteers would be able to get through. When this talk of abandoning the

Jack Donovan. One of the few Coloradoans at Beecher Island, Jack Donovan would suffer great hardship (as would Jack Stillwell, Allison J. Pliley, and Pierre Trudeau) to bring reinforcements to Beecher Island. *Courtesy Denver Public Library, Denver, Colorado, Western History Department.*

wounded reached Colonel Forsyth's ears he called us together and made a nice talk. It was very touching and soldierlike — so much so that I never heard any more talk about abandoning the wounded. Forsyth told us he expected us to stay with the command until the men he had sent out had time to get to the fort, and that it was our duty to the law of humanity to stick together at least that long. 'After that,' he concluded, 'I will have no further claim on you, and you can do the best you can to save your own lives.' We all then swore," Hurst recalled, "we never would desert the wounded, but would die with them if necessary."[27]

Forsyth, however, suffering from multiple wounds, remembered this episode differently, and somewhat more melodramatically, making himself and his men out (after the fact) to be a little more self-sacrificing than they probably were at the time. "On the evening of the sixth day I called the sound men around me," Forsyth later wrote for an admiring public, "and in a few words stated the facts of the case as they knew them. I told them that possibly the scouts who had been sent out from the command had failed to get through, and that we might not get the succor we hoped for. . . . Those of us who were wounded must take our chances. If relief came in time, well and good; if not we were soldiers, and knew how to meet our fate. For a few seconds there was dead silence, and then rose a hoarse cry of 'Never! Never! We'll stand by you, General, to the end!' and [Sergeant] McCall voiced sentiment of the men by saying, 'We've fought together, and, by heaven, if need be, we'll die together!' "[28]

George Washington Oaks remembered this incident much like Forsyth. " 'You men who aren't wounded can probably get to Wallace,'" he paraphrased Forsyth as saying. " 'You are at liberty to go. We'll make out somehow.' We could hardly believe our ears when we heard it," Oaks remembered.

" 'Walk away and leave our wounded to thim [sic] red devils,' said Martin Burke. 'What the hell would people think of us?'

" 'Yes,' I heard somebody say, 'that would be a fine thing to think about the rest of our days. . . . '

"Martin [Burke], who had been prowling around on the island the night before, had found an old tipi pole. He took off his sailor's blue jacket and tied it to the pole. Then he dug a hole in the sand and planted the staff. 'There,' says he; 'that's our flag of no surrender.' And so it was."[29]

After three days on the island, the wounded began to suffer miserably. The autumn weather fluctuated from broiling days to freezing nights and one morning there was a dusting of snow on the island. Surgeon Mooers died on the morning of the 20th. "Our mortally wounded were made as comfortable as possible before they died," Sigmund Shlesinger remembered. "As soon as possible we put our dead in the ground. Those that died at one end of the island were cared for by those in that vicinity, and others in their vicinity, so that one part of the island was not aware of the location of the corpses of the other part; at least I did not know where the bodies lay of those killed on the eastern end of the island. So one time, as I walked around among the pits, I noticed something red and round sticking out of the sand, like a half-buried red berry. I kicked it, but by so doing it was not dislodged; I kicked it again, but to no result. I then looked closer and discovered that it was the nose of a dead man."[30]

"As the days wore on," Forsyth remembered, "the wounded became feverish, and some of them delirious, gangrene set in, and I was distressed to find the wound in my leg infested with maggots."[31] The ball in Forsyth's right leg began to pain him excessively. He decided to extract it. "I appealed to several of the men to cut it out," he later wrote, "but as soon as they saw how close it lay to the artery, they declined doing so, alleging that the risk was too great. However, I determined that it should come out, as I feared sloughing, and then the artery would probably break in any event; so taking my razor from my saddle-pocket, and getting two of the men to press the adjacent flesh back and draw it taut, I managed to cut it out myself without disturbing the artery, greatly to my almost immediate relief."[32]

For some of the unwounded men, the nine-day ordeal on Beecher Island affected them in more gruesome ways. "On about the fifth day, as the Indians began leaving us, we began to walk about and look around," Sig Shlesinger remembered. "About fifteen or twenty feet from my pit I noticed a few of our men calling to the rest of us. I ran to the place, and there, against the edge of the island, I saw three dead Indians. Their friends evidently could not reach them to carry them off, which explained to us the persistent fighting in this direction. When I got there the Indians were being stripped of their equipments, scalps, etc. One of them was shot in the head and his hair was clotted with blood. I took hold of one of his braids and applied my knife to the skin above the ear to secure the scalp, but my hand coming in contact with the blood, I dropped the hair in disgust.

"Old Jim Lane saw my hesitation, and taking up the braid, said to me: 'My boy, does it make you sick?' Then inserting the point of the knife under the skin, he cut around, took up the other braid, and jerked the scalp from the [Indian's] head." On the fifth day of the ordeal on Beecher Island (September 21), the sensibilities of the young Hungarian immigrant from New York City still prevented him from accepting the crude customs prevalent on the western military frontier of 1868. By the end of the ordeal, however, Sigmund Shlesinger finally would participate in questionable practices bred from the racial hatred generated by the conflict.[33]

For most of the men hunger became the major concern. By the fourth day (September 20), Forsyth remembered the suffering to be intense. "It was very hot," he wrote, "our meat had become putrid, . . . and the stench from the dead horses lying close around us was almost intolerable."[34] "The men began to get discouraged," Howard Morton remembered. "There was no certainty that our men sent to the fort . . . had ever reached it. Some of our [healthy] men found prickly pears on the hills, which we ate with relish. We were a disconsolate looking crowd. It was cold and wet most of the time and one morning it snowed. We hovered over our little fires, [and] made soup from the strong horse meat, putting in [gun]powder to deaden the taste."[35]

"We had no salt," remembered John Hurst, "and our systems were crying for it. One of the men found a small piece of pork rind in his haversack and chewed it until he thought he had all the good out of it and spit it out; when another comrade took it up and chewed it for a while and spit it out; and then I took it and chewed it up and thought it tasted delicious."[36] On the 22nd, Sig Shlesinger wrote in his diary: "Killt [*sic*] a Coyote & eat him all up."[37] A rib and the brain were Shlesinger's portion.[38]

But most of the scouts' diet consisted of the putrid flesh of their horses and mules, which Shlesinger noted "soon told on our bowels."[39] After September 22, John Hurst remembered, "we had nothing to eat but the dead horses which were festering and decaying about us, and when we cut into this meat the stench was something frightful, and it had green streaks running all through it. The only way it was made at all available for eating was by sprinkling gunpowder over it while it was cooking, which partially took away the bad odor."[40] "On the morning of the sixth day [September 22]," Eli Ziegler remembered, "everything was quiet, except the howling of wolves and sour horse meat was so rotten and alive with maggots we thought we would try to find some game or something to live on so we rustled out a little and found nothing much but prickly pears. We soon found out they would not do entirely for food so we lingered along on our old butcher shop [the decaying horses and mules] until the eighth night."[41] On the seventh night (September 23), a note of desperation creeped into the diary entry of Chauncey B. Whitney: "Still looking anxiously for relief. Starvation is staring us in the face; nothing but horse meat."[42]

On the eighth day (September 24), as the Indians had left the immediate vicinity, some of the men began prowling the adjacent hills looking for food. They discovered a prairie dog town. John Hurst was determined to secure one of the rodents to give him sustenance. "I went out to the dog town and watched it for quite a while," he remembered, "but no dog came out [of its hole]. I had kept [my spirits] up pretty well until this time, but [now] I began to think I would starve to death."[43] On the night of September 24, Chauncey B. Whitney faced what seemed to be a real possibility of starvation when he wrote another anxious entry in his battlefield diary: "All fresh meat gone. Tried to kill some wolves last night, but failed. . . . Made some soup tonight from putrid horse meat. My God! Have you deserted us?"[44]

Relief and Retribution 9

God bless the Beecher Island men. They were a noble set of men.

— REUBEN WALLER
Former Private, Company H, 10th U.S. Cavalry
Eldorado, Kansas
July 23, 1929

On the morning of the ninth day on the island (September 25), Eli Ziegler sat by his small fire roasting a piece of rotten horse meat when Fletcher Vilott came up to him and said: "Eli, let's take a little walk and see what we can find."

"We took our guns and started north across the river," Ziegler remembered. "When we got across . . . Fletcher said to me, 'There is going to be a change today, that is why I wanted you to take a walk with me. I wanted to tell you about it.' " Questioning him further, Ziegler discovered that Vilott had convinced himself either the Indians would return that day to finish them off or the command would be relieved by troops from Fort Wallace. "As we got nearly to the top of the hill [slightly northwest of the island]," Ziegler remembered, "we came to a big rock and sat down a moment to rest. . . . We sat there talking a few moments; my eye caught an object on the far hills to the south. . . . We jumped to our feet and walked up the hill a little farther, where we could plainly see that [something was] coming over the hill toward us. . . . We could not make out what it was so we hurried back to camp in case it was Indians. We reported in camp that there was quite a large force of something coming over the hill from the south. The colonel said, 'Get the men all in [from the surrounding countryside] and we will be ready for anything.' "[1]

John Hurst was out in the prairie dog town trying to kill one of the rodents for breakfast. "I had not gone far when I saw some of the men running towards me and motioning for me to hurry [back to the island]," he remembered. "The thought that it was the Indians returning for another invasion of the island took possession of me and I started on a dead run for my comrades. I was too faint and exhausted, however, to run very far, and soon [I] fell to the ground, all in, and scarcely caring whether it was the Indians or not, so discouraged and disheartened was I. Happening to look up, I saw three horsemen riding toward me. "[2]

The scouts on the island could see the riders, too. One of the men near Forsyth's rifle pit sprang to his feet, shaded his eyes with his hand, and shouted, "There are some moving objects on the far hills."

"Instantly every man who could stand was on his feet," Forsyth remembered, "gazing intensely in the direction indicated."[3]

It was by then 10:00 A.M., and Howard Morton along with some of the other scouts took a pair of army field glasses to try to discern whether the riders were Indians or whites. They could not tell. "The horsemen kept coming," Morton recalled. "Everybody who could get up was watching them, our hearts in our mouths. They saw us and rode toward us on the run."[4]

Back on the prairie, at the base of the hills to the south where John Hurst had fallen down, the three horsemen approached rapidly. "I gazed long and earnestly at the advancing riders," Hurst remembered, "and soon saw they were white men. It proved to be Jack Donovan [with Jack Peate, a Forsyth Scout who had remained behind at Fort Wallace, and another unidentified man], and the relief party. Never before nor since, have I been so glad to see the face of a friend!" Hurst confessed. "The sudden transition from despair to safety was too much for my overtaxed nerves, and I broke down and wept like a child."[5]

After reporting to Forsyth, Eli Ziegler returned to the mainland to bring in two foraging scouts who he thought might have wandered out of sight of the island. "In a short while I saw a man at full gallop," Ziegler remembered. "When he got a little closer to my great surprise [I saw] it was my old friend Jack Peate."[6]

"How are the rest of the boys?" Peate asked.

Ziegler's reply reflected another urgency. "Have you anything to eat?" he asked. "[Peate] reached in his saddle pockets," Ziegler remembered, "and brought me out a hard tack and a little piece of bacon about an inch thick and about two inches long. Then he put spurs to his horse and rode on [toward] the island. I followed him up as close as I could," Ziegler admitted, "thinking he might drop another crumb that I could pick up."[7]

"Down that steep hill [now called Peate Hill] we rushed as fast as we could urge our horses," Peate remembered. "Soon we could see several men running toward us. Nearer us was a man running toward the island. We were fast overtaking him when he stopped and raised his gun to fire at us. We separated, waved our hats and he came running toward us. Soon we met the others, but . . . I put spurs to my horse and rode into that blood-stained island alone. . . . [Nobody] ne'er received so royal and hearty a welcome as I did. . . . Among those staunch-hearted men, who lifted me from my horse, embraced me and, strong men though they were, wept, as cheer upon cheer arose. How they cheered, again and again, while manly tears coursed down their cheeks."[8]

Sigmund Shlesinger was napping when he heard someone call attention to Peate and Donovan's arrival. When the youth realized it was the advance of a relief party, he could not control his emotions. "Enfeebled as I was," Shlesinger remembered, "I jumped up and joined in a lunatics' dance that was in progress all around us. Those on the hill must have seen us for there was a rush of horsemen down the hill toward us, followed by one or two ambulance wagons."[9]

"By the God above us, it's an ambulance!" Forsyth remembered one of the men shouting as the main body of the relief party followed Peate and Donovan over the hill. "And then went up a wild cheer," Forsyth recalled. "They grasped hands, and then flung their arms around each other, and laughed and cried, and fairly danced and shouted again in glad relief of their long-pent up feelings."[10]

The word "ambulance" jolted George Washington Oaks "wide awake," he remembered. "Those able to stand were doing a war dance," he later wrote, "and I joined them, sore hip and all."[11]

As more soldiers from the relief party poured onto the island at a gallop, near-chaos broke out among the Forsyth Scouts. "I noticed a soldier on a white horse coming full tilt," Sig Shlesinger remembered. "The momentum carried him past me, but in passing I grabbed his saddle-bag and was taken off my feet, but it would have taken more than one horse to drag me from my hold. I suspected some eatables in there, and as soon as he could stop, without dismounting, he assisted me to open that bag. With both hands I dived in, and with each hand I clutched some hardtack, but only one hand could reach my mouth; my other was in the grip of one of our men, who ravenously snatched the 'tacks' [away from me]. We ate, cried, laughed, and ate, all in a breath."[12]

It was immediately apparent to the Forsyth Scouts that they had been rescued by a troop of "Buffalo Soldiers" from Fort Wallace. Although great joy was in the heart of George Washington Oaks on September 25, 1868, he nevertheless did not quite avoid the pejorative sentiments of his culture when he later wrote his memoirs. The "troopers [in the relief column] were Negroes," Oaks wrote, "but boy, were we glad to see them! ... Schlesinger [sic] was walking around among the Negro troopers offering them some of our ripe horse meat seasoned with gunpowder. To show them his heart was in the right place, he said if the troopers didn't like horse meat, we had some mule meat that was riper still. The black boys held their noses and told him if he didn't get the hell out of there with his seasoned horse meat there would be one Hebrew less in this world in short order."[13]

That night Chauncey B. Whitney entered in his diary a notation of a different tone: "Oh, the unspeakable joy! Shouts of joy and tears of gladness were [today] freely comingled."[14]

Company H of the 10th Cavalry, seventy strong and under the command of Captain (Brevet Lieutenant Colonel) Louis H. Carpenter, had rescued Forsyth and his scouts. Other officers in the command included First Lieutenant Charles Banzhof, Second Lieutenant L. H. Orleman, and Surgeon Jenkins A. Fitzgerald. The company had with them seventeen scouts (including Peate and Donovan), thirteen supply wagons, and an ambulance.[15]

Jack Stillwell and Pierre Trudeau had been the first Forsyth Scouts safely to reach Fort Wallace, arriving on the evening of September 22.[16] Upon their arrival, the post was instantly "full of excitement" as the two

Captain (Brevet Lieutenant Colonel) Louis H. Carpenter. Forsyth's rescuer was an old friend from the Civil War, Captain L. H. Carpenter of the 10th Cavalry. His "Buffalo Soldiers" of Company H, 10th Cavalry, known as "Carpenter's Brunettes," were the first to reach the island on September 25. According to Carpenter's surgeon, a delay of one more day would have cost Sandy Forsyth his life. *Courtesy Denver Public Library, Denver, Colorado, Western History Department.*

exhausted scouts told their grim tale of the Beecher Island fight to the commandant, (Brevet) Colonel Henry Bankhead. Carpenter and Company H were already in the field on a scout along the Smoky Hill route, following up reported Indian depredations. That night, Bankhead dispatched a courier to find Carpenter and send him to Forsyth's rescue. Carpenter had departed Fort Wallace on the 21st, with Jack Peate as scout, under orders to camp sixty miles west of the fort near the Cheyenne Wells stage station located in present-day Cheyenne County, Colorado, and then scout in every direction in search of Indian raiders. Carpenter's "Buffalo Soldiers" eventually crossed Sand Creek and went into camp on Goose Creek, north of the Smoky Hill stage road, when Bankhead's dispatch caught up with them on September 23.

"The dispatch directed Carpenter to proceed at once to a point on the Dry Fork of the Republican [Arickaree Fork]," Jack Peate remembered, " 'about seventy-five or eighty miles north, northwest [from Fort Wallace], thirty or forty miles west by a little south from the forks of the Republican, with all possible dispatch.' Not a man in the company knew the country [to the] north," Peate recalled; "it [the Arickaree Fork] was so far from the usual routes of travel that it is doubtful if any white men had ever been there." Consequently, Carpenter's command had to move cautiously, scouting up each dry wash of the Republican. "We left the stage road at noon [September 23]," Peate later wrote, "going in a northerly direction. Our gait was an alternative walk and trot, making five or six miles an hour, a gait that seemed far too slow for those in the command who had friends on the island."[17]

Although Carpenter was under orders to return Dr. Fitzgerald to Fort Wallace, he kept the surgeon with his command in case he found the Forsyth Scouts before any other relief column did. Meanwhile, Bankhead left Fort Wallace on the 23rd with 106 men, who constituted one company of the 38th Infantry, a detachment from the 5th Infantry, one company of the 10th Cavalry, several scouts, and Assistant Surgeon Theophilus H. Turner. The command had with them two field artillery pieces. Jack Stillwell and Pierre Trudeau accompanied Bankhead's command back to the island; they rode in an ambulance wagon most of the way because of their fatigued condition. Bankhead had sent the news of Forsyth's plight to Sheridan, who ordered "that the greatest dispatch be used, and every means employed to succor Forsyth at once." Bankhead complied with the orders of his department commander fully.[18]

"Carpenter's Brunettes," as the men of Company H, 10th Cavalry, were called by many of the white soldiers on the Kansas frontier, reached the South Fork of the Republican on the afternoon of September 24. There the command discovered a "large, fresh trail over which at least 2,000 head of ponies had recently been ridden." Carpenter ordered his wagons to be corralled in case of attack, and he and several troopers rode to a nearby hill to reconnoiter their position. There the soldiers witnessed a chilling sight. "Having surveyed the landscape," Carpenter remembered, "our attention was directed to several Indian scaffoldings erected on the hill, upon which bodies were placed after the Cheyenne method of burial. A body was taken down, unrolled from the skins enveloping it, and it was discovered that the Indian warrior had evidently died from a recent gunshot wound. Another was examined with the same result, and another, and another. Five Indians all killed recently by bullet wounds. Everyone was satisfied that these men had met death in some fight fought at no great distance within the last few days, and as the Forsyth fight was the only one likely to have occurred, they had probably taken part in that affair."[19]

Across the valley Carpenter spied a white object in a ravine. "This turned out to be a wigwam or tepee built of freshly tanned white skins," Carpenter remembered. "Inside on a platform lay the body of an Indian warrior, evidently a chief or man of considerable consequence, wrapped in buffalo robes. An Indian drum, similar to those used by the Indians for medicine purposes, a shield and some other equipments were placed at the head and feet. This chief had also been killed recently by a bullet wound." For the time being, the Buffalo Soldiers left the bodies of the dead warriors where they found them and moved out to locate Forsyth.[20]

Carpenter's command camped on the South Fork of the Republican that night. Early on the morning of September 25, while the strikers were packing up in preparation to move out, "some mounted men appeared on the hills to the south," Carpenter recalled, "and rode rapidly towards us. We soon discovered that they were white men . . . a party of five, one of whom was . . . [Jack] Donovan."[21]

Donovan and Pliley had arrived at Fort Wallace shortly after Bankhead's departure with Stillwell and Trudeau on the 23rd. After taking food at a ranch on the Smoky Hill route, with their feet "swollen twice their normal size" from cactus spikes, the two scouts had caught a Wells Fargo stagecoach into Fort Wallace. There, finding the post almost deserted because most of its contingent was in the field looking for Forsyth, the two scouts split up, Pliley striking out to Frenchman's Fork of the Republican to alert another detachment of soldiers in the field out of Fort Sedgwick, Colorado Territory, under Lieutenant Colonel (Brevet Brigadier General) Luther P. Bradley of the 27th Infantry. Pliley arrived at Bradley's camp about 8:00 A.M. on the morning of September 25. Immediately Bradley dispatched two companies of the 2nd Cavalry in his command under Major James S. Brisbin to Forsyth's relief. Evidently Pliley was so entirely exhausted by his ordeal that after he reported to Bradley he returned immediately to the post hospital at Fort Wallace.[22]

Meanwhile, Donovan had collected "four adventurous spirits" and started off to find either Bankhead or Carpenter. "I borrowed a mule," Donovan recalled, "[because] all the horses had been taken — and sought [these] officers."[23] "Not knowing the trail," Carpenter later wrote, Donovan "had taken a wrong course, and [only] by a wonderful piece of luck had happened on my command. I gathered from a talk with Donovan that the fork or branch that Forsyth was on was probably more to the north." Company H started at once. "As we expected," Carpenter recalled, "the back trail of the Indians soon left the South Fork and led northward."[24]

About 10:00 A.M., following Donovan and Peate's directions, Carpenter's Buffalo Soldiers came to a ridge where they could clearly see both up and down the Arickaree. "After looking down the river a few moments," Peate recalled, "Donovan followed with his eye the stream to the west and said: 'I am not quite sure, but [I] think it (meaning the battle ground) is a little farther up the river.' Just at this moment," Peate remembered, "I was looking in a northeast direction and saw two objects that looked like men walking down a hill a mile and a half away. I called Donovan's attention to them and he said: 'Yes, by God! There is camp!' "[25]

Within minutes the activity on the island became the wild scene of celebration that Forsyth and his men would so long remember. "As we neared [the Forsyth Scouts]," Carpenter reminisced, "they recognized us and received us with evidences of the wildest joy. I could not help noting the haggard, wolfish look on their countenances, which indicated hunger and starvation, but [I] did not stop, rushing forward to where Forsyth was. He was lying in an excavation made in the sand, unable to move from the nature of his wounds."[26]

When Carpenter found him, Sandy Forsyth appeared to be complacently reading a tattered copy of *Oliver Twist* that one of the men had found in a saddlebag on a dead horse.[27] "When Colonel Carpenter rode up to me," Forsyth remembered, "as I lay half covered with sand in my rifle pit, I affected to be reading an old novel that one of the men had found in a saddle pocket. It was only affectation, though, for I had all I could do to keep from breaking down, as I was sore and feverish and tired and hungry, and I had been under a heavy strain from the opening of the fight until his arrival."[28]

"He maintained his nerve wonderfully," Carpenter remembered, "but [he] was much affected when he saw me." Then, in the stiff Victorian manner of addressing a fellow officer, Carpenter "grasped Forsyth's hand," he remembered, "and told him that I was sorry to see him in his present condition, but was glad to be able to render him assistance."[29] Having served with Forsyth on Sheridan's staff during the Wilderness Campaign and in the Shenandoah Valley during the Civil War, Carpenter was probably more pleased than his formal rhetoric may have indicated that he was commanding the first relief force to reach the island.[30]

Immediately Surgeon Jenkins A. Fitzgerald began attending the wounded. Carpenter's hostler, former slave Private Reuben Waller, never forgot the scene on the island. "And what a sight we saw," he recalled in 1929," 30 wounded and dead men [actually twenty-one or possibly twenty-two] right in the midst of 50 dead horses, that had lain in the hot sun for ten days. . . . The men were in a dying condition when Carpenter and myself dismounted and began to rescue them.

"By this time all the soldiers were in the pits and we began to feed the men from our haversacks. If the doctor had not arrived in time we would have killed them all by feeding them to death. The men were eating all we gave them, and it was a plenty. Sure, we never gave a thought that it would hurt them. You can imagine a man in starvation, and plenty suddenly set before him. He can't think of the results until too late. That is the condition that Company H, 10th Cavalry, fixed for the Beecher Island men. We were not aiming to hurt the boys. It was all done through eagerness and excitement."[31]

Soon First Lieutenant Charles Banzhof arrived with the supply train, and "in a short time," Carpenter recalled, "tents were erected on a grassy spot, a quarter of a mile from the island, in order to get away from the terrible stench which filled the air from the dead horses which lay in a circle outside the trenches. As soon as the tents were in shape the wounded were carried to them and made as comfortable as possible. Forsyth's men were soon cooking bacon, munching hard bread and drinking coffee," Carpenter remembered. "One of them showed me a piece of horse flesh that he had cut off to use for his dinner that day, but it was so offensive that I could not bear it near me."[32]

That night Surgeon Fitzgerald amputated the leg of scout Louis Farley. "I assisted all that I could in the operation," Carpenter recalled, "but the poor fellow was so far gone that he could not stand the shock and died the following morning." Dr. Fitzgerald also recommended taking off one of Forsyth's legs, but its owner "strenuously objected" and the operation did not take place. It was later Fitzgerald's opinion that had relief come twenty-four hours later, Major George A. Forsyth would not have survived.[33]

About noon on the tenth day on the island (September 26), Colonel Henry Bankhead arrived with his column. With the command was the assistant postmaster at Fort Wallace, Homer W. Wheeler, who along with a man named Richard Blake had been present in the Fort Wallace sutler's store at the very moment the stagecoach carrying Stillwell and Trudeau rolled into the post. Wheeler held a "special fondness" for First Lieutenant Frederick H. Beecher, whom he remembered frequenting the sutler's store, where he would trade tobacco to the Indians. Because Wheeler and

Private Reuben Waller, Company H, 10th Cavalry. An ex-slave, Private Waller was with Company H at the rescue of the Forsyth Scouts. Waller lived well into the twentieth century and wrote from his home in Eldorado, Kansas. He was one of few Buffalo Soldiers to leave a legacy of reminiscences regarding the experience of blacks in the Indian wars. *Courtesy Kansas State Historical Society, Topeka, Kansas.*

Drawing of the rescue. The relief of the Forsyth Scouts by Company H, 10th Cavalry, under Captain Louis Carpenter was one of the most dramatic rescues in the annals of the Indian wars. It was the opinion of Carpenter's surgeon that if relief had come twenty-four hours later, Major George A. Forsyth would have died of his wounds. *Courtesy Denver Public Library, Denver, Colorado, Western History Department.*

Blake had previously been to the Republican Valley with William Comstock, they were selected to assist the exhausted Stillwell and Trudeau in guiding Bankhead's command back to the island. Unfortunately, the column became temporarily lost along the forks of the Republican and arrived at the island twenty-six hours after Carpenter.[34]

As Bankhead's relief force came around a bend in the Arickaree, young Sig Shlesinger anxiously awaited to see if his friend Jack Stillwell was with them. "Nearly all of us ran out to meet the party," Shlesinger remembered. "Soon Jack jumped from his horse, and in his joy to see so many of us alive again, he permitted his tears [to] free flow down his good honest cheeks."[35]

The scouts embraced Stillwell and Trudeau. The elderly Trudeau, Homer Wheeler remembered, "had been the butt of everyone's jokes in the command, but after his daring trip was looked upon with great respect."[36]

When Bankhead arrived at Beecher Island, his command had already been joined by Major James S. Brisbin and the two troops of the 2nd Cavalry from Fort Sedgwick, Colorado Territory, which had been camped with Lieutenant Colonel Bradley on the Frenchman's Fork of the Republican. Brisbin had caught up with Bankhead about 3:00 A.M. on the 25th.[37]

Two days were spent nursing the wounded before the relief force evacuated the Forsyth Scouts to Fort Wallace on Sunday, September 27. During this period they dug deeper graves for the scouts who had lost their lives. "Today we are burying the dead and caring for the wounded," Major James S. Brisbin wrote in a letter to a friend in Cincinnati. "Dead Indians lay within fifteen feet of the breastworks, and the stench from their swollen and bloated bodies and the dead horses is terrible."[38]

Sigmund Shlesinger assisted in the final interment of First Lieutenant Frederick H. Beecher. "We [had] removed his boots, coat, etc. [when he first was wounded]," Shlesinger remembered, "and of course, these things were not replaced on the body after he was dead, but lay around unnoticed. My shoes were quite badly worn, especially after being used for digging in the sand, so when . . . we were preparing to leave the island, I put on his shoes, which were just about my size, and wore them even after I got back to New York City, leaving my old shoes in their stead on the island."[39]

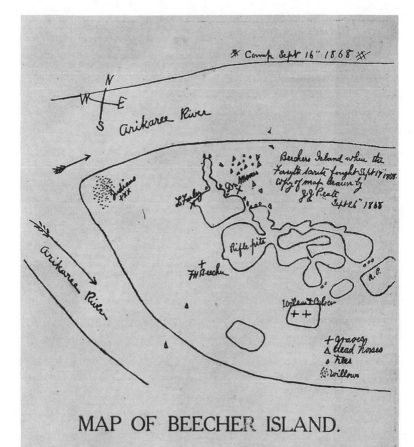

MAP OF BEECHER ISLAND.

The above map is reproduced from a copy drawn by J. J. Peate, of the Relief Expedition, at the time Forsyth and his scouts were rescued by Col. Carpenter's command.

The Island appears today as it did then excepting that the south channel of the river is closed and the trees and improvements, including the monument, appear as the Association has placed them.

Peate's map. Before leaving the island with the wounded for Fort Wallace, scout Jack Peate drew the only known firsthand sketch of the entrenchments on Beecher Island. A Labor Day flood washed the island from the Arikaree Fork forever in 1935. *Courtesy Denver Public Library, Denver, Colorado, Western History Department.*

Because the terrain of the prairie was rough, travel became uncomfortable for the wounded men riding in the ambulance wagons as the command moved away from the Arickaree. The unhurt scouts rode on mules. "The drivers of the ambulances picked out the best spots," George Washington Oaks remembered, "but it was just one bump after another for our wounded, and I was glad I could walk once in a while." [40]

Despite the pathos of the dramatic rescue, it is natural for modern observers to question the actions of the weary Forsyth Scouts who vented their frustrations along the route of march by pummeling anything "Indian" they encountered along the way. On September 27, the relief command moved back to Carpenter's old camp on the South Fork of the Republican. That day Jack Peate noted that he and some of the scouts "killed and scalped an Indian within a mile of camp." [41]

According to Jack Peate, it happened this way: Several of the scouts, including Pierre Trudeau and Jack Donovan, who were riding in advance of the command happened to be watering their horses and mules in the South Fork of the Republican when they noticed three stray horses in the river bottom. Soon four Indians jumped from concealment and three of them mounted the horses and "lashed them to their utmost speed." The fourth Indian, who failed to secure a mount, did what he could on foot to keep up with his friends. Mounted on mules (except probably for Peate), the scouts did not give chase to the mounted warriors but instead began chasing down the unmounted Indian. "Just before he [the warrior] came to the river," Jack Peate remembered, "he dropped a woman's white skirt, and soon after a calico dress; then, as the race grew warmer (we were on the rolling ground south of the river now), he dropped his blanket.

"The sport, to us, was now becoming exciting. The boys [were] shooting at the Indian whenever they could. The Indian was running very very fast, but we were gaining on him slowly. He would not run in a straight line; he would jump several times to the right, then back to the left, still rushing ahead. . . . [Our] bullets were striking the ground all around him.

"It looked as if the Indian would get to the deep cañon still a half mile away, where his comrades had passed out of sight, when a shot from a Henry rifle [more likely a Spencer] in the hands of Pierre Trudea[u] . . .

broke the Indian's right leg above the knee. . . . After hopping a few feet he sits down and faces the foe. The few hundred feet that still separate us is soon passed over. As soon as the Indian faces us he commences to fire, being armed with a Colt's navy revolver. . . . Then something seems to be the matter with his revolver; he looks into it and throws it on the ground. Not a shot was fired by our party while advancing after the Indian discarded his revolver."[42]

Knowing that their adversaries, the plains Indians, gave no quarter to white enemies in similar circumstances, the scouts showed no mercy to the wounded and unarmed warrior. As Peate, Trudeau, and Donovan rushed up to the seated Indian, Jack Peate noted that "he was a young man, perhaps twenty-five years of age, and was arrayed in the lovely simplicity of nature and a breech cloth. He was chanting a weird song and did not offer any resistance. He knew what his fate would be," Peate asserted, "and [he] showed no fear."

The scouts executed the unarmed warrior as he sat resignedly on the prairie singing his death song. Then they scalped him. "In examining the discarded revolver," Peate remembered after the killing, "we found that the cylinder would not revolve, and the cause was a bullet from a revolver the same size in the hand of Jack Donovan . . . going into the barrel of the Indian's revolver and about half of it passing into the cylinder, thereby stopping its revolving, and the Indian could not fire his last load."

The next morning Peate rode by where he and his comrades had left the dead man. "The wolves," Peate noted, "had held a banquet there and a few bones was all that remained of the warrior of yesterday."[43]

In the same vicinity of the Republican Valley where Peate, Trudeau, and Donovan killed the Indian, the command came upon, once again, the graves of the warriors killed at Beecher Island, which Carpenter had discovered on his way to Forsyth's relief. After their ordeal on the island, some of the Forsyth Scouts had no remorse in desecrating the graves of their enemies, especially the tomb of the warrior buried on the scaffold inside the white tepee.

Jack Peate joined his comrades in the desecration. "We went into the lodge and found that it was the tomb of a medicine man killed in the battle," Peate recalled in 1905. "The Indian was placed on a scaffold that was eight feet high. Fastened to the scaffold was his war bonnet and a large drum. He was wrapped in blankets and a buffalo robe and tied on the scaffold. The posts on one side of the scaffold were torn away by the boys so we could have a better look at the *good Indian* [emphasis mine]. The body was then rolled to the edge of the cañon and it rolled from there to the bottom."[44]

Perhaps the most revealing tale of intense emotion regarding the destruction of the Indian graves is the reminiscence of Sigmund Shlesinger. The young, impressionable immigrant from New York City, who only a few days previous was sickened by the sight of his comrades scalping three Indian corpses near the island, now demonstrated an eager, almost morbid, delight in looting an Indian grave in search of trophies. This story, which Shlesinger told almost half a century later, remained vivid and intense in his memory and betrays a developmental racial prejudice acquired during his experience at the Battle of Beecher Island.

"There were six [actually five] . . . scaffolds, composed of four poles stuck in the ground and a buffalo hide stretched across each pole; on top of each scaffold lay a corpse fully dressed and wrapped in blankets," Shlesinger remembered. "All the bodies were pulled down from their lofty perches. This may seem a wanton sacrilege, but not to those who have suffered bodily torture and mental anguish from these very cruel savages. I had no scruples in rolling one out of his blankets, that still were soaking in the blood from the wounds that evidently caused his death, and appropriating the top one that was least wet. This Indian had on a headdress composed of buckskin beautifully beaded and ornamented, with a polished buffalo horn on the frontal part and eagle feathers down the back. When I took this off, maggots were in the headpiece. I also pulled off his earrings and finger rings, which were of tin. He was so far decomposed that when I took hold of the rings the fingers came along, and these I shook out! I also got his beaded knife scabbard and other trinkets. The blanket, one earring and scabbard are still in my possession. I had great trouble in carrying my souvenirs away, owing to the awful stench. No one would tolerate me near him. When I was mounted I tied the bundle to the saddle girth under the mule's body, and when I rode in a wagon I tied it to the axle, but in spite of these expedients," Shlesinger continued, "I had to put up with remonstrances until we finally reached Fort Wallace, where I immediately soaked my trophies in a creek, weighing them down with stones.

"At Wallace we naturally were objects of interest . . . and our souvenirs no less so. My Indian headdress was an especial curiosity. Jack Donovan interceded for one of the officers and offered me $50 for it, but I refused to part with it. Next morning it was missing from my tent!"[45]

❊ ❊ ❊

The relief column arrived at Fort Wallace on September 29. It was later surmised that Sigmund Shlesinger had robbed the grave of Roman Nose, but this is not likely because Roman Nose's war bonnet contained no beadwork or anything of the white man's manufacture. Others thought that the Indian buried in the white tepee was Roman Nose, but it probably was the remains of the Dog Soldier warrior named Killed by a Bull.[46] So the Dog Soldiers and their allies moved south after the fight they called "Where Roman Nose Was Killed." Some of them soon joined friends and relatives for the winter, living south of the Arkansas. But most of the Dog Soldiers returned to the Republican Valley, where they would continue raiding in October.

The violation of the dead Cheyenne warriors' bodies was not as horrible as the white men thought it would be for the Indians, Ice (White Bull) recalled years later. The Cheyennes considered it a good thing that after warriors die bravely in battle the wolves, eagles, vultures, and other animals eat the flesh of their bodies and scatter their body parts across the prairie for the wind to carry to the four directions, where dwelled the "Sacred Persons," so revered by the People.[47]

Conclusions: The Last Days of the Dog Soldiers

One of the most remarkable defences [*sic*] ever made against overwhelming forces was that of Major Geo. A. Forsyth.

> — COLONEL RICHARD IRVING DODGE
> *Aide-de-Camp to General William T. Sherman*
> *1882*

The Indians agree that all that saved Forsyth and his command was that he got on the island and remained there.

> — GEORGE BIRD GRINNELL
> *1915*

*T*actically the Battle of Beecher Island accomplished little toward bringing lasting peace south of the Platte. At the same time that Forsyth began his movements toward the Arickaree, Major General Philip Sheridan ordered eight companies of the 7th Cavalry and one company of the 3rd Infantry, with a small field piece, under Lieutenant Colonel (Brevet Brigadier General) Alfred Sully, to operate out of Fort Dodge, Kansas, and attack the Southern Cheyennes and Arapahoes who were reputedly camping along the Cimarron River south of the Arkansas. This action, Sheridan hoped, would pull the Dog Soldiers down out of the Republican River country to help protect these exposed villages.

Although Sully had gained a reputation fighting Indians during the war with the Minnesota Sioux from 1863 to 1865, his campaign against the Southern Cheyennes in the fall of 1868 was a dismal failure. Along the banks of the North Canadian River in Indian Territory (Oklahoma), his supply wagons became mired in mud, he lost the confidence of his officers, and while Sully directed the campaign from the bed of an ambulance wagon Cheyenne war parties attacked his column relentlessly. On September 14, he ordered a general retreat. His command straggled into Fort Dodge on the 18th, the same day that the Forsyth Scouts were licking their wounds following the first day of fighting on the Arickaree.

After hearing of Forsyth's near miss with annihilation, Sheridan became frustrated. The two campaigns of Forsyth and Sully climaxed a dismal initiation to plains Indian warfare for the new commander of the Department of the Missouri. Sheridan biographer Paul Andrew Hutton stated, "Within the boundaries of Sheridan's command, since the Kansas raids of early August, 110 civilians had been killed, thirteen women had been raped, over a thousand head of stock stolen, farms, stage buildings and rolling stock destroyed, and unescorted travel stopped on all the major roads. His troops were engaged in numerous fights with the Indians, almost always being bested, and not once inflicting serious injury to the natives. . . . His aide-de-camp [Major George A. Forsyth] was critically wounded, and his company of scouts, of whom so much had been expected, had been badly shot up in their first engagement with the enemy."[1]

Although most of the individual Forsyth Scouts would soon be mustered out of service, Sheridan would place the unit itself under the command of Lieutenant Silas Pepoon of the 10th Cavalry. Others praised Forsyth's actions, but Sheridan was perhaps the one officer who truly appreciated that the objective of keeping the Indians on the run with a mobile scout unit had failed. Even some of Forsyth's own men had questioned on September 16 the validity of the march so far up the Republican, knowing full well that any action would likely be a defensive one against superior numbers of the enemy. But an assessment of the wisdom of Forsyth's actions was lost in the sensationalism of the nine days of suffering on the island and the dramatic rescue reported by a national press. Sheridan, however, had learned a bitter lesson. The perceived heroism of the scouts notwithstanding, he quietly made sure that the reorganized scout unit under Pepoon would never again be used for independent offensive operations.

Sheridan knew that if he were to successfully force the Dog Soldiers and other Cheyennes to return to the reservations and comply with the provisions of the Treaties of Medicine Lodge he would need additional troops. Already he had secured the transfer from the Department of the Platte of Lieutenant Colonel Luther P. Bradley's two companies of the 2nd Cavalry and six companies of the 27th Infantry. It had been troopers of the 2nd Cavalry under Major James S. Brisbin who had helped rescue Forsyth. Sheridan also secured the authority from divisional headquarters to allow Kansas governor Samuel J. Crawford to raise the 19th Kansas Volunteer Cavalry.

In November, the 19th Kansas would accompany the 7th Cavalry on the great winter campaign that culminated in the Battle of the Washita. Commanding Company A of the 19th Kansas was Captain Allison J. Pliley, fully recovered from his arduous trek with Jack Donovan to Fort Wallace in September to obtain relief for the Forsyth Scouts. Pliley was ready again for action against the Indians, as was his comrade from Beecher Island, Chauncey B. Whitney, who enlisted in the same company.[2]

Sheridan also secured the transfer of seven companies of the 5th Cavalry from duties in the Reconstruction South to service in Kansas. These companies were temporarily placed under the command of Major (Brevet Colonel) William B. Royall until such a time as Major (Brevet Major General) Eugene A. Carr could be released from staff duty in Washington to take over the regiment. Carr had a distinguished service record, having campaigned against the Sioux before the Civil War. For his gallantry in 1862, while commanding the 4th Division of the Army of the Southwest, he was later awarded the Medal of Honor for holding the Union line against the Confederates during the campaign that culminated in the Battle of Pea Ridge (Elkhorn Tavern) in northern Arkansas.[3]

In September, Royall's troops gathered at Fort Harker. On the 29th, the same day that the Forsyth Scouts, accompanied by Bankhead's relief forces, got back to Fort Wallace, Royall struck out toward the Republican Valley to hunt down the Indians who had attacked Forsyth at Beecher Island. Carr arrived at Fort Wallace on October 12 and moved out on the

14th to join his new command already in the field. His escort consisted
of about 120 troopers of the 10th Cavalry under Forsyth's rescuer, Captain
Louis H. Carpenter.

The chief scout for the expedition was Abner "Sharp" Grover, eager
for revenge against Tall Bull's Dog Soldiers. The day previous, October
13, instead of being discouraged by the death of their northern friend and
ally, Roman Nose, and unintimidated by the possibility of retribution for
Beecher Island, a group of warriors descended once again on the Kansas
settlements in the Solomon Valley. They left at least four settlers dead
and rode away with Anna Belle Morgan, who, along with Sarah White
the following spring, would be rescued in Medicine Arrows's village by
Custer's troopers and the 19th Kansas Volunteers. About the same time,
near the Arkansas River, Clara Blinn was captured by the southern
Indians, whom Sully was supposed to have checked. A little over a month
later she and her baby were slain at the Washita.

The number of Solomon raiders of October 1868 who had actually
fought at Beecher Island is unknown, but the defiant Dog Soldiers under
Tall Bull were in no hurry to turn south and join the Southern Cheyennes
on the reservation for the winter. To the contrary — they were leisurely
hunting buffalo between Beaver Creek and the Smoky Hill route in
northwestern Kansas. Carpenter's troops, with Major Carr, arrived on
Beaver Creek, scouting it for some fifty miles without finding Major Royall
and the balance of the 5th Cavalry. Royall was in fact farther south and
had been attacked by the Dog Soldiers near a station on the Union Pacific
Eastern Division on October 14, with the loss of two troopers and six
horses.[4]

So instead of finding the 5th Cavalry on Beaver Creek, Carpenter's
command found the Indians. There was at this time a medicine man in
the Dog Soldier camp named Bullet Proof (Wolf Man). He claimed that
by dressing the hides of young buffalo bulls in a secret manner with the
horns left on, he could make the wearers of the skins impervious to enemy
bullets. About the time that the Indians discovered Carpenter's soldiers,
Bullet Proof had convinced five young Dog Soldiers — Little Hawk, Bear
With Feathers, White Man's Ladder, Broken Arrow, and Bobtail Porcupine — that if they followed his instructions explicitly he could make

them safe from the soldiers' bullets. At dawn on October 17, a large war party of Dog Soldiers attacked Carpenter's command, forcing the 10th Cavalry into a defensive position. Bullet Proof convinced many of the warriors not to mass an attack on the soldiers until he could prove his medicine. Broken Arrow and Bobtail Porcupine wore the sacred buffalo robes that Bullet Proof had prepared for them. These two warriors followed up a charge made by their three comrades, who also believed in the power of Bullet Proof's medicine. As they charged the enemy position, the Buffalo Soldiers cut them down in order, wounding four of the Dog Soldiers and shooting their horses out from under them. When Broken Arrow and Bobtail Porcupine went down, many of the warriors returned to camp, disappointed in Bullet Proof's medicine. Later the Indians recalled that this was not really supposed to be a fight but rather they had intended it only as a demonstration by Bullet Proof to prove his medicine to disbelievers.[5]

After the Dog Soldiers withdrew, some of the black troopers in Carpenter's command scalped Broken Arrow and slit the throat of Bobtail Porcupine. According to George Bent, the warriors who remembered the fight insisted that Bobtail Porcupine had sustained only slight wounds when he was shot in the attack but that the soldiers opened a vein in his throat so that he would die slowly.[6] By autumn 1868 the brutal realities of racial hatred and war were evidenced in the behavior of at least a few of "Carpenter's Brunettes."

Carr joined his regiment and with five companies of the 5th Cavalry and Pepoon's Scouts he caught up with Tall Bull's Dog Soldiers once again on October 25. A running fight ensued for several days. The Indian rear guard screening the relocation of the entire village, put up such a good "bluff" that Carr was completely fooled. Carr dismounted his troops, threw up a skirmish line, and advanced on the rear guard, thus permitting the main village to escape. Carr could do nothing else but return to Fort Wallace while the Dog Soldiers broke into small bands and resumed attacking stage stations along the Smoky Hill route west of Fort Hays. Rather than forcing the determined Dog Soldiers south to the reservation, the actions in and around the Republican Valley during autumn 1868, beginning with Beecher Island and ending with Carpenter's and Carr's fights around Beaver Creek in October, had exactly the opposite effect. According to Two Crows, who had helped recover the mortally wounded Weasel Bear at Beecher Island, the Dog Soldiers held council with neighboring Sioux after these fights and decided *not* to move back south and join the Southern Cheyennes for the winter but to stay in northwestern Kansas and make raids. As the fighting in the central corridor ended for 1868, the Dog Soldiers became more determined than ever before to hold fast to their sacred lands in the Republican Valley.[7]

During the fighting of 1867 and 1868, the proud military establishment of the United States had been humiliated by a few thousand poorly armed Indians. The efforts of the Peace Commission had failed. The press and much of the public demanded decisive action. In October, with the capture of Clara Blinn and Anna Belle Morgan, and with a sympathetic public praising the highly publicized heroism of Forsyth at Beecher Island, Sheridan received final approval for his harsh winter campaign to punish the southern tribes for two years of raids. All Indians who did not report to Fort Cobb, Indian Territory, were to be considered "outlawed" and killed. Historian Paul Andrew Hutton asserted that "Sheridan was to launch a race war of vengeance — with no quarter asked or given."[8]

That war came on the bleak morning of November 27, when Custer's 7th Cavalry, to the sound of the regimental band playing the song "Garry Owen" completely surprised the unsuspecting village of Black Kettle. Although Sheridan's winter campaign was not completely decisive, the Battle of the Washita climaxed a total war of attrition that at least temporarily suppressed Indian militancy below the Arkansas. The troopers killed Black Kettle in the attack. In the wake of the campaign, Edward Wansear Wynkoop, good friend and agent to the Southern Cheyennes, resigned his post, disgusted with the actions of the government he served.[9] Although the Battle of the Washita finally persuaded many warriors to remain on the reservations that were agreed to at Medicine Lodge, the one group it completely failed to cripple was the most significant military power afforded the Southern Cheyennes, the proud Dog Soldiers of the Republican Valley. At the time of the Battle of the Washita, they were still camping in northwestern Kansas, concentrated under Tall Bull, and thus escaped Custer's avenging troops.[10]

But the free-roving days of the Dog Soldiers were numbered. On May 10, 1869, Dr. Thomas Durant's Union Pacific Railroad linked with Leland Stanford's Central Pacific at Promontory Point, Utah Territory, thus completing the nation's first transcontinental link. At its annual stockholders' meeting, held in Lawrence, Kansas, on April 5, 1869, the Union Pacific Eastern Division changed its name to the Kansas Pacific Railway Company and selected Colorado entrepreneur William Jackson Palmer as its director. With visions of linking Kansas and Colorado to both the Pacific and Mexico City, the Kansas Pacific announced its intentions to complete its rail to Denver by the following year. The favored buffalo ranges of the Cheyenne Dog Soldiers and their Sioux and Arapahoe allies in and around the Republican Valley would, within months, be flanked by the white man's greatest arteries of advancing civilization.[11]

Nevertheless, by May 1869 Tall Bull with approximately 165 lodges of Dog Soldiers were camped along Beaver Creek in the Republican Valley, determined to make a stand for their independence. On May 1, Major Carr and his 5th Cavalry moved from Fort Lyon, Colorado Territory, to Fort McPherson, Nebraska, to force the Dog Soldiers back to the Oklahoma reservations agreed upon at Medicine Lodge. With the 5th Cavalry was Carr's chosen chief scout, William F. "Buffalo Bill" Cody. About twelve days later, Carr's command discovered the main village of Dog Soldiers and attacked it in force. The Dog Soldiers had about five hundred warriors in the village and Carr's troopers killed twenty-five of them who were defending their women and children. Carr lost four dead and three wounded. The white soldiers pursued the Indians into Nebraska, where the warriors turned and feinted on Carr's advance guard and then broke into small bands, forcing Carr to abandon pursuit.[12]

In retaliation for Carr's attack on their village, the Dog Soldiers once again rode eastward out of the Republican Valley and slashed through the Kansas settlements along the frontier line in the Saline and Solomon valleys. For eight days following May 21, the warriors unleashed a violent retribution on the whites that left thirteen dead in its wake. It was during this raid that the warriors tore up two miles of Kansas Pacific railroad track near Fossil Creek Station (Russell, Kansas), which resulted in the derail-ment of a passenger train.[13] The situation became so serious that an itinerant Presbyterian circuit rider complained that although he had an appointment to preach up the Solomon in June, he would only go "with [a] revolver at my side and [a] rifle on my back."[14]

In one of the more devastating of these raids, which occurred on Spillman Creek near present-day Denmark, Kansas, the Dog Soldiers plundered a group of farms being homesteaded by recent German and Scandinavian immigrants. The Dog Soldiers killed Mr. and Mrs. Eskild Lauritzen and horribly mutilated their bodies in front of their sod house on May 30. They also killed Otto Peterson, Fred Meigherhoff, and George Weichell as these homesteaders tried to defend their farms. The Indians captured Mrs. Maria Weichell, described as an attractive woman about twenty years old. The Weichells had been in the United States only a few weeks.[15]

On this same day, tragedy struck two former Forsyth Scouts. On the Saline River, near Lincoln, Kansas, and not far from where the Indians had captured Mrs. Weichell, Thomas Alderice, who had survived the Battle of Beecher Island unscathed, left for Salina to get supplies, leaving at home his wife, Susanna, and their four children. Susanna Alderice was the sister of Forsyth Scout Eli Ziegler. While Susanna was visiting a neighbor family, that of Nicholas Whalen, the Dog Soldiers descended on the Whalen homestead. Susanna, pregnant with her fifth child and burdened with an infant in her arms, was unable to outrun the Indians. The Dog Soldiers took her and her baby prisoner, killed two other children, and severely wounded a third child.[16]

Tom Alderice became almost paralyzed with grief upon returning home to the Whalen farm to discover one of his children, six years of age, "dead on the ground with six bullets in his body" and another dead, "shot with five arrows. A third child had five arrow wounds in his body, one entering his back to the depth of five inches." Alderice took the wounded boy to the home of his brother-in-law, Eli Ziegler, where the lad eventu-ally recovered.[17] To rescue Maria Weichell and Susanna Alderice, and to punish the Indians for the Kansas raids, once again Major Eugene Asa

Carr with eight companies of the 5th Cavalry left Fort McPherson in search of the Dog Soldier village. Brigadier General (Brevet Major General) C. C. Augur, commander of the Department of the Platte, ordered Carr to "clear the Republican country of Indians."[18]

By June, the Dog Soldiers, along with some Sioux, were back in the Republican Valley, camping on a tributary stream called Cherry Creek. So too was Carr and the 5th Cavalry. With them were 150 of the Pawnee Scouts under Major Frank J. North. The soldiers would call the campaign the Republican River Expedition. With Tall Bull's people were Mrs. Alderice and Mrs. Weichell. Before they had returned to the Republican Valley, the Indians had killed the Alderice infant because of its incessant crying.[19]

For two weeks, the Dog Soldiers and Carr's forces played a cat-and-mouse game up the Republican and into Colorado Territory. Then Tall Bull relocated his village to a place called Summit Springs, about twelve miles south and four miles east of present Sterling, Colorado, in Logan County. It was Tall Bull's intent to cross the South Platte to escape Carr's relentless pursuit, but because the river was still swollen with runoff he decided to make camp at Summit Springs. Tall Bull said to his followers: "We will stop here for two days; then we will rush across the South Platte."[20] The decision to wait was disastrous for the Dog Soldiers.

On the night of July 10, after a forced march, the troopers and Pawnee Scouts of the Republican River Expedition camped within twenty miles of Tall Bull's village. Before sunrise on July 11, they moved out with three hundred men and followed a faint trail toward the Platte. Shortly after noon the command spotted eighty-five lodges, which constituted Tall Bull's village. Carr divided his command into two attack wings under Major F. W. Crittenden and himself respectively. About 3:00 P.M. the bugler sounded the charge. Lieutenant George F. Price, who was in the first wave to hit the village, later described it as "one of the most superb charges ever made by the Fifth Cavalry."[21]

Two Crows, one of the heroes of Beecher Island, was sitting in a lodge talking to friends when he heard someone outside shout: "People are coming." Soon the sound of shooting began close to the camp. Two Crows ran out of the tepee and saw the advance wave of Carr's charge, the

Pawnee Scouts, stripped for battle. Only the south side of the village offered escape for the Dog Soldiers. Confusion reigned in the Dog Soldier camp as horses ran in every direction and warriors tried desperately to catch their mounts and spring onto their backs. Many others were running away on foot, some toward the south, some toward nearby bluffs. The surprise attack was complete. Two Crows started out on foot, running as hard as he could. He saw a loose horse herd running away and shouted out to another warrior: "Turn the horses toward me." Two Crows had just enough time to slip the bridle over the neck of a fine black horse belonging to Tall Bull and make his escape.[22]

Many of the People ran into a nearby deep ravine with some of the women and children. They thought they could hide there from the soldiers. Among them was Tall Bull himself, accompanied by his wife and daughter on his horse. After locating a place where his family would be out of the line of fire, Tall Bull returned to the head of the ravine and stabbed his horse in the foreleg so that he could use the animal as a barricade. This was where Tall Bull intended to die. Soon the Pawnee Scouts surrounded the ravine and poured a deadly fire into the hiding Indians. Frank and Luther North were directing the actions of the Pawnee Scouts at the ravine when a bullet came whizzing by the head of Major Frank North while his horse galloped past the ravine. North dismounted and marked the spot where he had seen an Indian fire the shot. He dropped on his knee and, taking a knee rest, aimed his rifle at the spot where he had seen the Indian. A moment later he saw a rifle appear over the edge of the bank of the ravine, and then he saw a head rise in preparation for a shot. Major North the trigger of his Spencer carbine. The warrior's rifle remained on the bank, but no more shots came from it. After the fighting, the body of Dog Soldier chief Tall Bull was discovered at that place in the ravine. He had been shot cleanly through the forehead.[23]

During the fight at the ravine, a Dog Soldier warrior whose name was Wolf With Plenty of Hair staked himself out with a dog rope. There he prepared to die fighting unless another man would come along and risk his life by pulling up Wolf With Plenty of Hair's picket pin and strike him like a dog with his quirt in order to drive the brave warrior from the field before he was killed. When the fighting ended, soldiers found the body of Wolf With Plenty of Hair still tethered by the dog rope and the picket pin still sticking in the ground.

Wolf With Plenty of Hair was reputedly the last Dog Soldier ever to "stake himself out" in a battle with the whites.[24] After the battle, some of the Pawnee Scouts discovered the body of Mrs. Susanna Alderice lying on a buffalo robe inside a tepee, soaked in her own blood. She had been tomahawked, some said, by Tall Bull, or possibly by Tall Bull's wife. Carr's men discovered Mrs. Maria Weichell alive, though severely wounded. A bullet had gone through her breast, struck a bone, and was deflected. She had been a captive for forty-two days.[25] The next morning at 8:00 a detail buried Susanna Alderice in front of the assembled command. They wrapped her body in buffalo robes and placed it in a grave that was marked with a wooden headboard. Major Carr renamed the spot "Susanna Springs" but the name did not endure.[26]

Carr officially reported one soldier wounded, fifty-two Indians killed, and seventeen women and children captured. Carr also captured 274 horses and 144 mules as well as a large quantity of food and weapons. Carr's report did not specify how many of the "dead Indians" were warriors and how many were women and children. Carr's men recovered a sizable amount of cash in the Dog Soldier village. It was given to Maria Weichell. Before leaving the field for Fort Sedgwick, Colorado Territory, Carr ordered all of the Indian lodges burned.[27]

The Battle of Summit Springs was dramatic and decisive. Some of the survivors of Tall Bull's band went north to live with Sioux or Northern Cheyenne relatives. Some of them would participate in the campaigns of the 1870s on the northern plains. Others went south to live with the Southern Cheyennes on the reservation. In 1874, White Horse and some of the old Dog Soldiers fought one last time with the People in the actions climaxed by the Battle of Adobe Walls and the Red River War. By the 1870s, however, most of the old warriors of the once defiant Dog Soldier society resigned themselves to life on the reservation. Some even accepted assimilation. The Dog Soldier peace chief Bull Bear became one of the first Cheyennes to put his children into the white man's schools under Quaker tutelege. As an independent military organization of the

Southern Cheyennes, after the Battle of Summit Springs the Dog Soldier society effectively ceased to exist. "With the destruction of Tall Bull's village," George Bent remembered, "and the consequent breaking up of the Dog Soldiers as a band, some going to the Northern Cheyennes and others to the south, the power of this famous society was broken and never since have they been a factor in the wars of the Cheyenne tribe."[28] For only a little over twenty-six months, from April 19, 1867, when Hancock burned their village on Red Arm Creek, to July 11, 1869, with Carr's victory at Summit Springs, the Dog Soldiers played out their hand with the whites over possession of the Smoky Hill country and the Republican Valley.

In an ironic mimicry of its significance, the flamboyant showman William Frederick "Buffalo Bill" Cody, who had been Carr's chief scout on the Republican River Expedition, recognized the theatrical qualities, if not the symbolism and finality, of the fight at Summit Springs. For years, the climax to his extravaganza, called "The Wild West Show," was a reenactment of the charge on Tall Bull's village. The reenactment played to both European and American audiences. As late as 1907 the charge at Summit Springs was still part and parcel of Cody's show when he appeared at New York's Madison Square Garden.[29]

But perhaps more symbolic and final was the recovery from the Summit Springs battlefield of a weathered ledger book. In it were a number of sketches made by the Cheyennes. The drawings provide a pictorial history of warfare with the whites during the 1860s and provide a fitting dramatization of the free-roving days of the Cheyenne Dog Soldiers up to their last independent action with the whites. The sketch-book was given to the Colorado Historical Society.[30]

The Battle of Beecher Island had only an indirect, largely emotional, effect on the events that led to the final defeat of the Dog Soldiers. Even before their rescue by Carpenter and the 10th Cavalry, the Forsyth Scouts were front-page news around the nation. Basing its stories only on information delivered to Fort Wallace by Stillwell and Trudeau, which immediately hit the wire service to the east, the *New York Times* picked up on the human drama being played out on the faraway Arickaree Fork of the Republican River in Colorado Territory. "All are lying there," the

Times reported, "with Indians all around them, eating their horseflesh and waiting for relief. Cols. Bankhead and Carpenter will reach them to-night."[31] Throughout the country the journalists played on the reader's sympathies for the plight of the Forsyth Scouts. "The rations were all gone," exclaimed the *Times and Conservative*, "and their only dependence was the horse and mule meat, and courage."[32]

In Denver, the highly sensational *Rocky Mountain News* proclaimed "Colonel Forsyth's Command Exterminated. Forsyth Reported Mortally Wounded."[33] Soon after the Forsyth Scouts returned to Fort Wallace, DeBenneville Randolph Keim rushed to the bedside of the wounded to report their harrowing stories of the fight on the Arickaree for the *New York Herald*. He perhaps more than any other journalist began the process of enshrining the Forsyth Scouts as national heroes.[34]

Arguably the sensationalism generated by the press over the Beecher Island fight had an immediate psychological impact on public opinion regarding the so-called Indian problem. To be sure, after a sympathetic public read about the ordeal of the Forsyth Scouts there was no doubt that the efforts of the Peace Commission had failed. Sentiment to transfer the Indian Bureau to the War Department gained support. And Major General Philip Sheridan had little trouble securing final approval for his requested additional troop strength and planned winter campaign. From 1868 forward the policy of striking villages during both the winter and summer months with a sizable force — destroying lodges, ponies, and provisions — would become the tactical fixture that would ultimately defeat the plains tribes. But it is probable that these events would have occurred anyway, had the Battle of Beecher Island never been fought.[35]

Indeed, the more far-reaching significance of the Battle of Beecher Island is the impact it has had through the years, beginning almost immediately after the scouts' relief, on the public imagination. After Keim proclaimed the scouts' actions to be a "brilliant and heroic achievement," George Armstrong Custer adulated Forsyth in 1874 in *My Life on the Plains*. Others soon followed. In 1879 James B. Fry published a book entitled *Army Sacrifices*. One of its features was a highly sensationalized account of the Battle of Beecher Island: "The ground was strewed with dead and dying warriors. . . . In advance of them all lay the superb but lifeless form of Roman Nose, the red tide from his hot veins saturating the crimson sash which encircled his naked body."[36]

Even Roman Nose was depicted as a larger-than-life symbol, wearing a white buffalo robe, a taboo that George Bird Grinnell discredited at length.[37] In Fry's nationalistic narrative, Major George A. Forsyth was undoubtedly a heroic figure. Fry inferred that the gallant Forsyth, ignoring his wounds, towered over his men shouting encouragement such as "We will yet win the fight or sell our lives dearly in the attempt."[38] Forsyth did win a brevet of brigadier general for the action on the Arickaree, and the government awarded Captain Louis H. Carpenter the Medal of Honor for the rescue of the Forsyth Scouts and for his fight on Beaver Creek in autumn 1868. The award came thirty years later, in 1898.[39]

In 1895 Forsyth himself succumbed to his celebrated status as symbolic hero when he wrote his account of the engagement for *Harper's Monthly Magazine*. The article was entitled "A Frontier Fight." Although some of these reminiscences are accurate and corroborated by others, and most of his narrative can be accepted in substance, when he described the Indians' first massed charge on the island his writing became romanticized. Forsyth mistakenly put Roman Nose at the head of the charging warriors early in the day. Because Forsyth was suffering from wounds, it is arguable how much he actually remembered about the first day of fighting at Beecher Island. Nevertheless, his narrative, which he later republished in his book *Thrilling Days in Army Life* (1902), was laced with such tantalizing rhetoric as "Crash! Can I believe my eyes? Roman Nose is down! He and his horse lie dead together on the sand, and for an instant the column shakes; but a hundred yards more and they are upon us!"[40]

Forsyth identified Roman Nose as having led the first massed charge because chief scout Abner "Sharp" Grover supposedly saw Roman Nose during the assault. Many other writers who composed their accounts *after* "A Frontier Fight" appeared in print also accepted Grover's identification of Roman Nose as leading the charge. Although Allison J. Pliley remembered seeing Roman Nose at Medicine Lodge, it is doubtful that either Forsyth or Grover had ever before seen the famous warrior, and thus it is unlikely that they would have been able to recognize him in the battle.[41]

Some of the Forsyth Scouts subtly admitted that Forsyth romanticized his account of the charge. In a letter written to a friend in 1922, E. A. Brininstool, who first studied the battle in depth by interviewing some of the surviving Forsyth Scouts, wrote: "All of the men [Forsyth Scouts] I have talked with say that Col. Forsythe's [sic] story of the fight is pretty much exaggerated, so far as the fighting was concerned."[42] In essence, until the late nineteenth century the focus on Beecher Island was one of praise for the heroic exploits of the Forsyth Scouts.[43] In Major George A. Forsyth, other young officers saw themselves; like Forsyth, they would stand fast before insurmountable odds and survive. No one dared to raise the questions, What was Forsyth doing so far up the Republican, knowing as he did that many Indians were nearby, and despite advice from experienced scouts, why was he so determined to have a fight against such odds?

That Sandy Forsyth wished to gain what recognition and possible glory he could in combat against Indians before returning to staff duty is undeniable. The conspicuous belief that a much smaller force of trained, disciplined whites could whip a larger, even much larger, force of experienced plains warriors was not uncommon on the military frontier and this belief illuminates Forsyth's actions.

Adulation was also given to some of Forsyth's men. In 1879 a poem appeared in Fry's book *Army Sacrifices* praising the exploits of the young Hungarian immigrant from New York City, Sigmund Shlesinger. Although the poem may seem patronizing to modern readers, Fry meant it to be nothing less than a tribute to Shlesinger's bravery at Beecher Island.

When the foe charged on the breastworks
  With the madness of despair,
And the bravest souls were tested,
  The little Jew was there.

When the weary dozed on duty,
  Or the wounded needed care,
When another shot was called for,
  The little Jew was there.

With the festering dead around them,
  Shedding poison in the air,
When the crippled chieftain ordered,
  The little Jew was there.[44]

Suddenly everyone wanted Shlesinger's story. Much of Cyrus Townsend Brady's mostly accurate, but highly nationalistic, account of the
Battle of Beecher Island in *Indian Fights and Fighters* (1904) was written
from correspondence received from Sigmund Shlesinger. The heroic
actions of the Forsyth Scouts appealed greatly to the Progressive-era
audiences of the United States following the Spanish-American War. By
the 1920s, however, the Beecher Island story had flattened out even more
into nostalgia; its focus was now on trivia and minutiae — reconstructing
specific but comparatively minor incidents of the battle. This effort is
illustrated in the information Shlesinger gave to E. A. Brininstool for his
several tracts on the Battle of Beecher Island.

After the publication of Grinnell's *The Fighting Cheyennes*, later
writers said much regarding numbers of casualties. It is certain that five
scouts were killed. They were First Lieutenant Frederick H. Beecher,
Surgeon J. H. Mooers, G. W. Culver, William Wilson, and Louis Farley.
About eighteen sustained wounds. Forsyth reported thirty-two dead Indians. Later he claimed that an old warrior who had been in the fight told
him that at least seventy-five Indians had been killed. Grinnell and Bent
agreed on only nine Indians dead out of a sizable number of Indian
participants. They were Roman Nose, Prairie Bear (Northern Cheyennes), Dry Throat, White Thunder, Weasel Bear, Killed by a Bull (Dog
Soldiers), Little Man (Northern Arapahoe), and two unidentified Sioux.
There are no accurate estimates of the number of Indians wounded.[45]
Estimates of the number of Indian participants in the fight range from
three hundred (Bent) to six hundred (Grinnell) to over a thousand
(various white sources). Discrepancies in casualty figures and numbers of
participants, as with other conflicts of the Indian wars, will probably never
be resolved. Today a monument at Beecher Island Battleground lists the
names of most of the uninjured Forsyth Scouts. Five separate stones
around the monument commemorate the individual scouts who died in
the battle. Except for a stone marker on the hill northwest of the

battleground designating it as "Roman Nose Ridge," there are no separate monuments commemorating individual Indians who fought at Beecher Island.

Beginning in 1898, the scouts held reunions at the battleground. By the reunion of 1905, when they dedicated the battle monument, Robert Lynam and former scout Jack Peate of the Beecher Island Battle Memorial Association had collected as many accounts as they could from the survivors of the battle for a publication entitled *The Beecher Island Annual*. That year Colonel Forsyth spoke at the reunion.[46]

In December 1868 a detachment was sent to the island to recover the bodies of the scouts buried there. The remains of Culver and Farley were recovered but not those of the others. The detachment assumed that the graves had been violated.[47] Henry Ward Beecher attempted to organize a party to recover his nephew's body but the effort failed. There arose a fascination with finding the remains of the missing men. Finally, at the 1900 reunion celebration, Ed Christy, who had been at Forsyth's relief, along with former Forsyth Scout Fletcher Vilott, went to Beecher Island and found Lieutenant Beecher's bones at the request of Beecher's family in Boston. Both men had dug his final grave in 1868. They found one "yellowed rib, a vertebra, one knee cap, a forearm, and two leg bones." A deformity, caused by a wound, in one of the leg bones identified it as belonging to Frederick H. Beecher (Beecher had received such a wound in the Civil War).[48]

During the 1905 reunion, old Howard Morton, who had lost an eye to a Cheyenne bullet during the battle, spotted a youngster digging in the sand of the Arickaree. Morton quipped to the lad: "If you find an eye in there, young fellow, it's mine. I lost one hereabouts."[49] As late as the 1990s, annual celebrations have been held at the battleground on the weekend closest to September 17.

Most of the old veterans of the Forsyth Scouts died with the hero status that writers had given them. A number of artists and illustrators immortalized them. Robert Lindneux, Maynard Dixon, and even Frederic Remington found inspiration in Forsyth's stand on the Arickaree when creating their stylized, arguably mythical, image of the Indian-fighting army of the western frontier. Forsyth went on to participate in the Apache campaigns of the 1880s in New Mexico Territory. He served along the border with the 4th Cavalry at Fort Huachuca, Arizona Territory. He retired in 1904 with the rank of colonel and died September 12, 1915, at the age of seventy-seven. Most of the old scouts from the Saline and Solomon valleys proved up their homesteads and lived to see Kansas settled.[50] Some, such as Isaac Thayer, Fletcher Vilott, and Allison J. Pliley, retired to the comforts of Kansas City. Jack Donovan saw Denver grow into a great city. Jack Stillwell went on to become a judge in Texas. George Washington Oaks became a prominent citizen of Tucson. "Sharp" Grover was killed by a gunfighter. Sigmund Shlesinger returned to New York City shortly after Beecher Island and later migrated to Cleveland, where he entered the cigar and tobacco business and lived to the age of seventy-eight.

One day "Buffalo Bill" Cody's Wild West Show came to Cleveland and Shlesinger went out to the fairground to see if he could find anyone he knew and renew old friendships. He walked up to an old man who looked to Shlesinger like "a typical frontiersman" and asked: "Beg pardon, did you live in Kansas in 1868, and if so, do you know any of Forsyth's Scouts?" "Yes," the old-timer replied. "I was at Forsyth's rescue." The man's name was John Nelson. After reminiscing awhile about the vanquished frontier, Nelson invited Shlesinger into an Indian tepee set up on the fairground.

"Sitting [inside the tepee] on a buffalo robe on the ground was an old squaw surrounded by pappooses [sic]," Shlesinger remembered. "She was his wife. He said something to her in the Indian tongue, whereupon she looked up at me, grunted, started up towards me and grabbed my hands. Although the manifestation seemed friendly, I got scared," Shlesinger admitted. Upon questioning Nelson further, Shlesinger learned what all the commotion was about. "She is glad to see you," Nelson said, "for she was on the north hill [Squaw Hill at Beecher Island] watching your fight with her people." Later the woman prevailed upon her husband to ask Shlesinger an important question. She wanted to know which one of the Forsyth Scouts wore a new buckskin shirt. "I reflected a moment," Shlesinger recalled, "and remembered that Jack Stillwell brought such a garment to camp before we started from Fort Hays. I helped him hem a seam around the collar." Shlesinger became puzzled and inquired of Nelson what the Indian woman wished to know.

"Do you remember the three dead Indians your people scalped on the edge of the island?" Nelson replied. "One of them was a relative of my wife, and a man wearing a buckskin shirt was seen to shoot and kill this Indian. All these years my wife and her people have been under the impression that I was with you during the fight, and accuse me because I happened to be there with the rescue party; and because I usually wore a buckskin shirt that was conclusive evidence that I was the guilty one. It would please me very much," Nelson beseeched Shlesinger, "if you would testify to my innocence."[51]

By the turn of the century, many of the old hatreds of the past had tempered. One year after the Battle of Summit Springs, and throughout the decade of the 1870s, there was a rush for Kansas lands that eclipsed all previous immigrations. Within three years after that decisive engagement the settlements reached the Colorado border. Western Kansas reported a population of fewer than 30,000 in 1870. The census of 1880 revealed a population in the state of nearly 400,000. During the 1880s that population spilled over onto the plains of eastern Colorado. Gone were the hordes of buffalo observed by DeB. Randolph Keim. Gone too were the free lands of the old Dog Soldiers in the Republican Valley.[52] Much of the bitter hatred characteristic of racial war was gone as well. Most of the newly arrived immigrants never had a personal encounter with Indians. To be sure, the war for the Smoky Hill country and the Republican Valley had attained "savage" porportions. Depredations were committed by both red and white. But the war was not a conflict of a "good" society versus an "evil" society; it was a clash of totally uncompromising visions for the future.

Early in the twentieth century, Rev. Cyrus Townsend Brady clipped an article from an unidentified newspaper. The writer's depth of perception was surprisingly modern. "To-day cattle stand knee-deep in the Arickaree," he wrote. "The water no longer ripples around the island, as the shifting sands have filled the channel to the south. But if one digs under the cottonwoods he can find bullets, cartridges, and knives. And near at hand is the simple white shaft that tells where Beecher and Roman

Nose, typifing all that is brave in white man and red, forgot all enmity in the last sleep that knows no dreams of racial hatred."[53]

In 1935 a ravaging flood swept away the island in the Arickaree forever. Gone too by that date were most of those who fought there. The story of Beecher Island and the Dog Soldiers' struggle for their homelands had passed from memory into the realm of myth and imagination.[54]

Notes

Introduction

1. General Nelson A. Miles, *Personal Recollections and Observations of General Nelson A. Miles* (Chicago: Werner Publishing, 1896), 145; General Nelson A. Miles, "Jack Stilwell's Daring Achievement," *The Trail* (v. 18, no. 3, Aug. 1925): 11.
2. George E. Hyde, *Life of George Bent: Written From His Letters* (Norman: University of Oklahoma Press, 1968), 305; George Bird Grinnell, *The Fighting Cheyennes* (New York: Charles Scribner's Sons, 1915), 278–281; Peter John Powell, *People of the Sacred Mountain: A History of the Northern Cheyenne Chiefs and Warrior Societies, 1830–1879, With an Epilogue, 1969–1974,* v. 1 (San Francisco: Harper & Row, 1981), 581.
3. Many early accounts stressed the heroism of the scouts with little consideration for the significance of the battle in the history of the Indian wars on the central and southern plains. Typical are James B. Fry, *Army Sacrifices* (New York: D. Van Nostrand, 1879), 32–45; and Cyrus Townsend Brady, *Indian Fights and Fighters* (Lincoln: University of Nebraska Press, 1971) (first published in 1904), 72–122.
4. Homer E. Socolofsky and Huber Self, *Historical Atlas of Kansas,* 2nd edition (Norman: University of Oklahoma Press, 1988), 29.
5. Forsyth, in his official report to Sheridan, estimated the number of Indians to be 450. Other scouts estimated no less than 750. For years, writers (and later Forsyth himself) accepted the report of Forsyth's chief of scouts, Abner S. "Sharp" Grover, which estimated the number to be between eight hundred and nine hundred. See Fry, *Army Sacrifices,* 44–45; Winfield Freeman, "The Battle of the Arickaree," *Transactions of the Kansas Historical Society* (v. 6, 1897–1900): 357. From Indian informants Grinnell placed the number at six hundred, while Bent asserted that the estimates by white informants of the number of Indians engaged has always been "grossly exaggerated." He gave the figures as about "300 or 350." Grinnell, *The Fighting Cheyennes,* 291; Hyde, *Life of George Bent,* 300; Bent to Hyde, February 23, 1904, Bent Letters, Coe Collection, Yale University Library. More modern accounts have cited a diversity of estimates, which has resulted in a confusingly wide range of Indian participants in this fight, usually between four hundred and one thousand. Such a discrepancy could have a significant impact on the interpretation of the events at Beecher Island. A good example is George M. Heinzman, "Don't Let Them Ride Over Us," *American Heritage: The Magazine of History* (v. 18, no. 2, Feb. 1967): 45.
6. Illustrating the discrepancy always encountered in measuring Indian casualties during the wars with white soldiers, four early accounts of the battle estimated casualties as follows: Forsyth, in his official report, estimated thirty-two killed. Later, from information obtained from Indian informants, Forsyth escalated his estimate to seventy-five killed. In 1900 Freeman gave the figure at about 750. Contrast these figures with both Grinnell and Bent, who emphatically placed the number killed at nine and then proceeded to name each of the casualties. A more recent student, Lonnie J. White, accepted Forsyth's original figures of thirty-two killed and about three times that number wounded. See George A. Forsyth, "A Frontier Fight," *Harper's New Monthly Magazine* (v. 91, June 1895): 62; Freeman, "The Battle of the Arickaree," 357; Grinnell, *The Fighting Cheyennes,* 279; Hyde, *Life of George Bent,* 305; and Lonnie J. White, "The Battle of Beecher Island: The Scouts Hold Fast on the Arickaree," *Journal of the West* (v. 5, no. 1, 1966): 19.
7. Henry M. Stanley, *My Early Travels and Adventures in America and Asia,* v. 1 (London: S. Low, Marston, 1895), 29–47.

8. Robert M. Utley, *The Indian Frontier of the American West, 1846–1890* (Albuquerque: University of New Mexico Press, 1984), 124.

9. Quoted in *ibid.*, 125.

10. *Ibid.*

11. Paul Andrew Hutton, *Phil Sheridan and His Army* (Lincoln: University of Nebraska Press, 1985), 48.

12. George A. Custer, *My Life on the Plains, or, Personal Experiences With Indians* (Norman: University of Oklahoma Press, 1962), 143.

13. Quoted in W. A. Graham, *The Custer Myth: A Source Book of Custeriana* (New York: Bonanza Books, 1953), 316.

14. Cyrus Townsend Brady, among others, gathered information from surviving scouts, Sigmund Shlesinger in particular, and then popularized their stories with the general reading public. See Brady, *Indian Fights and Fighters*, 72–122. The Dog Soldiers later asserted that after Beecher Island they decided to remain in the Republican Valley and resume raids eastward against the Kansas settlements. See Hyde, *Life of George Bent*, 311.

15. Robert Lynam, editor, *The Beecher Island Annual: Sixty-Second Anniversary of the Battle of Beecher Island*, September 17–18, 1868 (Wray, Colo.: Beecher Island Battle Memorial Association, 1930), 93–94.

16. A. P. Gaines, "The Battle of Beecher's Island," *Denver Westerners Monthly Roundup* (v. 25, no. 7–8, July–Aug. 1969): 123–124.

17. Arthur Chapman, "The Indian Fighters of the Arickaree," *Harper's Weekly* (July 26, 1913): 9.

18. *Ibid.*

19. For example, see Stuart R. Carswell, "Twenty to One," *Cavalry Journal* (v. 46, Jan.–Feb. 1937): 9–55. There were other fights on the Indian frontier that are, arguably, more deserving of the image. One of the best known is the so-called Wagon Box Fight of August 1867, a similar defensive action against the Sioux in the Powder River country. As at Beecher Island, the whites possessed superior weaponry and were rescued, here in the nick of time, by a relief column. For a good concise sketch see Jerry Keenan, *The Wagon Box Fight* (Sheridan, Wyo.: Fort Phil Kearny/Bozeman Trail Association, 1988).

20. Grinnell, *The Fighting Cheyennes*, 279. For a comprehensive bibliography of primary and secondary sources on the Cheyennes prior to 1980, see Peter John Powell, *The Cheyennes, Ma.he.o's People: A Cultural Bibliography* (Bloomington: Indiana University Press, 1980).

21. E. A. Brininstool, *Fighting Red Cloud's Warriors: True Tales of Indian Days When the West Was Young* (Columbus, Ohio: Hunter-Trader-Trapper Co., 1926), 97, 99.

22. Hyde, *Life of George Bent*, 305.

23. Powell, *People of the Sacred Mountain*, v. 1, 583.

24. David Fridtjof Halaas, "America's Blurred Vision: A Review Essay on Indian-White Histories," *Colorado Heritage* (Colorado Historical Society, Issue 3, 1983): 44.

25. *Ibid.*, 45.

26. Robert M. Utley in particular is highly esteemed in the field of military history of the Indian wars. For his analysis of Beecher Island, see Utley, *The Indian Frontier*, 122–125; and Utley, *Frontier Regulars: The United States Army and the Indian, 1866–1891* (New York: Macmillan, 1973), 142–148. For an objective overview of the Beecher Island fight, see Ralph K. Andrist, *The Long Death: The Last Days of the Plains Indians* (New York: Collier Books, 1964), 145–166. See also James Hutchins, *Great Western Indian Fights* (Lincoln: University of Nebraska Press, 1960), 165–175. An excellent study of the regular army in the nineteenth century is Edward M. Coffmann, *The Old Army: A Portrait of the American Army in Peacetime, 1784–1898* (New York and Oxford: Oxford University Press, 1986).

27. Halaas, "America's Blurred Vision," 46–47.

28. Two concise, understandable overviews that evoke the philosophy and viewpoints of the so-called New Western History are Historical Commentary, "Western History, Why the Past May Be Changing: Four Essays by Patricia Nelson Limerick, Michael P. Malone, Gerald Thompson, and Elliot West," *Montana: The Magazine of Western History* (v. 40, no. 3, Summer 1990): 60–76. See also Patricia Nelson Limerick, Clyde A. Milner II, and Charles E. Rankin,

eds., *Trails Toward a New Western History* (Lawrence: University Press of Kansas, 1991). Although not well documented as to specific sources, a comprehensive synthesis of the West from the so-called new perspective is Richard White, *It's Your Misfortune and None of My Own: A New History of the American West* (Norman and London: University of Oklahoma Press, 1991). For popular impressions of the revisionism of the late 1980s and 1990s, see "How the West Was Really Won," *U.S. News and World Report* (May 21, 1990): 56–67.

29. Patricia Nelson Limerick, *The Legacy of Conquest: The Unbroken Past of the American West* (New York and London: W. W. Norton & Company, 1987), 216–217.
30. Quoted in Halaas, "America's Blurred Vision," 47.
31. William Cronon and Richard White, "Indians in the Land, A Conversation Between William Cronon and Richard White," *American Heritage* (v. 37, no. 5, Aug.–Sep. 1986): 20.
32. Halaas, "America's Blurred Vision," 47.
33. *Ibid.*, 46.
34. Sherry L. Smith, *The View From Officers' Row: Army Perceptions of Western Indians* (Tucson: University of Arizona Press, 1990), 184.
35. Quoted in *ibid.*, 134–135. For other interpretations of Social Darwinism and its applicability to the late nineteenth century, see Richard Hofstadter, *Social Darwinism in American Thought*, revised edition (Boston: Beacon Press, 1955).
36. Gerald D. Nash, *Creating the West: Historical Interpretations, 1890–1990* (Albuquerque: University of New Mexico Press, 1991), vii–xi.
37. Limerick, *The Legacy of Conquest*, 221.

Chapter 1

1. Colonel Henry Inman, *Tales of the Trail* (Topeka, Kans.: Crane & Company, 1898), 1.
2. *Ibid.*, 2.
3. *Ibid.*
4. *Ibid.*, 3.
5. *Ibid.*
6. DeB. Randolph Keim, *Sheridan's Troopers on the Borders: A Winter Campaign on the Plains* (Lincoln and London: University of Nebraska Press, 1985) (first published in 1885), Introduction to the Bison Book Edition by Paul Andrew Hutton.
7. *Ibid.*
8. *Ibid.*, ix–x.
9. *Ibid.*
10. *Ibid.*, 37.
11. *Ibid.*, 38–40.
12. *Ibid.*, 40.
13. *Ibid.*, 49–50.
14. Oliver Knight, *Following the Indian Wars: The Story of the Newspaper Correspondents Among the Indian Campaigners* (Norman: University of Oklahoma Press, 1960), 77.
15. Keim's dispatches back East brought national attention to the fight on the Arickaree. These reports not only gave Sheridan support for his winter campaign but also embarrassed the congressional members of the "Blue Ribbon" Peace Commission who had secured the Treaty of Medicine Lodge in October 1867.
16. Keim, *Sheridan's Troopers*, 50.
17. Mrs. Frank C. Montgomery, "Fort Wallace and Its Relation to the Frontier," *Collections of the Kansas State Historical Society* (v. 17, 1926–1928): 232.
18. Keim, *Sheridan's Troopers*, 59.
19. For the Washita campaign see Stan Hoig, *The Battle of the Washita* (Lincoln and London: University of Nebraska Press, 1976). For Carr's campaign in 1869 and the Battle of Summit

Springs, see James T. King, *War Eagle: A Life of General Eugene A. Carr* (Lincoln: University of Nebraska Press, 1963).

20. Republican presidential candidate Ulysses S. Grant was especially influenced by the Beecher Island battle in his desire to subordinate the Indian Bureau to the War Department. See Utley, *The Indian Frontier*, 124–125.

21. West of the one hundredth meridian, the lands of the shortgrass prairie receive less than the average twenty inches of annual rainfall necessary to grow the usual cereal crops of wheat, corn, and barley. Machinery and large landholdings were necessary. See Gilbert C. Fite, *The Farmers' Frontier, 1865–1900* (Albuquerque: University of New Mexico Press, 1974), 1–14.

22. Ray Allen Billington and Martin Ridge, *Westward Expansion: A History of the American Frontier*, 5th edition (New York: Macmillan, 1982), 629–643.

23. William Frank Zornow, *Kansas: A History of the Jayhawk State* (Norman: University of Oklahoma Press, 1957), 162.

24. *Ibid.*, 163.

25. Socolofsky and Self, *Historical Atlas of Kansas*, 39.

26. *Osborne County Farmer*, July 22, 1880. For an excellent discussion of the Indian impact on western Kansas from the settlers' point of view, see Craig Miner, *West of Wichita: Settling the High Plains of Kansas, 1865–1890* (Lawrence: University Press of Kansas, 1986), 14–25.

27. *Osborne County Farmer*, July 1880; Miner, *West of Wichita*, 15.

28. Socolofsky and Self, *Historical Atlas of Kansas*, 29.

29. Lieutenant General Philip H. Sheridan, *Outline of Posts: Descriptions of the Posts in the Military Division of the Missouri* (Chicago: Military Division of the Missouri, 1876), 5; Miner, *West of Wichita*, 15.

30. Sheridan, *Outline of Posts*, 70; Miner, *West of Wichita*, 15.

31. Carl Abbott, Stephen J. Leonard, and David McComb, *Colorado: A History of the Centennial State*, revised edition (Boulder: Colorado Associated Press, 1982), 74.

32. Grinnell, *The Fighting Cheyennes*, 137–138.

33. *Ibid.*, 145; Hyde, *Life of George Bent*, 131–134. See also Donald J. Berthrong, *The Southern Cheyennes* (Norman: University of Oklahoma Press, 1963), 186–187.

34. *Rocky Mountain News*, August 10, 1864.

35. For the Hungate Massacre, see Henry Littleton Pitzer, *Three Frontiers: Memories and a Portrait of Henry Littleton Pitzer as Recorded by His Son Robert Clarbourne Pitzer* (Muscatine, Iowa: Pioneer Press, 1938), 162–163.

36. Grinnell, *The Fighting Cheyennes*, 137–148.

37. "The Sand Creek Massacre: Report of the Secretary of War": *Senate Executive Document*, 39th Cong., 2nd sess., 1867, no. 26, 216–217. See also Stan Hoig, *The Peace Chiefs of the Cheyennes* (Norman: University of Oklahoma Press, 1980), 86.

38. For an analysis of the original sources pertaining to the causes and effects of the Sand Creek Massacre, see Stan Hoig, *The Sand Creek Massacre* (Norman: University of Oklahoma Press, 1961).

39. Socolofsky and Self, *Historical Atlas of Kansas*, 29.

40. For the "Great Raids" of revenge see Hyde, *Life of George Bent*, 164–201. See also Eugene F. Ware, *The Indian War of 1864* (New York: St. Martin's, 1960), 324–327.

41. Utley, *The Indian Frontier*, 102.

42. Quoted in *ibid.*

43. *Ibid.*, 103.

44. Hyde, *Life of George Bent*, 247–249.

45. *Ibid.*

46. Ezra J. Warner, *Generals in Blue: Lives of the Union Commanders* (Baton Rouge: Louisana State University Press, 1964), 454.

47. *Ibid.*, 108–109.

48. William H. Leckie, *The Buffalo Soldiers: A Narrative of the Negro Cavalry in the West* (Norman: University of Oklahoma Press, 1967), 8–18. See also William Loren Katz, *The Black West*, 3rd edition (Seattle: Open Hand Publishing, Inc., 1987), 199–244.

49. Reuben Waller, to the Beecher Island Battle Memorial Association, in Lynam, "History of a Slave Written by Himself at the Age of 89 Years," *The Beecher Island Annual,* 115–118.
50. William Winsor and James Scarbrough, "History of Jewell County, Kansas, Written in 1878," *Collections of the Kansas State Historical Society* (v. 17, 1926–1928): 391.
51. Montgomery, "Fort Wallace," 206.
52. Hyde, *Life of George Bent,* 253–254.
53. Marvin H. Garfield, "Defense of the Kansas Frontier, 1866–1867," *Kansas Historical Quarterly* (v. 1, no. 4, Aug. 1932): 329.
54. Samuel J. Crawford, *Kansas in the Sixties* (Chicago: A. C. McClurg and Co., 1911), 326–327. See also William H. Leckie, *The Military Conquest of the Southern Plains* (Norman: University of Oklahoma Press, 1963), 37.
55. Garfield, "Defense of the Kansas Frontier," 329.
56. *Army and Navy Journal* (v. 4, April 6, 1867): 518. See also Leckie, *Military Conquest,* 38.
57. Dee Brown, Foreword to the Bison Book Edition, 1982, in Stanley, *My Early Travels and Adventures,* v–xi.
58. *Ibid.,* xvi.
59. *Ibid.,* v–xi.
60. *Ibid.,* 4.
61. *Ibid.,* 18–23.
62. *Ibid.,* 24.
63. Warner, *Generals in Blue,* 202–203.
64. Glenn Tucker, *Hancock the Superb* (Indianapolis: Bobbs-Merrill, 1960), 303.
65. Grinnell, *The Fighting Cheyennes,* 248. Grinnell may be overstating his case. Infantry were frequently used during the Indian wars, occasionally with great success, as evidenced by such engagements as Wolf Mountains in the Great Sioux War of 1876–1877.
66. Hyde, *Life of George Bent,* 272–276.

Chapter 2

1. Hancock's campaign and his meetings with Roman Nose are well documented. See George Bent to George E. Hyde, Correspondence, William Robertson Coe Collection, Yale University Library, June 5 and 12, 1906; *Report, Commissioner of Indian Affairs,* 1867, 310–312; Custer, *My Life on the Plains,* 25–28; Hyde, *Life of George Bent,* 244–266; Grinnell, *The Fighting Cheyennes,* 245–253; and Stanley, *My Early Travels and Adventures,* 26–40. Secondary sources include Berthrong, *The Southern Cheyennes,* 266–280; and Powell, *People of the Sacred Mountain,* v. 1, 462–474.
2. Apparently Hancock retained his composure and stood his ground when Roman Nose struck him with his quirt. Bent to Hyde, June 5, 1906; Powell, *People of the Sacred Mountain,* v. 1, 470. Grinnell, who was told of this incident by interpreter Ed Guerrier, mentions Roman Nose staring at Hancock but not counting coup on him. See Grinnell, *The Fighting Cheyennes,* 250.
3. Hyde, *Life of George Bent,* 259; Grinnell,*The Fighting Cheyennes,* 258.
4. Hyde, *Life of George Bent,* 259; Grinnell, *The Fighting Cheyennes,* 248.
5. Bent to Hyde, June 5, 1906; Powell, *People of the Sacred Mountain,* v. 1, 462.
6. Hyde, *Life of George Bent,* 255–256; Berthrong, *The Southern Cheyennes,* 273; Powell, *People of the Sacred Mountain,* v. 1, 464.
7. Hyde, *Life of George Bent,* 255–256; Berthrong, *The Southern Cheyennes,* 273; Powell, *People of the Sacred Mountain,* 464.
8. Stanley, *My Early Travels and Adventures,* 29.
9. *Ibid.*
10 *Ibid.,* 30–33. Stanley gives a full account of Hancock's speech and Tall Bull's reply.
11. *Ibid.,* 32. For a discussion of the role of a Cheyenne peace chief see Hyde, *Life of George Bent,* 294.

12. Hyde, *Life of George Bent*, 257–258.
13. *Cincinnati Commercial*, October 24, 1867; Stanley, *My Early Travels and Adventures*, 34; quoted in Hoig, *Peace Chiefs*, 92.
14. Hyde, *Life of George Bent*, 258; Bent to Hyde, June 5, 1906; Grinnell, *The Fighting Cheyennes*, 249–250.
15. Hyde, Bent, and Grinnell agreed that the Indians were prepared for war should Hancock show any hostile intent. The chiefs of the Dog Soldiers were very intent upon keeping the peace and planned only for defensive actions. Hancock, however, interpreted the Indian line of defense to indicate hostility on the part of the warriors. See Winfield Scott Hancock, *Reports of Major General Hancock Upon Indian Affairs With Accompanying Exhibits*, Washington, D.C., 1867, 20–21.
16. Stanley, *My Early Travels and Adventures*, 37; Powell, *People of the Sacred Mountain*, v. 1, 469; Berthrong, *The Southern Cheyennes*, 275; Hancock, however, reported the Indian numbers at "several hundred" in *Reports of Major General Hancock*, 21. Correspondent Theodore Davis listed the Indian numbers at 329 in "A Summer on the Plains," *Harper's New Monthly Magazine* (v. 36, no. 213, Feb. 1868): 295.
17. Custer related a vivid picture of the confrontation on Red Arm Creek (Pawnee Fork) in Custer, *My Life on the Plains*, 33–39.
18. Hyde, *Life of George Bent*, 259.
19. Bent to Hyde, June 5, 1906.
20. Hyde, *Life of George Bent*, 265.
21. *Ibid.*, 306.
22. Cheyenne historian Peter John Powell claimed Roman Nose was born circa 1823. See Powell, *People of the Sacred Mountain*, v. 1, 1426.
23. Hyde, *Life of George Bent*, 306.
24. It is beyond the scope of this book to examine in depth Cheyenne religion and spiritualism. For an excellent explanation of the significance of the Medicine Arrow renewal cermony and its place in Cheyenne culture, see E. Adamson Hoebel, *The Cheyennes: Indians of the Great Plains* (New York: Holt, Rinehart & Winston, 1960), 6–11. For the importance of the sacred Buffalo Hat, see John Stands in Timber and Margot Liberty, *Cheyenne Memories* (Lincoln and London: University of Nebraska Press, 1972), 74–78; for the related story of the deity "Sweet Medicine," see George Bird Grinnell, *The Cheyenne Indians*, v. 2 (New Haven: Yale University Press, 1923), 345–381.
25. Bent's description of Roman Nose's quiet nature among his own people contrasts sharply with his actions as a warrior. Actually this seeming dichotomy fits well with Hoebel's description of the Cheyenne worldview and personality. Warriors were expected to exercise self-control in all matters, including sexual activity. Such pent-up emotions were considered most valuable when released in combat with enemies. See Hoebel, *The Cheyennes*, 84.
26. It is a misconception that counting coup always resulted in conservation of life. During intertribal conflict, belligerents often tried to annihilate each other. Of course warriors would do likewise to white soldiers when they held a decisive advantage. For the coup ritual see Grinnell, *The Cheyenne Indians*, 29–38.
27. Circa 1860 is Powell's date. See Powell, *People of the Sacred Mountain*, v. 1, 229.
28. For White Bull's (Ice's) description of making Thunder's war bonnet for Roman Nose, see Grinnell, *The Cheyenne Indians*, 119–121.
29. *Ibid.*, 120.
30. *Ibid.*
31. The standard work on the Red Buttes fight and the Platte Bridge fight is J. W. Vaughn, *The Battle of Platte Bridge* (Norman: University of Oklahoma Press, 1963).
32. The classic account of the Red Buttes fight and Roman Nose's activities during the battle was given by George Bent, who rode with the Cheyennes in the engagement. See Hyde, *Life of George Bent*, 214–222. That the mutilation of the whites was more for revenge for Sand Creek rather

than common social-spiritual practice is claimed by Powell, *People of the Sacred Mountain*, v. 1, 342.

33. Hyde, *Life of George Bent*, 239–240. The classic source for this fight is Bent.
34. Anthony McGinnis, *Counting Coup and Cutting Horses: Intertribal Warfare on the Northern Plains, 1738–1889* (Evergreen, Colo.: Cordillera Press, 1990), 114.
35. Because Roman Nose came south in 1866 and remained there until his death at Beecher Island in 1868, he has often been called a "Southern" Cheyenne. In fact he had close friends among the Dog Soldiers and Suhtais (especially Bull Bear and Black Shin) and camped with them for long periods. It is probable that he remained in the south after 1866 because he sympathized with the struggle of the Dog Soldiers to hold on to their lands in deference to the Treaty of the Little Arkansas and the Treaty of Medicine Lodge concluded in 1867.
36. Berthrong, *The Southern Cheyennes*, 262–263.
37. Davis, "A Summer on the Plains," 295. Grinnell, however, qualified Davis's description of Roman Nose. He asserted, "Obviously, if Roman Nose was so well provided with firearms as was said, he had no ammunition for them, or else he would have carried a firearm in his hands" (in Grinnell, *The Fighting Cheyennes*, 250). Stanley stated only that Roman Nose was "dressed magnificently" (in Stanley, *My Early Travels and Adventures*, 37).
38. Stanley, *My Early Travels and Adventures*, 38.
39. *Ibid.*; Hyde, *Life of George Bent*, 259.
40. Stanley, *My Early Travels and Adventures*, 38.
41. Hyde, *Life of George Bent*, 260.
42. *Ibid.*; Grinnell, *The Fighting Cheyennes*, 251.
43. Bent to Hyde, June 5, 1906. Custer wrote his wife that morning stating that he was to pursue the Indians and engage them if they did not come back and were disposed to fight. See Elizabeth B. Custer, *Tenting on the Plains; or, General Custer in Kansas and Texas* (New York: C. L. Webster and Company, 1887), 560–561. See also Berthrong, *The Southern Cheyennes*, 277.
44. Stanley, *My Early Travels and Adventures*, 39–40; Custer, *My Life on the Plains*, 64; *Reports of Major General Hancock*, 23. Berthrong asserted that the accusation that soldiers raped the girl was an attempt by agent Wynkoop to discredit the army's relations with the Cheyennes during 1867. Army officers thoroughly discredited this notion. Powell, however, claimed that during the treaty councils at Medicine Lodge, Kansas, during fall 1867 White Head stated that he was the last man to leave the village and that at his departure no one had harmed the girl. It seems unlikely that Cheyenne warriors would have committed such an act given their strict codes of sexual behavior toward chaste women of their tribe. See Powell, *People of the Sacred Mountain*, v. 1, 472.
45. Grinnell, *The Fighting Cheyennes*, 254.
46. Hyde, *Life of George Bent*, 261; Berthrong, *The Southern Cheyennes*, 278. Grinnell asserted that two men were killed at Fossil Station, which is today Russell, Kansas. Grinnell, *The Fighting Cheyennes*, 253–254.
47. Berthrong, *The Southern Cheyennes*, 279.
48. Grinnell, *The Fighting Cheyennes*, 253.
49. *Ibid.* Much controversy exists about when Hancock decided to burn the village. According to Grinnell, Wynkoop claimed that he made up his mind the night of April 15. Hancock, however, asserted that it was not until he learned from Custer that the Indians had committed depredations along the Smoky Hill Road. Stanley claimed that Hancock made up his mind to burn the village on the night of April 14 and the following morning. See Stanley, *My Early Travels and Adventures*, 40.
50. Grinnell, *The Fighting Cheyennes*, 253; Stanley, *My Early Travels and Adventures*, 46; Berthrong, *The Southern Cheyennes*, 279; Powell, *People of the Sacred Mountain*, v. 1, 473.
51. *Ibid.*, Powell, *People of the Sacred Mountain*, v. 1, 473–475.

Chapter 3

1. Winsor and Scarbrough, "Jewell County," 392–393.
2. Bent and Grinnell both attributed Hancock's burning of the Dog Soldier village on Red Arm Creek as the immediate cause of the war. There were, however, both Sioux from the north and Spotted Tail's Indians who, it is fairly certain, were involved in raiding in western Kansas during this time. By summer 1868, the Arapahoes joined in the war in sizable numbers, creating panic in Colorado.
3. *Rooks County Record,* March 29, 1912.
4. Figures tabulated by the Kansas State Historical Society. See Mark A. Plummer, *Frontier Governor: Samuel J. Crawford of Kansas* (Lawrence/Manhattan/Wichita: University Press of Kansas, 1971), 114.
5. Berthrong, *The Southern Cheyennes,* 266–307.
6. *Annual Report of the Secretary of War, 1868–1869* (Washington, D.C.: Government Printing Office, 1869), 4.
7. Mrs. Olive A. Clark, "Early Days Along the Solomon Valley," *Collections of the Kansas State Historical Society,* (v. 17, 1926–1928): 724.
8. *Ibid.*
9. *Ibid.*
10. *Kansas State Record* (Topeka), August 19, 1868. For a thorough accounting of women captives, see Lonnie J. White, "White Women Captives of Southern Plains Indians, 1866–1875," *Journal of the West* (v. 8, no. 3, July 1969): 327–354. Powell suggested that some of these Indians could have remembered their own ravished women at Sand Creek and thus took out revenge on the women of the Kansas settlements during these raids. See Powell, *People of the Sacred Mountain,* v. 1, 568.
11. Winsor and Scarbrough, "Jewell County," 395.
12. *Kansas State Record* (Topeka), September 2, 1868.
13. White, "Women Captives," 338. White claimed that the exact identity of this raiding party is not known. James Morgan, whose wife, Anna Belle, was captured by these Indians, believed they were from Black Kettle's village. Others thought the war party was Sioux. In any event, Anna Belle Morgan soon wound up in a Dog Soldier camp, possibly having been traded to them.
14. *Weekly Union* (Junction City), December 26, 1868; David L. Spotts, *Campaigning With Custer, 1868–1869* (Los Angeles: Wetzel Publishing Company, 1928), 207–210.
15. *Weekly Union* (Junction City), December 26, 1868; Spotts, *Campaigning With Custer.*
16. *Times and Conservative* (Leavenworth), December 23, 1868.
17. Keim, *Sheridan's Troopers on the Borders,* 119. The exact circumstances of the Blinns' deaths have become controversial. Former Kiowa agent Jesse Leavenworth testified before a Senate committee on Indian affairs that troopers shot Mr. Blinn by mistake. Because Mrs. Blinn's body and that of her son, Willie, were found near where Kiowas were concentrated, some writers have blamed that tribe while others accuse the Arapahoes. For an overview of this controversy see Hoig, *Battle of the Washita,* Appendix E, 210–213. See also White, "Women Captives," 339 and 353 (note 36), for a complete bibliography of this well-known episode of the plight of Mrs. Blinn.
18. *Weekly Union* (Junction City), April 10, 1869.
19. Spotts, *Campaigning With Custer,* 159.
20. *Ibid.*
21. Emily Haines Harrison, "Reminiscences of Early Days in Ottawa County," *Collections of the Kansas State Historical Society* (v. 10, 1907–1908): 627–628. For Anna Belle Morgan's tribulations after her release, see also Joanna L. Stratton, *Pioneer Women: Voices From the Kansas Frontier* (New York: Touchstone, 1981), 123–125.
22. Clark, "Along the Solomon Valley," 728. Although George Bent asserted that women captives were "invariably well treated and adopted into the tribe" and that "it was considered a disgrace to the tribe to ill-treat these prisoners," the examples he gave are for other Indian captives and for Hispanic children. He admitted that when it came to customs of warfare (scalping, turning

the faces of the slain toward the earth, and so on) when whites were concerned, sometimes these customs were not practiced. The objective was sheer disrespect for the whites. Sexual repression among Cheyenne males is well known. So is the renowned chastity of Cheyenne women. But for the unchaste woman, the behavior exhibited by the "superego" of the Cheyenne warrior was quite different. Hoebel documented four cases in which unchaste Cheyenne wives were, according to custom, "put on the prairie. The outraged husband," wrote Hoebel, "invites all the unmarried members of his military society (excepting his wife's relatives) to a feast on the prairie. There the woman is raped by each of them in turn." As with the laxity of following custom in dealing with white combatants, treatment of white women captives, or white women abducted in their own homes during raids, may have been quite different from that of female Native American prisoners, especially after the Sand Creek Massacre. In any case, Mrs. Morgan's treatment by her Cheyenne "husband" was obviously disturbing to her given her reactions after she was released. See Bent, *Life of George Bent*, 296–297; and Hoebel, *The Cheyennes*, 95–96.

23. Clark, "Along the Solomon Valley," 728.
24. *Ibid.*
25. Harrison, "Early Days in Ottawa County," 628.
26. Spotts, *Campaigning With Custer*, 210–215.
27. Sandra L. Myres, *Westering Women and the Frontier Experience, 1800–1915* (Albuquerque: University of New Mexico Press, 1982), 38. Myres asserted "that the opinion that all women hated and feared Indians was a view held primarily by men."
28. Miner, *West of Wichita*, 25.
29. For this reason the Union Pacific Eastern Division Railroad locomotives were frequently halted when huge buffalo herds were near the tracks. Passengers would often take sport in shooting the animals from the seats of the passenger cars. For a good account, see Keim, *Sheridan's Troopers on the Borders*, 37–41.
30. Clark, "Along the Solomon Valley," 720.
31. Julia Chase, "Mother Bickerdyke," *Collections of the Kansas State Historical Society* (v. 7, 1902–1903): 189–193.
32. Clark, "Along the Solomon Valley," 729.
33. Sarah C. Brooks to Captain A. J. Pliley, February 8, 1914, reproduced in Alan W. Farley, ed., "Reminiscences of Allison J. Pliley, Indian Fighter," *The Trail Guide* (Kansas City Posse, the Westerners: v. 2, no. 2, June 1957): 13.
34. Homer E. Socolofsky, *Kansas Governors* (Lawrence: University Press of Kansas, 1990), 89.
35. *Ibid.*, 91.
36. Plummer, *Frontier Governor*, 115.
37. Crawford, *Kansas in the Sixties*, 263.
38. Plummer, *Frontier Governor*, 115.
39. *Ibid.*, 119.
40. *Weekly Leader* (Topeka), August 27, 1868.
41. The best account of the activities of the 19th Kansas during the winter campaign of 1868–1869 is Spotts, *Campaigning With Custer*.
42. Robert G. Athern, "Colorado and the Indian War of 1868," *Colorado Magazine* (v. 33, no. 1, Jan. 1956): 46.
43. Frank Hall, *History of the State of Colorado* (Chicago: Blakely Printing Company, 1889), 458–459.
44. Athern, "Indian War of 1868," 45. Fort Reynolds was built in 1867 in Pueblo County, Colorado, on the south bank of the Arkansas.
45. *Ibid.*, 49.
46. Although a member of Sheridan's staff, Forsyth held a line commission in the 9th Cavalry, while Beecher held a commission in the 3rd Infantry.
47. Frank Petree, "The Battle of Beecher island and Recollections of Some of the Men Engaged in It," in Lynam, ed., *The Beecher Island Annual*, 109.
48. *Ibid.*, 110.
49. Robert Lynman, ed., "The Forsyth Scouts at Beecher Island," *The Beecher Island Annual*, 88.

50. *National Tribune* (Fletcher Vilott's account), November 5, 1896. Lynman, ed., "Death of an Old Resident," *The Beecher Island Annual*, 102.

Chapter 4

1. Powell, *People of the Sacred Mountain*, v. 1, 479.
2. Leckie, *Military Conquest of the Southern Plains*, 46–47.
3. Custer, *My Life on the Plains*, 66.
4. *Ibid.*, 69.
5. Davis, "A Summer on the Plains," 301.
6. Hyde, *Life of George Bent*, 372.
7. Custer, *My Life on the Plains*, 78.
8. *Ibid.*, 82–85.
9. Hyde, *Life of George Bent*, 266. Custer claimed that more Indians were killed in this fight. See Grinnell, *The Fighting Cheyennes*, 258.
10. Stanley, *My Early Travels and Adventures*, 129.
11. Custer, *My Life on the Plains*, 101–109.
12. Hyde, *Life of George Bent*, 274–275; Grinnell, *The Fighting Cheyennes*, 260–261.
13. Custer, *My Life on the Plains*, 111–112.
14. Leckie, *Military Conquest of the Southern Plains*, 55–56. Much has been written about Custer's behavior at the time of the Hancock campaign and his resultant court-martial. Two excellent biographies covering this period are Jay Monaghan, *Custer: The Life of General George Armstrong Custer* (Lincoln: University of Nebraska Press, 1971), 279–303; and Robert M. Utley, *Cavalier in Buckskin: George Armstrong Custer and the Western Military Frontier* (Norman: University of Oklahoma Press, 1988), 36–56. For the court-martial, see Lawrence A. Frost, *The Court-Martial of General George Armstrong Custer* (Norman: University of Oklahoma Press, 1968).
15. Berthrong, *The Southern Cheyennes*. 282.
16. *Harper's Weekly*, July 27, 1867.
17. Lynam, *Beecher Island Annual*, 57–58.
18. Montgomery, "Fort Wallace and Its Relation to the Frontier," 206–207.
19. Robert M. Utley, ed., *Life in Custer's Cavalry: Diaries and Letters of Albert and Jennie Barnitz, 1867–1868* (New Haven: Yale University Press, 1977), 70.
20. Grinnell, *The Fighting Cheyennes*, 260.
21. Utley, *Life in Custer's Cavalry*, 73.
22. *Harper's Weekly*, July 27, 1867; Hyde, *Life of George Bent*, 276.
23. *Harper's Weekly*, July 27, 1867; Hyde, *Life of George Bent*, 276.
24. *Harper's Weekly*, July 27, 1867.
25. Montgomery, "Fort Wallace and Its Relation to the Frontier," 210.
26. Garfield, "Defense of the Kansas Frontier," 334–335.
27. George B. Jenness, "The Battle of Beaver Creek," *Transactions of the Kansas State Historical Society* (v. 9, 1905–1906): 443–444.
28. Joseph Snell and Robert Richmond, "When the Union and Kansas Pacific Built Through Kansas," *Kansas Historical Quarterly* (v. 32, 1966): 346.
29. George A. Armes, *Ups and Downs of an Army Officer* (Washington, D.C., 1900), 230–232. This fight is sometimes called the Battle of the Saline River.
30. *Johnson County Democrat* (Kansas), April 7, 1922. Farley, "Reminiscences of Allison J. Pliley," 2–3.
31. *Ibid.*, 3.
32. *Ibid.*, 4.
33. Jenness, "The Battle of Beaver Creek," 446.
34. *Ibid.* There is some confusion as to where this fight took place. Jenness placed it on Beaver Creek, while Pliley, who knew the country well, stated that it was on a tributary of Prairie Dog Creek

near where Phillipsburg, Kansas, is now located. Pliley's account of the fight differs somewhat from Jenness's. The most complete secondary source is Lonnie J. White, "The Battles of the Saline River and Prairie Dog Creek," *Hostiles and Horse Soldiers: Indian Battles and Campaigns in the West* (Boulder: Pruett, 1972), 49–67.

35. Farley, "Reminiscences of Allison J. Pliley," 5.
36. *Ibid.*
37. Davis, "A Summer on the Plains," 305; *Daily Conservative* (Leavenworth), August 23, 1867. Quoted in White, "The Battles of the Saline River and Prairie Dog Creek," 62.
38. Jenness, "The Battle of Beaver Creek," 447–452.
39. White, "The Battles of the Saline River and Prairie Dog Creek," 63. White made a logical argument regarding the feud between Moore and Armes over the "blame" for this battle.
40. Moore to Crawford, August 31, 1867, Governor's Papers (Crawford), Kansas State Historical Society, Topeka, Kans.
41. Leckie, *The Buffalo Soldiers*, 25.
42. Stanley, *My Early Travels and Adventures*, 133.
43. *Ibid.*, 129–130.

Chapter 5

1. Stands in Timber and Liberty, *Cheyenne Memories*, 173.
2. Powell, *People of the Sacred Mountain*, v. 1, 488.
3. Grinnell, *The Fighting Cheyennes*, 266.
4. Stands in Timber and Liberty, *Cheyenne Memories*, 174.
5. Grinnell, *The Fighting Cheyennes*, 266–267. Porcupine told this story to Grinnell early in the twentieth century. He claimed that there were only two men on the handcar. In actuality there were six including William Thompson. See Stanley, *My Early Travels and Adventures*, 156.
6. Grinnell, *The Fighting Cheyennes*, 266–267; Stanley, *My Early Travels and Adventures*, 156.
7. Grinnell, *The Fighting Cheyennes*, 267–268.
8. Hyde, *Life of George Bent*, 277.
9. Powell, *People of the Sacred Mountain*, v. 1, 491.
10. Stands in Timber and Liberty, *Cheyenne Memories*, 176.
11. Hyde, *Life of George Bent*, 277.
12. Stanley, *My Early Travels and Adventures*, 158.
13. For an excellent sketch of the Pawnee Scouts, see Donald F. Danker, ed., *Man of the Plains: Recollections of Luther North, 1856–1882* (Lincoln: University of Nebraska Press, 1961), 58–60, 73–74.
14. George Bird Grinnell, *Two Great Scouts and Their Pawnee Battalion: The Experiences of Frank J. North and Luther H. North, Pioneers in the Great West, 1856–1882, and Their Defense of the Building of the Union Pacific Railroad* (Lincoln: University of Nebraska Press, 1973), 145–146.
15. Hyde, *Life of George Bent*, 278.
16. Stanley, *My Early Travels and Adventures*, 155.
17. *Ibid.*, 155–156.
18. Powell, *People of the Sacred Mountain*, v. 1, 670.
19. John Stilgoe, *Metropolitan Corridor: Railroads and the American Scene* (New Haven: Yale University Press, 1983), ix–xii.
20. Miner, *West of Wichita*, 26.
21. John H. Putnam, "A Trip to the End of the Union Pacific in 1868," *Kansas Historical Quarterly* (v. 13, no. 3, Aug. 1944): 196–203.
22. Quoted in Miner, *West of Wichita*, 27.
23. Stands in Timber and Liberty, *Cheyenne Memories*, 176.
24. *Osborne County Farmer*, July 22, 1880.
25. Miner, *West of Wichita*, 17.

26. *Hays Sentinel,* January 18, 1878.
27. A. Roenigk, "Railroad Grading Among Indians," *Collections of the Kansas State Historical Society* (v. 8, 1904): 384–390.
28. Wallace County Historical Society, *History of Wallace County* (Sharon City, Kans.: Wallace County Historical Society, 1979), 7.
29. *Harper's New Monthly Magazine,* November 1875, 830.
30. *Lawrence Weekly Tribune* (Lawrence), July 30, 1868.
31. *Kansas City Commonwealth* (Topeka), August 4, 1869. For Sheridan, Kansas, see also Daniel Fitzgerald, *Ghost Towns of Kansas: A Traveler's Guide* (Lawrence: University Press of Kansas, 1988), 241–246.
32. George L. Anderson, *Kansas West* (San Marino, Calif.: Golden West Books, 1963), 67.
33. Keim, *Sheridan's Troopers on the Borders,* 42, 44–45.
34. E. A. Brininstool, ed., *Fighting Red Cloud's Warriors* (Columbus, Ohio: Hunter-Trader-Trapper Co., 1926), 79–84; E. A. Brininstool, "The Beecher Island Fight," *Winners of the West* (October 1942): 5; see also John H. Monnett and Michael McCarthy, *Colorado Profiles: Men and Women Who Shaped the Centennial State* (Evergreen, Colo.: Cordillera Press, 1987), 33–41. Scout Eli Ziegler was possibly seventeen or eighteen years old at the time of the Beecher Island fight.
35. Leckie, *Military Conquest of the Southern Plains,* 58.
36. *House Executive Documents, 40th Congress, 2nd sess., no. 97,* 1.
37. *Annual Report of the Commissioner of Indian Affairs for the Year 1867,* 27–28.
38. Alfred A. Taylor, "Medicine Lodge Peace Council," *Chronicles of Oklahoma* (v. 11, March 1924): 99.
39. Hyde, *Life of George Bent,* 278–279; Grinnell, *The Fighting Cheyennes,* 270–273. Berthrong disagrees that agent Leavenworth was principally responsible for assembling the Indians on Medicine Lodge Creek. See Berthrong, *The Southern Cheyennes,* 290n.
40. *New York Tribune,* October 23, 1867.
41. Stanley, *My Early Travels and Adventures,* 227–229.
42. *Ibid.,* 283.
43. Quoted in Leckie, *Military Conquest of the Southern Plains,* 60n.
44. Stanley, *My Early Travels and Adventures,* 224.
45. Hyde, *Life of George Bent,* 284.
46. Farley, "Reminiscences of Allison J. Pliley," 6.
47. Grinnell, *The Fighting Cheyennes,* 273.
48. Hyde, *Life of George Bent,* 284.
49. Stanley, *My Early Travels and Adventures,* 231.
50. *New York Tribune,* October 23, 1867.
51. Charles J. Kappler, *Indian Affairs: Laws and Treaties* (Washington, D.C.: Government Printing Office, 1903), 980–981, 984–989.
52. There is some question that the Dog Soldiers were not told truthfully what they were signing at Medicine Lodge. At the beginning of the council their behavior was haughty, even threatening, yet for once their chiefs signed the treaty. See Hyde, *Life of George Bent,* 284; Leckie, *Military Conquest of the Southern Plains,* 62; Douglas C. Jones, *The Treaty of Medicine Lodge* (Norman: University of Oklahoma Press, 1966), 178. Jones presents one of the most complete, although arguable, interpretations of the Medicine Lodge councils.
53. E. E. Lindquist, "Indian Treaty Making," *Chronicles of Oklahoma* (v. 24, Winter 1948–1949): 427–430.
54. Garfield, "Defense of the Kansas Frontier," 454.
55. *Annual Report of the Commissioner of Indian Affairs for the Year 1868,* 63–68.
56. *Ibid.,* 72; *New York Tribune,* August 15, 1868. The Solomon Valley raids are recounted vividly in Leckie, *Military Conquest of the Southern Plains,* 70–73.
57. Jones, *Treaty of Medicine Lodge,* viii.
58. Hyde, *Life of George Bent,* 285.

Chapter 6

1. *Rocky Mountain News*, September 7, 1867.
2. Hutton, *Phil Sheridan and His Army*, 27–28.
3. *Ibid.*, xiii. Hutton's book is by far the best biography of Sheridan's career in the West following the Civil War.
4. *Annual Report of the Secretary of War for the Year 1868*, I:38.
5. *Ibid.*, I:736–737.
6. Quoted in Robert Athern, *William Tecumseh Sherman and the Settlement of the West* (Norman: University of Oklahoma Press, 1956), 207–208.
7. Utley, *Life in Custer's Cavalry*, 115.
8. Hyde, *Life of George Bent*, 290.
9. P. H. Sheridan, *Personal Memoirs of P. H. Sheridan, General, United States Army*, 2 vols. (New York: Charles L. Webster & Co., 1888), II:299; Hutton, *Phil Sheridan and His Army*, 36–37.
10. Roll 1339, RG 94, Fort Wallace: Post Returns, Letters sent, August 19, 1868, National Archives Records Service, hereafter referred to as NARS. *Harper's Weekly Magazine* (v. 17, Sept. 19, 1868): 606.
11. *Annual Report of the Secretary of War for the Year 1868*, II: 4–5.
12. Leckie, *Military Conquest of the Southern Plains*, 74.
13. Hutton, *Phil Sheridan and His Army*, 39.
14. Hutton, *Phil Sheridan and His Army*, 41–42.
15. *Boston Globe*, September 13, 1915; "George A. Forsyth," *Denver Westerners' Roundup* (Sept. 1969): 23–25.
16. Dennis Collins, *The Indians' Last Fight or the Dull Knife Raid* (Girard, Kans.: Press of the Appeal to Reason, 1934), 170.
17. George A. Forsyth, *The Story of the Soldier* (New York: D. Appleton and Co., 1900), 200.
18. George A. Forsyth, *Thrilling Days in Army Life* (New York: Harper & Brothers, 1902), 9. The story of the Beecher Island fight in this book first appeared in 1895 as an article. See George A. Forsyth, "A Frontier Fight," *Harper's New Monthly Magazine* (v. 91, June 1895): 41–67. As with many of his scouts who later published their recollections of the Beecher Island fight, Forsyth reconstructed his conversations "in substance" as best as he remembered them.
19. Forsyth, "A Frontier Fight"; Forsyth, *Thrilling Days*, 9–10.
20. Forsyth, Thrilling Days, 10–11; Roster of Forsyth Scouts, *The Beecher Island Annual*, 60.
21. George Washington Oaks, recorded by Ben Faastad, ed., and annotated by Arthur Woodward, *Man of the West: Reminiscences of George Washington Oaks* (Tucson: Arizona Pioneers Historical Society, 1956), 29.
22. Forsyth, *Thrilling Days*, 12.
23. *Ibid.*, 14–15.
24. F. C. Stilbeboyer, ed., *Nebraska Pioneers: The Story of Sixty–five Years of Pioneering in Southwest Nebraska* (Grand Rapids, Mich.: Wm. Eerdmans, 1944), 25.
25. Brininstool, *Fighting Indian Warriors*, 86.
26. Oaks, *Man of the West*, 29.
27. *Ibid.*
28. Brininstool, *Fighting Indian Warriors*, 86.
29. *Ibid.*, 87. There is some confusion over Shlesinger's age. In 1952, historian Merrill J. Mattes listed Shlesinger's year of birth as 1848, making him nearly twenty at the time of the Beecher Island fight. Shlesinger's personal reminiscences, however, were directly given over the years by Sig to writer E. A. Brininstool. In one of the earliest published accounts, *Fighting Red Cloud's Warriors* (1926), Shlesinger states that he was sixteen in 1865, making him eighteen at the time of the Battle of Beecher Island. In a later, somewhat more "popular," account, *Fighting Indian Warriors* (1953), Shlesinger states: "Well, there I was, 'Sig' Shlesinger, a friendless, seventeen-year-old boy . . . during that summer of 1868." Brininstool, who knew him better than anyone else who recorded his story, placed Shlesinger's age at seventeen in 1868, as did several of Sig's fellow

scouts. In any event, most participants agreed he was the youngest member of the Forsyth Scouts, with Eli Ziegler possibly being a few months older and Jack Stillwell one year older.

30. Adolph Roenigk, *Pioneer History of Kansas* (Lincoln, Kans., 1933), 133.
31. Obituary, *The Beecher Island Annual*, 105.
32. A. J. Pliley, "The Journey of Pliley and Donovan to Fort Wallace for Relief," *The Beecher Island Annual*, 74–75.
33. *Ibid.*, 74.
34. Obituary, *Ibid.*, 104
35. John Hurst, "The Beecher Island Fight," *Collections of the Kansas State Historical Society* (v. 15, 1919–1922): 530. Hurst's account is also told in "The Beecher Island Fight," *Winners of the West* (Feb. 16, 1925): 1, 4, 7–8; and the *Beecher Island Annual*, 68–73.
36. Obituary, *The Beecher Island Annual*, 105.
37. Thomas J. Cormack, "Charley Cormack, Forsyth Scout," *Frontier Times* (v. 53, no. 6, Oct.–Nov. 1979): 25.
38. Forsyth, *Story of a Soldier*, 211.
39. Forsyth, *Thrilling Days*, 20.
40. Brininstool, *Fighting Red Cloud's Warriors*, 85.
41. Brininstool, *Fighting Indian Warriors*, 89.
42. Merrill Mattes, ed., "The Beecher Island Battlefield Diary of Sigmund Shlesinger," *Colorado Magazine* (v. 29, no. 3, July 1952): 161–169; Chauncey B. Whitney, "Diary of Chauncey B. Whitney," *Collections of the Kansas State Historical Society* (v. 12, 1911–1912): 296.
43. Thomas B. Murphy, "The First Day of the Battle of the Arickaree," *The Beecher Island Annual*, 66.
44. *Ibid.*, 67.
45. Hurst, "The Beecher Island Fight," 531.
46. Forsyth, *Story of a Soldier*, 214.
47. William M. Wells, *The Desert's Hidden Wealth* (Topeka, Kans., 1934), 71.
48. Forsyth, *Story of a Soldier*, 214–215.
49. Forsyth, *Thrilling Days*, 24.
50. Brininstool, *Fighting Indian Warriors*, 90.
51. *Rocky Mountain News*, April 22, 1900. Actually, the command may have been marching away from the nearby Indian villages by the time some of the scouts urged Forsyth to reconsider marching forward in pursuit.
52. Forsyth, *Thrilling Days*, 26; Hurst, "The Beecher Island Fight," 531.
53. Forsyth, *Thrilling Days*, 26; Hurst, 531.
54. Oaks, *Man of the West*, 30.
55. *Ibid.*
56. Eli Zeigler, "Story of the Beecher Island Battle as Told by Scout Eli Ziegler," *The Beecher Island Annual*, 61.
57. John Hurst, "Scout John Hurst's Story of the Fight," in *ibid.*, 69.
58. Mattes, *Diary of Sigmund Shlesinger*, 169.
59. Forsyth, *Thrilling Days*, 30.
60. Powell, *People of the Sacred Mountain*, v. 1, 573.
61. Brininstool, "The Beecher Island Fight," 6.

Chapter 7

1. William MacLeod Raine, *Famous Sheriffs & Western Outlaws* (Garden City & New York: Doubleday, Doran & Co., 1929), 177–178.
2. Ziegler's account, *Beecher Island Annual*, 61.
3. Raine, *Famous Sheriffs*, 178–179.

4. Forsyth, *Thrilling Days*, 32.
5. *Ibid.*
6. Brininstool, *Fighting Red Cloud's Warriors*, 88, 90.
7. There is some controversy over whose idea it was to fall back on the island to make a defensive stand. Shlesinger "believed" it was Stillwell. So did Hurst. Forsyth did not acknowledge either scout in his accounts but instead gave himself credit for the decision. Thomas Murphy, however, in a letter written to a friend after the battle, was obviously aggravated by Forsyth's claim to the decisive judgment. Murphy paraphrased George Washington Oaks as stating something to the effect that "Forsyth claimed credit for everything, that it was you [Murphy] and Jack Stillwell that called [out] 'go on to the island'. . . . Forsyth never . . . gave a command to go on the island[.] That he [Forsyth] knew nothing about the western country or Indians or Indian warfare [was obvious]." See Thomas Murphy to J. G. Masters (undated letter), Western History Department, Denver Public Library.
8. John Hurst, "The Beecher Island Fight," *Collections of the Kansas State Historical Society* (v. 15, 1919–1922): 532.
9. Ziegler's account given to Winfield Freeman of the Kansas State Historical Society in Roenigk, *Pioneer History of Kansas*, 136.
10. Ziegler's account, *Beecher Island Annual*, 61, 63.
11. Hurst, "The Beecher Island Fight," 533.
12. Raine, *Famous Sheriffs*, 180–181.
13. Thomas Murphy, "The First Day of the Battle of the Arickaree," in *Beecher Island Annual*, 67–68.
14. Robert McReynolds, *Thirty Years on the Frontier* (Colorado Springs: El Paso Publishing Co., 1906), 241.
15. Brininstool, *Fighting Indian Warriors*, 95.
16. Ziegler's account, *Beecher Island Annual*, 63.
17. Hurst, "The Beecher Island Fight," 533.
18. Frank Harrington, Obituary, *Beecher Island Annual*, 38.
19. H. H. Tucker, Obituary, *Beecher Island Annual*, 104.
20. Frank Petree, "The Battle of Beecher Island and Recollections of Some of the Men Engaged in It," in *Beecher Island Annual*, 108.
21. Forsyth, *Story of a Soldier*, 220–221. A compilation of the scouts' casualities is listed by Freeman, "The Battle of Arickaree," 354.
22. Hyde, *Life of George Bent*, 22–23; Grinnell, *The Fighting Cheyennes*, 284. Most of the scouts in their accounts, as well as Forsyth, accepted Grover's mistaken identification of Roman Nose in the first charge. One of the only scouts to get it right was George Washington Oaks. See Oaks, *Man of the West*, 30–33.
23. Brininstool, *Fighting Indian Warriors*, 97.
24. Hurst, "The Beecher Island Fight," 534.
25. Ziegler's account in Roenigk, *Pioneer History*, 137.
26. Hurst, "The Beecher Island Fight," 535.
27. *Ibid.*, 533.
28. *Ibid.*, 534. Bent vividly described Bad Heart or Wolf Belly's ride over the island. See Hyde, *Life of George Bent*, 301.
29. Interview with Chalmers Smith, January 18, 1913, Walter Camp manuscripts, Lilly Library, University of Indiana, Bloomington. Quoted in Hutton, *Phil Sheridan*, 47.
30. Louis McLoughlin, "The Forsyth Scouts at Beecher Island," *Beecher Island Annual*, 88.
31. Forsyth, *Story of a Soldier*, 225. At this point in the battle all of Forsyth's accounts become confused and melodramatic. He placed Roman Nose at the head of the warriors during the first charge, which is based on the erroneous identification of "Sharp" Grover. See note 22. His directions are turned around. Possibly his wounds clouded his recollections. Hurst's account (up to the second charge by the Indians) and Ziegler's accounts along with the Indians' accounts, meticulously collected by Grinnell and Hyde, are far more reliable after the point in the fighting where Forsyth was wounded. The notable exception is Forsyth's recollections of Beecher's and Mooer's deaths, which are corroborated in detail by several of the scouts in their writings.

In a letter to a friend, Brininstool stated: "All the men I have talked to say that Col. Forsythe's [sic] story of the fight is pretty much exaggerated, as far as the fighting was concerned." See E. A. Brininstool, ed., "Survivors Tell of the Forsyth Fight," *The Chicago Westerners Brand Book* (v. 29, no. 4, June 1972): 26.

32. Forsyth, *Thrilling Days*, 45–46.

33. *Ibid.*, 54–55. George Washington Oaks claimed Beecher was mortally wounded about noon when "an Indian sharpshooter fired across the neck of the horse and struck Beecher at the base of the backbone." Raine, *Famous Sheriffs*, 184; McLoughlin's account, *Beecher Island Annual*, 86.

34. Grinnell, *The Fighting Cheyennes*, 284.

35. Although Grinnell claimed that there were no women near the battlefield, this is doubtful because an overwhelming majority of the scouts who left accounts independently related almost exact tales regarding their presence. See Forsyth, *Thrilling Days*, 57, and *Story of the Soldier*, 228–229; Ziegler in Roegnik, *Pioneer History*, 141; Oaks, *Man of the West*, 32–33; Hurst, "Battle of the Arickaree," 535, Shlesinger in Brininstool, *Fighting Red Cloud's Warriors*, 91; and Murphy's account, *Beecher Island Annual*, 68.

36. Hurst, "Battle of the Arickaree," 533. Forsyth claimed the remark was distinctly heard by the whole command. Herbert Myrick, in "The Mysterious Renegade," *Pearson's Magazine* (v. 12, 1906): 96, claimed that two whites were with the Indians at Beecher Island. One was a man named Nisbi, and the other was supposedly John Clybor, a 7th Cavalry deserter. Myrick claimed the Indians had a bugle, which Clybor taught them to use in the battle. See Hurst, "Battle of the Arickaree," 533, n. 5. Dee Brown accepted this story in Dee Brown, "The Battle of the Arickaree," *American History Illustrated* (v. 2, no. 5, Dec. 1967): 8.

37. Farley, "Reminiscences of Allison J. Pliley," 8.

38. Brininstool, *Fighting Red Cloud's Warriors*, 91.

39. Sigmund Shlesinger, "The Beecher Island Fight," *Collections of the Kansas State Historical Society* (v. 15, 1919–1922): 544.

40. Ziegler's account in Roenigk, *Pioneer History*, 136; Grinnell, *The Fighting Cheyennes*, 284; Hyde, *Life of George Bent*, 301. Forsyth did not identify any of the men who entrenched on the riverbank, but several of the scouts as well as George Bent, who later interviewed Stillwell, confirmed that it was Jack Stillwell who took that position.

41. Grinnell, *The Fighting Cheyennes*, 285; Hyde, *Life of George Bent*, 301–302.

42. Grinnell, *The Fighting Cheyennes*, 285.

43. *Ibid.*, 282–283.

44. Powell, *People of the Sacred Mountain*, v. 1, 574–575.

45. Grinnell, *The Fighting Cheyennes*, 284.

46. Hyde, *Life of George Bent*, 301.

47. Grinnell, *The Fighting Cheyennes*, 285–286.

48. *Ibid.*, 288–290; Hyde, *Life of George Bent*, 304. John Stands in Timber related the same story from oral tradition except that he claimed it was Roman Nose who was dragged away. Bent, however, corroborated Grinnell's assertion told to him by Cheyenne participants that it was Weasel Bear who was recovered. See Stands in Timber and Liberty, *Cheyenne Memories*, 176–178.

49. The story of Yellow Haired Woman was told by herself to George Bird Grinnell on September 24, 1908. It is recounted in Powell, *People of the Sacred Mountain*, v. 1, 577–578.

50. *Ibid.*, 578.

51. Stands in Timber and Liberty, *Cheyenne Memories*, 177–178.

52. Grinnell, *The Fighting Cheyennes*, 286. Grinnell did not mention Eagle Feather as party to this council. Because White Contrary's speech to Roman Nose is so similar to that of Eagle Feather's speech, possibly they are the same warrior recounted by John Stands in Timber.

53. *Ibid.* Grinnell related that Roman Nose repeated the telling of this story twice, White Contrary joining the group after he had first told it to the Dog Soldier chiefs.

54. *Ibid.*, 287.

55. Powell, *People of the Sacred Mountain*, v. 1, 579.

56. Hyde, *Life of George Bent*, 303. John Stands in Timber asserted that Roman Nose fell from his horse on the riverbank and that it was he, rather than Weasel Bear, who was recovered by Two Crows. See note 478. Grinnell also claimed that Roman Nose fell from his horse, crawled away, and was later rescued. He treated this event as a separate incident from that of Weasel Bear, however. Powell accepted Bent's version of the story, that of Roman Nose riding under his own power to the rear. See Powell, *People of the Sacred Mountain*, v. 1, 579.
57. Grinnell, *The Fighting Cheyennes*, 290–291.
58. *Ibid.*, 291. Powell gave a vivid description of Roman Nose's scaffold burial. See Powell, *People of the Sacred Mountain*, v. 1, 582.

Chapter 8

1. Forsyth, *Thrilling Days*, 59.
2. *Ibid.*, 60.
3. Hurst, "Battle of the Arickaree," 536; Ziegler's account, *Beecher Island Annual*, 64.
4. Hurst, "Battle of the Arickaree," 536; Ziegler's account, *Beecher Island Annual*, 64.
5. Brininstool, *Fighting Red Cloud's Warriors*, 94.
6. *Ibid.*, 93–94.
7. Brady, *Indian Fights and Fighters*, 117; Oaks, *Man of the West*, 36.
8. Forsyth, *Thrilling Days*, 62.
9. Oaks, *Man of the West*, 34.
10. Ziegler's account in Roenigk, *Pioneer History of Kansas*, 145.
11. Freeman, "The Battle of the Arickaree," 354–356; Miles, *Personal Recollections*, 148; Brady, *Indian Fights and Fighters*, 98–100. Miles and Brady disagree whether Stillwell and Trudeau were hiding in a buffalo carcass (Miles) or a wallow (Brady) when they encountered the snake.
12. Chauncey B. Whitney, "Diary of Chauncey B. Whitney," 298.
13. Merrill Mattes, ed., "The Beecher Island Battlefield Diary of Sigmund Shlesinger," 169.
14. Hurst, "Battle of the Arickaree," 536.
15. Ziegler's account, *Beecher Island Annual*, 64.
16. Forsyth, *Thrilling Days*, 62, 63.
17. Oaks, *Man of the West*, 34.
18. Shlesinger, "The Beecher Island Fight," 544.
19. Hurst, "Battle of the Arickaree," 536.
20. Whitney, "Diary," 298.
21. Allison J. Pliley, "The Journey of Pliley and Donovan to Fort Wallace for Relief," in *Beecher Island Annual*, 74.
22. Lucille Hagus Imherr, *Donovan Family Papers* (unpublished manuscript, Western History Department, Denver Public Library, 1968), 14.
23. Farley, "Reminiscences of Allison J. Pliley," 8.
24. Imherr, *Donovan Family*, 14. Pliley did not relate this incident in either of his accouts of the battle. Donovan's granddaughter later stated: "The accounts of scout Pliley and John Vincent Donovan differ. It may be that time diminished memory." Which scout's memory? She does not speculate. Farley, "Reminiscences of Allison J. Pliley," 15.
25. J. J. Donovan to nephew, June 25, 1905, in "Eli S. Ricker Interviews" (unpublished manuscript, Tablet 6, Eli S. Ricker Collection, Nebraska State Historical Society, Lincoln, Nebraska), 77–86.
26. Pliley's account in *Beecher Island Annual*, 74–75. Pliley made this statement to the Beecher Island Battle Memorial Association on October 29, 1905. See "Ricker Interviews," 63–76.
27. Hurst, "Battle of the Arickaree," 537.
28. Forsyth, *Thrilling Days*, 71.
29. Oaks, *Man of the West*, 35. Oaks did not speculate why a tepee pole was on Beecher Island or how it got there. No one else on the island remembered and wrote about the "flag of no surrender" incident.

30. Brady, *Indian Fights and Fighters*, 120.
31. Forsyth, *Thrilling Days*, 70–71.
32. *Ibid.*, 67; Oaks, *Man of the West*, 35.
33. Brady, *Indian Fights and Fighters*, 118. Shlesinger told this story to the Reverend Cyrus Townsend Brady about 1903. In his diary entry for September 21, however, he wrote without an explanation of his role in the incident: "scalpt 3 Indians which were found about 15 Feet from my hole consealt in Grass." See Mattes, "Shlesinger Diary," 169. These Indians may have been Sioux and Arapahoe. If we accept Grinnell's contention that only nine Indians were killed, by this time most of the Cheyenne bodies had been recovered.
34. Forsyth, *Thrilling Days*, 66–67.
35. Morton's account in *Beecher Island Annual*, 100.
36. Hurst's account in *Beecher Island Annual*, 72.
37. Mattes, "Shlesinger Diary," 169.
38. Brady, *Indian Fights and Fighters*, 119.
39. *Ibid.*
40. Hurst, "Battle of the Arickaree," 537.
41. Ziegler's account in *Beecher Island Annual*, 65.
42. Whitney, "Diary," 298.
43. Hurst's account in *Beecher Island Annual*, 72.
44. Whitney, "Diary," 298.

Chapter 9

1. Ziegler's account in *Beecher Island Annual*, 65–66.
2. Hurst, "Battle of the Arickaree," 537.
3. Forsyth, *Thrilling Days*, 72.
4. Morton's account in *Beecher Island Annual*, 100.
5. Hurst, "Battle of the Arickaree," 537.
6. Ziegler's account in *Beecher Island Annual*, 66. Jack Peate of Beverly, Kansas, had previously enlisted in the Forsyth Scouts but because of a mix-up in orders had not arrived at Fort Wallace in time to join the expedition to the Arickaree. See *Beecher Island Annual*, 89.
7. Ziegler's account in *Beecher Island Annual*, 66.
8. Jack Peate, "J. J. Peate Tells of the Relief," *Beecher Island Annual*, 90.
9. Brady, *Indian Fights and Fighters*, 119.
10. Forsyth, *Thrilling Days*, 72.
11. Oaks, *Man of the West*, 36.
12. Brady, *Indian Fights and Fighters*, 119–120.
13. Oaks, *Man of the West*, 36–37.
14. Whitney, "Diary," 298.
15. National Archives (NARS), Record Group 94, Roll 1339, Fort Wallace: Post Returns, Letters sent, October 5, 1868; Peate's account in *Beecher Island Annual*, 89.
16. According to Berthrong, the two scouts met two troopers of Company H, 10th Cavalry, along the Smoky Hill route on September 22. They then went on to Fort Wallace while the troopers reported to Carpenter. Carpenter did not mention this incident in his memoirs. See Berthrong, *Southern Cheyennes*, 312.
17. Peate's account in *Beecher Island Annual*, 90.
18. For a complete account of the role of Company H, 10th Cavalry, in the rescue of the Forsyth Scouts, see L. H. Carpenter, "The Story of a Rescue," *Journal of Military Service Institution of the United States* (v. 17, no. 67, Sept. 1895): 267–276 (reprinted in *Winners of the West*, February 16, 1925, 6–7, and *English Westerners Brand Book* [London: English Westerners Society, v. 19,

no. 1, Oct. 1966): 1–10]), hereafter referred to as "Rescue." See also E. A. Brininstool, "The Rescue of Forsyth's Scouts," *Collections of the Kansas State Historical Society* (v. 17, 1926–1928): 845–851; and the *National Tribune*, September 13, 1923.

19. Carpenter, "Rescue," 5.
20. *Ibid.*
21. *Ibid.*, 6.
22. Pliley's statement in "Ricker Interviews," 6: 71–73.
23. Imherr, *Donovan Family*, 14.
24. Carpenter, "Rescue," 6.
25. Peate's account in *Beecher Island Annual*, 90.
26. Carpenter, "Rescue," 7.
27. Brady, *Indian Fights and Fighters*, 107.
28. Forsyth, *Thrilling Days*, 73.
29. Carpenter, "Rescue," 7.
30. *Ibid.*, 3.
31. "Trooper of the Tenth Cavalry Claims to Be the First Man to the Rescue at Beecher Island," *Winners of the West*, August 8, 1925, 5; Reuben Waller, "History of a Slave Written by Himself at the Age of 89 Years," *Beecher Island Annual*, 116.
32. Carpenter, "Rescue," 7.
33. *Ibid.*
34. Homer W. Wheeler, *Buffalo Days: Forty Years in the Old West; The Personal Narrative of a Cattleman, Indian Fighter and Army Officer* (Indianapolis: Bobbs-Merrill, 1923), 16–19.
35. Brady, *Indian Fights and Fighters*, 122.
36. Wheeler, *Buffalo Days*, 18. Brady claimed that Trudeau remained behind at Fort Wallace and died shortly thereafter. Brady is mistaken, however. Wheeler was with Bankhead's column and remembered Trudeau going back to the island with the column along with Stillwell. Wheeler claimed that Trudeau was afterward employed at Fort Wallace in the quartermaster's corral for "many months, but finally went to Arizona."
37. James S. Brisbin is best remembered for his book *The Beef Bonanza; or, How to Get Rich on the Plains* (1881) (facsimile [Norman: University of Oklahoma Press, 1959]), a booster publication that unrealistically inspired the corporate phase of the open-range cattle business on the northern plains.
38. *The Republican* (Chicago), October 8, 1868; See also Harry H. Anderson, ed., "Stand at the Arickaree," *Colorado Magazine* (v. 41, no. 4, Fall 1964): 342.
39. Brady, *Indian Fights and Fighters*, 120.
40. Oaks, *Man of the West*, 38.
41. Peate's account in *Beecher Island Annual*, 91.
42. *Ibid.*, 92. What the warrior was doing carrying a woman's skirts and wearing a blanket when he was trying to run as fast as he could, in competition with three others to capture and escape on only three horses, is unknown. This aspect of Peate's story seems like a fabrication in order to justify the fact that the scouts killed the defenseless Indian.
43. *Ibid.*
44. *Ibid.*, 91.
45. Shlesinger, "Battle of the Arickaree," 546.
46. See Powell, *People of the Sacred Mountain*, v. 1, 678–679, n. 13. Powell asserted that the warrior buried in the tepee was Killed by a Bull. He also claimed that several Cheyennes and some Sioux of this time had war bonnets with single buffalo horns protruding from the forehead. As Powell stated, "The mystery remains."
47. Ice (White Bull) to George B. Grinnell, retold in *Ibid.*, v. 1, 582.

Chapter 10

1. Hutton, *Phil Sheridan and His Army*, 48–49.
2. Spotts, *Campaigning With Custer*, 16. For the history of the 19th Kansas Volunteers, see James A. Hadley, "The Nineteenth Kansas Cavalry and the Conquest of the Plains Indians," *Collections of the Kansas State Historical Society* (v. 17, 1926–1928): 429–456.
3. Hutton, *Phil Sheridan and His Army*, 50. The best biography of Major Eugene Asa Carr is King, *War Eagle*.
4. Hutton, *Phil Sheridan and His Army*, 50; King, *War Eagle*, 86–87.
5. Hyde, *Life of George Bent*, 310–311; Grinnell, *The Fighting Cheyennes*, 293–296.
6. Grinnell, *The Fighting Cheyennes*, 293–296; Hyde, *Life of George Bent*, 311.
7. Two Crows to George Bent, in Hyde, *Life of George Bent*, 311.
8. Hutton, *Phil Sheridan and His Army*, 52–53.
9. House Executive Document, 41st Cong., 2nd Sess., no. 240, 1868, 4–5.
10. Sources differ as to how many Dog Soldiers came south that winter. In one of his articles, historian Lonnie White has Tall Bull living in the south that winter and in another article he has Tall Bull spending the winter with Northern Cheyennes and Sioux in the Powder River country, all during the same winter. In any event, the Dog Soldiers were not crippled by the Washita campaign because Tall Bull assembled 165 lodges in the Republican Valley in spring 1869. Berthrong, *The Southern Cheyennes*, 340.
11. Anderson, *Kansas West*, 25.
12. Berthrong, *The Southern Cheyennes*, 340.
13. *Ibid.*
14. *Daily Tribune* (Lawrence), June 16, 1869.
15. Garfield, "Defense of the Kansas Frontier," 469.
16. White, "Women Captives," 344.
17. *Times and Conservative* (Leavenworth), June 20, 1869. See also Lonnie J. White, "Indian Raids on the Kansas Frontier," *Kansas Historical Quarterly* (v. 38, no. 4, Winter 1972): 369–388; and Lonnie J. White, "The Cheyenne Barrier on the Kansas Frontier, 1868–1869," *Arizona and the West* (v. 4, no. 1: Spring 1962): 51–64.
18. Quoted in Berthrong, *The Southern Cheyennes*, 341.
19. Garfield, "Defense of the Kansas Frontier," 468–469.
20. Grinnell, *The Fighting Cheyennes*, 311.
21. Jack D. Filipiak, "The Battle of Summit Springs," *Colorado Magazine* (v. 41, no. 4, Fall 1964): 350–351.
22. Grinnell, *The Fighting Cheyennes*, 312–313.
23. *Ibid.*, 313. There is some controversy over who actually killed Tall Bull. "Buffalo Bill" Cody also claimed the honor. Historian James T. King stated wryly that "the circumstances of the death of Tall Bull have given rise to one of the longest continuing, one of the most involved, and perhaps one of the least important controversies in frontier history." See King, *War Eagle*, 113; Filipiak, "Summit Springs," 351.
24. Hyde, *Life of George Bent*, 359.
25. Ray G. Sparks, *Reckoning at Summit Springs* (Kansas City: Lowell Press, 1969), 49.
26. Filipiak, "Summit Springs," 352.
27. James T. King, "The Battle of Summit Springs," *Nebraska History* (v. 41, 1960): 290–292.
28. Hyde, *Life of George Bent*, 340.
29. Filipiak, "Summit Springs," 344.
30. See *ibid.*, 343–353.
31. *New York Times*, September 24, 1868.
32. *Times and Conservative* (Leavenworth), September 25, 1868.
33. *Rocky Mountain News*, September 25, 1868.
34. Keim, *Sheridan's Troopers on the Borders*, 50–57.
35. See Utley, *The Indian Frontier*, 123–125.

36. Fry, *Army Sacrifices*, 35.
37. Grinnell, *The Fighting Cheyennes*, 292.
38. Quoted in Fry, *Army Sacrifices*, 37.
39. Filipiak, "Summit Springs," 342, n. 8.
40. Forsyth, *Thrilling Days*, 53.
41. Grinnell, *The Fighting Cheyennes*, 292.
42. Brininstool, "Survivors Tell of Forsyth Fight," 26.
43. For example see Fry, *Army Sacrifices*, 44.
44. *Ibid.*
45. Grinnell, *The Fighting Cheyennes*, 291; Hyde, *Life of George Bent*, 305. There may have been a sixth Forsyth Scout, Bernard Day, who later died of wounds at Forth Wallace. Forsyth mentioned him in his reports as being "mortally wounded" on the first day of fighting on the island. No mention of his death was reported by anyone else, including Forsyth, after that time. In any event, Day was not buried on the island with the other five scouts who died there.
46. A. P. Gaines, "The Battle of Beecher Island," *Denver Westerners Monthly Roundup* (v. 25, no. 7–8, July–August 1969): 123.
47. National Archives (NARS), Record Group 393, Captain C. Butler to Lieutenant A. Lewis, December 20, 1869; Assistant Surgeon T. A. Turner to Captain E. Butler, December 23, 1868, Division of the Missouri, Fort Wallace: Post Records, 1868.
48. *Denver Post*, September 19, 1900.
49. Quoted in *Denver Post* September 8, 1968.
50. Although the scouts were technically civilians during their enlistments, they or their heirs were nevertheless awarded government pensions. See National Archives (NARS), Record Group 15, Roll 1–7, T 316, Old War Index to Pension Files, 1815–1926.
51. Shlesinger, "The Beecher Island Fight," 547. These bodies, mentioned by both Shlesinger and Brisbin, must have been the Sioux and Arapahoes, as most of the Cheyennes killed were recovered during the fight.
52. W. D. Street, "The Victory of the Plow," *Collections of the Kansas State Historical Society* (v. 9, 1905–1906): 39–40.
53. Brady, *Indian Fights and Fighters*, 111.
54. For an account of the flood and a recent attempt to recover the missing portions of the monument, which was swept away, see Thomas A. Witty, "Investigations to Locate Missing Sections of the Beecher Island Monument," Archaeological Report 5YM–Beecher Island, Kansas State Historical Society, 1985.

Bibliography

Manuscript Collections

Bent, George, to George E. Hyde. Correspondence, William Robertson Coe Collection, Yale University Library, New Haven, Connecticut.

Bent, George. Letters to George E. Hyde, Colorado State Historical Society, Denver, Colorado.

Camp, Walter. Manuscripts, Lilly Library, University of Indiana, Bloomington, Indiana.

Crawford, Samuel J. Governor's Papers — Crawford, Kansas State Historical Society, Topeka, Kansas.

Hancock, Winfield Scott. Reports of Major General Hancock Upon Indian Affairs With Accompanying Exhibits, Washington, D.C., 1867.

Imherr, Lucille Hagus. Donovan Family Papers, Western History Department, Denver Public Library, Denver, Colorado, 1968.

Murphy, Thomas, to J. G. Masters. Undated letter, Western History Department, Denver Public Library, Denver, Colorado.

National Archives (NARS), Washington, D.C., Record Group 15, Records of the Veterans Administration.

——. Record Group 94, Records of the Adjutant General's Office, 1780s–1917.

——. Record Group 393, Records of the United States Army Continental Commands, 1821–1920.

Ricker, Eli S. Interviews, 1900–1905, Tablet 6, Nebraska State Historical Society, Lincoln, Nebraska.

Witty, Thomas A. "Investigations to Locate Missing Sections of the Beecher Island Monument." Archaeological Report 5YM-Beecher Island, Kansas State Historical Society, Topeka, Kansas, 1985.

Government Documents

Annual Reports of the Commissioner of Indian Affairs, 1867–1868.

Annual Reports of the Secretary of War, 1868–1869 Washington, D.C.: Government Printing Office.

Chronological List: Action With Indians. Washington, D.C.: Adjutant General's Office, 1891.

House Executive Documents, 40th Cong., 2nd sess., 1868, 1, no. 97.

——. 40th Cong., 3rd sess., 1868, v. 3, serial 1412.

——. 41st Cong., 2nd sess., 1868, v. 2, serial 1412.

Kappler, Charles J., *Indian Affairs: Laws and Treaties*. Washington, D.C.: Government Printing Office, 1903.

"The Sand Creek Massacre: Report of the Secretary of War": *Senate Executive Document*. 39th Cong., 2nd sess., 1867, no. 26.

Sheridan, Lieutenant General Philip H., *Outline of Posts: Descriptions of the Posts in the Military Division of the Missouri*. Chicago: Military Division of the Missouri, 1876.

———. *Records of Engagements With Hostile Indians Within the Military Division of the Missouri From 1868–1882*. Washington, D.C.: Government Printing Office, 1882.

Newspapers and Weekly News Periodicals

Army and Navy Journal

Boston Globe

Cincinnati Commercial

Daily Conservative (Leavenworth)

Denver Post

Harper's New Monthly Magazine

Harper's Weekly

Hays Sentinel

Johnson County Democrat (Kansas)

Kansas City Commonwealth (Topeka)

Lawrence Daily Tribune (Kansas)

Lawrence Weekly Tribune (Kansas)

National Tribune

New York Times

New York Tribune

Osbourne County Farmer (Kansas)

Rocky Mountain News

Rooks County Record (Kansas)

The Republican (Chicago)

Times and Conservative (Leavenworth)

Topeka State Record (Kansas)

U.S. News and World Report

Weekly Leader (Topeka)

Weekly Union (Junction City)

Periodical Articles and Publications of Learned Societies

Anderson, Harry H., ed. "Stand at the Arickaree," *Colorado Magazine* 41, #4 (Fall 1964).

Athern, Robert G. "Colorado and the Indian War of 1868," *Colorado Magazine* 33, #1 (Jan. 1956).

Brininstool, E. A., ed. "The Beecher Island Fight," *Winners of the West* (Oct. 1942).

———. "The Rescue of Forsyth's Scouts," *Collections of the Kansas State Historical Society* 17 (1926–1928).

———. "Survivors Tell of the Forsyth Fight," *The Chicago Westerners Brand Book* 29, #4 (June 1972).

Brown, Dee A. "The Battle of the Arickaree," *American History Illustrated* 2, #8 (Dec. 1967).

Carpenter, L. H. "The Story of a Rescue," *English Westerners Brand Book* 19, #1 (Oct. 1976).

———. "The Story of a Rescue," *Journal of Military Service Institution of the United States* 17, #67 (Sept. 1895).

———. "The Story of a Rescue," *Winners of the West* (Feb. 16, 1925).

Carswell, Stuart R. "Twenty to One," *Cavalry Journal* 46, (Jan.–Feb. 1937).

Chapman, Arthur. "The Indian Fighters of the Arickaree," *Harper's Weekly* (July 26, 1913).

Chase, Julia. "Mother Bickerdyke," *Collections of the Kansas State Historical Society* 7 (1902–1903).

Clark, Mrs. Olive. "Early Days Along the Solomon Valley," *Collections of the Kansas State Historical Society* 17 (1926–1928).

Cormack, Thomas J. "Charley Cormack, Forsyth Scout," *Frontier Times* 53, #6 (Oct.– Nov. 1979).

Cronon, William, and Richard White. "Indians in the Land: A Conversation Between William Cronon and Richard White," *American Heritage* 37, #5 (Aug.– Sept. 1986).

Davis, Theodore. "A Summer on the Plains," *Harper's New Monthly Magazine* 36, #213 (Feb. 1868).

Farley, Alan W., ed. "Reminiscences of Allison J. Pliley, Indian Fighter," *Trail Guide* 2, #2 (Kansas City Posse, the Westerners, June 1957).

Filipiak, Jack D. "The Battle of Summit Springs," *Colorado Magazine* 41, #4 (Fall 1964).

Forsyth, George A. "A Frontier Fight," *Harper's New Monthly Magazine* 91 (June 1895).

Freeman, Winfield. "The Battle of the Arickaree," *Transactions of the Kansas State Historical Society* 6 (1897–1900).

Gaines, A. P. "The Battle of Beecher Island," *Denver Westerners Monthly Roundup* 25, #7–8 (July– Aug. 1969).

Garfield, Marvin H. "Defense of the Kansas Frontier, 1866-1867," *Kansas Historical Quarterly* 1, #4 (Aug. 1932).

———. "Defense of the Kansas Frontier, 1868–1869," *Kansas Historical Quarterly* 1, #5 (Nov. 1932).

Hadley, James A. "The Nineteenth Kansas Cavalry and the Conquest of the Plains Indians," *Collections of the Kansas State Historical Society* 17 (1926–1928).

Halaas, David Fridtjof. "America's Blurred Vision: A Review Essay on Indian-White Histories," *Colorado Heritage* (Colorado Historical Society) #3 (1983).

Harrison, Emily Haines, "Reminiscences of Early Days in Ottawa County," *Collections of the Kansas State Historical Society* 10 (1907–1908).

Heinzman, George M. "Don't Let Them Ride Over Us," *American Heritage* 18, #2 (Feb. 1967).

Historical Commentary. "Western History, Why the Past May Be Changing: Four Essays by Patricia Nelson Limerick, Michael P. Malone, Gerald Thompson, and Elliot West," *Montana: The Magazine of Western History* 40, #3 (Summer 1990).

Hurst, John. "The Beecher Island Fight," *Collections of the Kansas State Historical Society* 15 (1919–1922).

———. "The Beecher Island Fight," *Winners of the West* (Feb. 16, 1925).

Jenness, George B. "The Battle of Beaver Creek," *Transactions of the Kansas State Historical Society* 9 (1905–1906).

King, James T. "The Battle of Summit Springs," *Nebraska History* 41 (1960).

Lindquist, E. E. "Indian Treaty Making," *Chronicles of Oklahoma* 24 (Winter 1948–1949).

Mattes, Merrill, ed. "The Beecher Island Battlefield Diary of Sigmund Shlesinger," *Colorado Magazine* 29, #3 (July 1952).

Miles, Nelson A. "Jack Stilwell's Daring Achievement," *The Trail* 18, #3 (Aug. 1925).

Montgomery, Mrs. Frank C. "Fort Wallace and Its Relation to the Frontier," *Collections of the Kansas State Historical Society* 17 (1926–1928).

Myrick, Herbert. "The Mysterious Renegade," *Pearson's Magazine* 12 (1906).

Petman, Theodore B., ed. "Survivors Tell of Forsyth Fight," *Chicago Westerners Brand Book* 29, #4 (June 1972).

Putnam, John H. "A Trip to the End of the Union Pacific in 1868," *Kansas Historical Quarterly* 13, #3 (Aug. 1944).

Roenigk, A. "Railroad Grading Among Indians," *Collections of the Kansas State Historical Society* 8 (1904).

The Roundup 9, #9 (Western Writers of America, Sept. 1961).

Shlesinger, Sigmund. "The Beecher Island Fight," *Collections of the Kansas State Historical Society* 15 (1919–1922).

Snell, Joseph, and Robert Richmond. "When the Union and Kansas Pacific Built Through Kansas," *Kansas Historical Quarterly* 32 (1966).

Street, W. D. "The Victory of the Plow," *Collections of the Kansas State Historical Society* 9 (1905–1906).

Taylor, Alfred A. "Medicine Lodge Peace Council," *Chronicles of Oklahoma* 11 (March 1924).

"Trooper of the Tenth U.S. Cavalry Claims to Be the First Man to the Rescue at Beecher Island," *Winners of the West* (Aug. 8, 1925).

White, Lonnie J. "The Battle of Beecher Island: The Scouts Hold Fast on the Arickaree," *Journal of the West* 5, #1 (1966).

———. "The Cheyenne Barrier on the Kansas Frontier, 1868–1869," *Arizona and the West* 4, #1 (Spring 1962).

———. "Indian Raids on the Kansas Frontier," *Kansas Historical Quarterly* 38, #4 (Winter 1972).

———. "White Women Captives of Southern Plains Indians, 1866–1875," *Journal of the West* 8, #3 (July 1969).

Whitney, Chauncey B. "Diary of Chauncey B. Whitney," *Collections of the Kansas State Historical Society* 12 (1911–1912).

Winsor, William, and James Scarbrough. "History of Jewell County, Kansas, Written in 1878," *Collections of the Kansas State Historical Society* 17 (1926–1928).

Books and Pamphlets

Abbott, Carl, Stephen J. Leonard, and David McComb. *Colorado: A History of the Centennial State*. Rev. ed. Boulder, Colorado Associated University Press, 1982.

Anderson, George L. *Kansas West.* San Marino, Calif., Golden West Books, 1963.

Andrist, Ralph K. *The Long Death: The Last Days of the Plains Indians.* New York, Collier Books, 1964.

Armes, George A. *Ups and Downs of an Army Officer.* Washington, D.C., 1900.

Athern, Robert G. *William Tecumseh Sherman and the Settlement of the West.* Norman, University of Oklahoma Press, 1956.

Berkhofer, Robert F., Jr. *The White Man's Indian: Images of the American Indian From Columbus to the Present.* New York, Alfred A. Knopf, 1978.

Berthrong, Donald J. *The Southern Cheyennes.* Norman, University of Oklahoma Press, 1963.

Billington, Ray Allen, and Martin Ridge. *Westward Expansion: A History of the American Frontier,* 5th edition. New York, Macmillan, 1982.

Brady, Cyrus Townsend. *Indian Fights and Fighters.* Lincoln, University of Nebraska Press, 1971.

Brininstool, E. A. *Fighting Indian Warriors: True Tales of the Wild Frontiers.* Harrisburg, Pa., Stackpole Company, 1953.

————. *Fighting Red Cloud's Warriors: True Tales of Indian Days When the West Was Young.* Columbus, Ohio, Hunter-Trader-Trapper Company, 1926.

Brisbin, James S. *The Beef Bonanza; or, How to Get Rich on the Plains.* Norman, University of Oklahoma Press, 1959.

Coffman, Edward M. *The Old Army: A Portrait of the American Army in Peacetime, 1784–1898.* New York and Oxford, Oxford University Press, 1986.

Collins, Dennis. *The Indians' Last Fight or the Dull Knife Raid.* Girard, Kans., Press of the Appeal to Reason, 1934.

Crawford, Samuel J. *Kansas in the Sixties.* Chicago, A. C. McClurg and Company, 1911.

Custer, Elizabeth B. *Tenting on the Plains; or, General Custer in Kansas and Texas.* New York, C. L. Webster and Company, 1887.

Custer, George A. *My Life on the Plains; or, Personal Experiences With Indians.* Norman, University of Oklahoma Press, 1962.

Danker, Donald F., ed. *Man of the Plains: Recollections of Luther North, 1856–1882.* Lincoln, University of Nebraska Press, 1961.

Dodge, Richard Irving. *Our Wild Indians: Thirty-Three Years Personal Experience Among the Red Men of the Great West.* New York, Archer House, 1959.

Fite, Gilbert C. *The Farmers' Frontier, 1865–1900.* Albuquerque, University of New Mexico Press, 1974.

Fitzgerald, Daniel. *Ghost Towns of Kansas: A Traveler's Guide.* Lawrence, University Press of Kansas, 1988.

Forsyth, George A. *The Story of a Soldier.* New York, D. Appleton and Company, 1900.

————. *Thrilling Days in Army Life.* New York, Harper & Brothers, 1902.

Frost, Lawrence A. *The Court-Martial of General George Armstrong Custer.* Norman, University of Oklahoma Press, 1968.

Fry, James B. *Army Sacrifices.* New York, D. Van Nostrand, 1879.

Graham, W. A. *The Custer Myth: A Source Book of Custeriana.* New York, Bonanza Books, 1953.

Grinnell, George Bird. *The Cheyenne Indians,* v. 2. New Haven, Yale University Press, 1923.

————. *The Fighting Cheyennes.* New York, Charles Scribner's Sons, 1915.

————. Two Great Scouts and Their Pawnee Battalion: The Experiences of Frank J. North and Luther H. North, Pioneers in the Great West, 1856–1882, and Their Defense of the Building of the Union Pacific Railroad. New York, Arthur H. Clark Company, 1928.

Hall, Frank. History of the State of Colorado. Chicago, Blakely Printing Company, 1889.

Hoebel, E. Adamson. The Cheyennes: Indians of the Great Plains. New York, Holt, Rinehart & Winston, 1960.

Hofstadter, Richard. Social Darwinism in American Thought, revised edition. Boston, Beacon Press, 1955.

Hoig, Stan. The Battle of the Washita. Lincoln and London, University of Nebraska Press, 1976.

————. The Peace Chiefs of the Cheyennes. Norman, University of Oklahoma Press, 1980.

————. The Sand Creek Massacre. Norman, University of Oklahoma Press, 1961.

Hutchins, James S. Great Western Indian Fights. Lincoln, University of Nebraska Press, 1960.

Hutton, Paul Andrew. Phil Sheridan and His Army. Lincoln and London, University of Nebraska Press, 1985.

Hyde, George E. Life of George Bent:Written From His Letters. Norman, University of Oklahoma Press, 1968.

Inman, Henry. Tales of the Trail. Topeka, Kans., Crane & Company, 1898.

Jones, Douglas C. The Treaty of Medicine Lodge. Norman, University of Oklahoma Press, 1966.

Katz, William Loren. The Black West. 3rd ed. Seattle, Open Hand Publishing, 1987.

Keenan, Jerry. The Wagon Box Fight. Sheridan, Wyo., Fort Phil Kearney/Bozeman Trail Association, 1988.

Keim, DeB. Randolph. Sheridan's Troopers on the Borders: A Winter Campaign on the Plains. Lincoln and London, University of Nebraska Press, 1985.

King, James T. War Eagle: A Life of General Eugene A. Carr. Lincoln, University of Nebraska Press, 1963.

Knight, Oliver. Following the Indian Wars: The Story of the Newspaper Correspondents Among the Indian Campaigners. Norman, University of Oklahoma Press, 1960.

Leckie, William H. The Buffalo Soldiers: A Narrative of the Negro Cavalry in the West. Norman, University of Oklahoma Press, 1967.

————. The Military Conquest of the Southern Plains. Norman, University of Oklahoma Press, 1963.

Limerick, Patricia Nelson. The Legacy of Conquest: The Unbroken Past of the American West. New York and London, W. W. Norton & Company, 1987.

Limerick, Patricia Nelson, Clyde A. Milner II, and Charles E. Rankin, eds. Trails Toward a New Western History. Lawrence, University Press of Kansas, 1991.

Lynam, Robert, ed. The Beecher Island Annual: Sixty-Second Anniversary of the Battle of Beecher Island, September 17–18, 1868. Wray, Colo., Beecher Island Battle Memorial Association, 1930.

McGinnis, Anthony. Counting Coup and Cutting Horses: Intertribal Warfare on the Northern Plains, 1738–1889. Evergreen, Colo., Cordillera Press, 1990.

McReynolds, Robert. Thirty Years on the Frontier. Colorado Springs, El Paso Publishing Company, 1906.

Miles, Nelson A. Personal Recollections and Observations of General Nelson A. Miles. Chicago, Werner Publishing, 1896.

Miner, Craig. *West of Wichita: Settling the High Plains of Kansas, 1865–1890.* Lawrence, University Press of Kansas, 1986.

Monaghan, Jay. *Custer: The Life of General George Armstrong Custer.* Lincoln, University of Nebraska Press, 1971.

Monnett, John H., and Michael McCarthy. *Colorado Profiles: Men and Women Who Shaped the Centennial State.* Evergreen, Colo., Cordillera Press, 1987.

Myres, Sandra L. *Westering Women and the Frontier Experience, 1800–1915.* Albuquerque, University of New Mexico Press, 1982.

Nash, Gerald. *Creating the West: Historical Interpretations, 1890–1990.* Albuquerque, University of New Mexico Press, 1991.

Pitzer, Henry Littleton. *Three Frontiers: Memories and a Portrait of Henry Littleton Pitzer as Recorded by His Son Robert Clarbourne Pitzer.* Muscatine, Iowa, Pioneer Press, 1938.

Plummer, Mark A. *Frontier Governor: Samuel J. Crawford of Kansas.* Lawrence/Manhattan/Wichita, University Press of Kansas, 1971.

Powell, Peter John. *The Cheyennes, Ma.he.o's People: A Critical Bibliography.* Bloomington, Indiana University Press, 1980.

———. *People of the Sacred Mountain: A History of the Northern Cheyenne Chiefs and Warrior Societies, 1830–1879, With an Epilogue, 1969–1974.* 2 vols. San Francisco, Harper & Row, 1981.

Prucha, Francis Paul. *The Great Father: The United States Government and American Indians,* abridged edition. Lincoln, University of Nebraska Press, 1984.

Raine, William MacLeod. *Famous Sheriffs & Western Outlaws.* Garden City, N.Y., Doubleday, 1929.

Roenigk, Adolph. *Pioneer History of Kansas.* Kansas City, 1933.

Sheridan, P. H. *Personal Memoirs of P. H. Sheridan, General, United States Army.* 2 vols. New York, Charles L. Webster & Co., 1888.

Smith, Sherry L. *The View From Officers' Row: Army Perceptions of Western Indians.* Tucson, University of Arizona Press, 1990.

Socolofsky, Homer E. *Kansas Governors.* Lawrence, University Press of Kansas, 1990.

Socolofsky, Homer E., and Huber Self. *Historical Atlas of Kansas,* 2nd ed. Norman, University of Oklahoma Press, 1988.

Sparks, Ray G. *Reckoning at Summit Springs.* Kansas City, Lowell Press, 1969.

Spotts, David L. *Campaigning With Custer, 1868–1869.* Los Angeles, Wetzel Publishing Company, 1928.

Stands in Timber, John, and Margot Liberty. *Cheyenne Memories.* Lincoln and London, University of Nebraska Press, 1972.

Stanley, Henry M. *My Early Travels and Adventures in America and Asia,* v. 1. London, S. Low, Marston, 1895.

Stilbeboyer, C., ed. *Nebraska Pioneers: The Story of Sixty-Five Years of Pioneering in Southwest Nebraska.* Grand Rapids, Mich., Wm. Eerdmans, 1944.

Stilgoe, John. *Metropolitan Corridor: Railroads and the American Scene.* New Haven, Yale University Press, 1983.

Stratton, Joanna L. *Pioneer Women: Voices From the Kansas Frontier.* New York, Touchstone Books, 1981.

Tucker, Glenn. *Hancock the Superb.* Indianapolis, Bobbs-Merrilll, 1960.

Utley, Robert M. *Cavalier in Buckskin: George Armstrong Custer and the Western Military Frontier*. Norman, University of Oklahoma Press, 1988.

———. *Frontier Regulars: The United States Army and the Indian, 1866–1891*. New York, Macmillan, 1973.

———. *The Indian Frontier of the American West, 1846–1890*. Albuquerque, University of New Mexico Press, 1984.

———. ed. *Life in Custer's Cavalry: Diaries and Letters of Albert and Jennie Barnitz, 1867–1868*. New Haven, Yale University Press, 1977.

Vaughn, J. W. *The Battle of Platte Bridge*. Norman, University of Oklahoma Press, 1963.

Wallace County Historical Society. *History of Wallace County*. Sharon City, Kans., Wallace County Historical Society, 1979.

Ware, Eugene F. *The Indian War of 1864*. New York, St. Martin's, 1960.

Warner, Ezra J. *Generals in Blue: Lives of the Union Commanders*. Baton Rouge, Louisana State University Press, 1964.

Wells, William M. *The Desert's Hidden Wealth*. Topeka, 1934.

Wheeler, Homer W. *Buffalo Days: Forty Years in the Old West; The Personal Narrative of a Cattleman, Indian Fighter and Army Officer*. Indianapolis, Bobbs-Merrilll, 1925.

White, Lonnie J. *Hostiles and Horse Soldiers: Indian Battles and Campaigns in the West*. Boulder, Pruett Publishing Company, 1972.

White, Richard. *It's Your Misfortune and None of My Own: A New History of the American West*. Norman and London, University of Oklahoma Press, 1991.

Woodward, Arthur, ed. *Man of the West: Reminiscences of George Washington Oaks, 1840–1917*. Tucson, Arizona Pioneers Historical Society, 1956.

Zornow, William Frank. *Kansas: A History of the Jayhawk State*. Norman, University of Oklahoma Press, 1957.

Index